Do You Know What You Look Like?

Do You Know What You Look Like?
Interpersonal Relationships in Education

Edited by

Theo Wubbels and Jack Levy

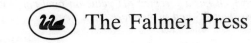 The Falmer Press

(A Member of the Taylor & Francis Group)
London · Washington, D.C.

UK   The Falmer Press, 4 John St., London WC1N 2ET
USA   The Falmer Press, Taylor & Francis Inc., 1900 Frost Road, Suite 101, Bristol, PA 19007

First published 1993

Library of Congress Cataloging-in-Publication data are available on request

A catalogue record for this book is available from the British Library

ISBN 0750 70 216 8 cased
ISBN 0750 70 217 6 paper

Cover design by Caroline Archer

Set in 9.5/11pt. Times by
Graphicraft Typesetters Ltd., Hong Kong

Printed in Great Britain by Burgess Science Press, Basingstoke on paper which has a specified pH value on final paper manufacture of not less than 7.5 and is therefore 'acid free'.

Contents

v

Contents

List of Figures and Tables

Acknowledgments

Many people have contributed to the work described in this book. We first need to acknowledge the 30,000-plus students and teachers who allowed us to enter their classrooms. We especially appreciate their cooperation and hope our relationship will continue in the future.

The editors and authors have been working in various groups on the research and development presented in these chapters. This cooperation — especially between the Dutch authors and the editors — was often so close that individual contributions are not separately visible, and they may not always coincide with the distribution of authors over the chapters. Since most of the book represents a cooperative effort, we feel that the identification of individual entrees is not critically important. The pronoun 'we' in each chapter might therefore refer to a larger group than the authors of that segment, and should be thought of as describing something like an extended family.

Some people who contributed to this work participated for only a short while, or completed tasks which did not result in their names appearing in any of the chapters. Their efforts, however, were essential. Our thanks for computer programming and statistical analyses go to Remko van den Dool, Marcel Galema, Albert Moes, Yvonne Sweers, Pierre Verweij and Rob Wiedemeyer. Rob Houwen was indispensable in helping us with graphics and statistical analyses. Crucial secretarial assistance was provided by Thea Strötbaum and, until 1990 Jenny Andriese. Finally, we recognize that without the patience and support of our families the book could not have been written.

Introduction

Focus on the Teacher

This year (1992) has been proclaimed 'The Year of the Teacher' in Europe. This recognition is part of the increasing global evidence that respect for teaching is on the rise. Reports such as The Holmes Group's (1986) *Tomorrow's Teachers*, or *Restructuring the Education of Teachers* (Association of Teacher Educators, 1991), are other indications that policy makers are focusing on the quality of teachers and their work life. This outlook represents a change from recent decades. If we compare the *Third Handbook of Research on Teaching* with the two preceding volumes it is evident that far more attention was devoted to the teacher in the 1980s than in the 1950s and 1960s. Throughout the last decade educational leaders were driven by a need to understand the 'effective teacher'.

An effective teacher is usually described as one who can produce high student scores on standardized tests. Fortunately, other criteria on effectiveness have crept into the literature in the last few years, and we've begun to see measurements based on supervisor and peer judgments. In the past, these two approaches — student outcomes and peer review — were not often combined, leaving the field with an incomplete understanding of effective teaching. Peer review alone is limited in scope, while sole reliance on tests doesn't allow for the ability to create and maintain a positive relationship with students. According to some researchers the latter element is at the heart of classroom teaching and learning (e.g., Kagan and Tippins, 1991).

The search for 'the effective teacher' has been conducted for more than a century (Borich, 1988). In the 1800s the effective teacher was usually thought of as someone who was a good person, an honorable citizen, well-educated and hardworking. They had high morale and were respected for their knowledge, friendliness and dedication. No special skills other than being well organized, disciplined and authoritative and dedicated to children were necessary. In the first half of this century literally thousands of studies were conducted to find that special personality trait which would predict teaching effectiveness (Getzels and Jackson, 1963). Ryans (1960), for example, claimed that teachers were mild in their judgment of others, very interested in culture and art, loved to interact with children, and were flexible, independent and not aggressive. Although the research designs and lack of recommendations for improving the field were properly criticized, these analyses probably produced some common-sense truths.

Attitudes, as measured by questionnaires, appeared to be a slightly better predictor of teacher effectiveness than personality traits. For example, good and bad teachers appeared to divide over the amount of empathy and caring they showed. Teaching style also became an important focus of the effectiveness research. Lewin, Lippitt and White's work (1939) on authoritarian, democratic and *laissez faire* leadership was one of the original contributions in this area. Flanders' research (1970) into direct and indirect teaching style also belonged in this category. These studies documented teaching style on a molecular and molar level. By investigating teacher behaviors during very short (molecular) time periods and combining them into extended (molar) patterns, descriptions of teaching styles emerged.

In the 1960s and 1970s process-product research revealed teacher competencies and strategies at both the molecular and molar levels which contributed to student achievement. These investigations demonstrated how some teachers excel in asking questions, monitoring student progress, organizing and managing the classroom and building appropriate lesson structures.

Interpersonal Teacher Behavior

The process-product analyses primarily focused on the methodological aspect of teacher behavior. This refers to the plethora of technical strategies such as choice and organization of teaching materials and instructional methods, motivational strategies and assessment. There is another aspect of teacher behavior which we believe is equally important. It has to do with the interpersonal actions which create and maintain a positive classroom atmosphere. These two aspects of teacher behavior are interconnected. The methodological element is evident in an analysis of content presentation, whereas the interpersonal can be seen in the affective climate. Naturally, however, when a teacher lectures for an hour it usually has important consequences for the climate; similarly, when the class is racked by disorder, the methodological aspect is of little relevance. This interpersonal element is vitally important for beginning teachers, and sometimes becomes a prerequisite for their survival. If the quality of the classroom environment does not meet certain basic conditions the methodological aspect loses its significance.

As you probably noted from the title, this book will discuss interpersonal teacher behavior, or communication style. We want to emphasize at the outset that this is not a study of teacher personality, though some of the descriptions might'lend that impression. We may say that a particular teacher is friendly, caring or humorous, or that another is authoritarian, aggressive or dull. We use these expressions to refer to patterns of teacher behavior rather than to stable, unchangeable traits. While an interpersonal style describes someone's manner of interacting it is not the only way that he or she can behave. People's actions are also influenced by their partners in the communication. Thus, how someone behaves will vary across different relationships and depends on the interpersonal styles of the people involved. Leary (1957) has said that the person with the smallest behavioral repertoire will most influence the nature of the relationship that evolves. From modern research we know, however, that someone's behavior is a result of personality, attitudes and environmental factors (Magnusson and Endler, 1977). It is therefore obvious that any attempt to predict teachers' behavior and effectiveness solely on the basis of their characteristics will meet with little success.

Origin of the Book

Much of the work in this book originated from a long-term research project called 'Education for Teachers' at Utrecht University in The Netherlands. Since 1980, educational researchers in the United States, Australia and Israel have joined in this effort.

When the research began in the 1970s our main goal was to investigate beginning teachers' experiences in order to improve our pre-service program. We designed a project to examine the problems of beginning teachers (Hooymayers *et al.*, 1978). The results were in keeping with a meta-analysis of the induction literature published by Veenman (1984). Beginning teachers' problems with classroom discipline were well-known. What had not received much attention was their need and desire for guidance, caused by the lack of an induction strategy.

We therefore developed and offered to schools an induction program for beginning teachers. The offer included a request for collaboration in research activities to better understand the population. Because of our desire to improve teacher education we focused on teacher behavior rather than other factors that may contribute to beginning teachers' problems, such as poor school organization and heavy teaching loads. After extensive observations, interviews, analyses of supervision conferences and action research activities (Wubbels, Créton, and Hooymayers, 1987), we arrived at the idea that interpersonal behavior was a key factor in the discipline problems of beginning teachers.

In this book, interpersonal teacher behavior will be analyzed from the participants' viewpoints, and especially from the secondary students' perspective. This is in keeping with a series of studies of learning environment (e.g., Fraser, 1986). There are three basic reasons for measuring aspects of the learning environment through students' perceptions. First, many teacher behaviors only become meaningful when they are perceived as cues by the students (Winne and Marx, 1977). Students' perceptions can thus be considered an important mediator between instructional characteristics and academic achievement (Walberg, 1976). Next, students' perceptions generally provide insight into 'usual' teacher behavior (Borich and Klinzing, 1984), as compared to snapshot data gathered through observations. Finally, it is possible to measure more idiosyncratic features of teacher behavior through students' perceptions, since some signals that are familiar to students may not be measured by observational instruments (Helmke, Schneider and Weinert, 1986).

There is sufficient evidence that students' perceptions of the learning environment can be useful in educational research and teacher improvement (Fraser, 1986). Waxman and Eash (1983) refer, among others, to research by Peck, Blattstein and Fox (1978), Peck, Olsson and Green (1978) and Stallings, Needels and Stayrook (1979) which described experienced observers' and students' agreement on teacher-behavior ratings. From comparisons of teachers', students' and observers' perceptions, it appears that the students and observers usually agree, but they differ from teachers (Ehman, 1970; Steele, House and Kernins, 1971;

Hook and Rosenshine, 1979). Based on the similarity of students' perceptions and observational data Marsh (1984) concludes from several meta-analyses that class means of students' perceptions are reliable and reasonably valid.

Overview of the Book

The first two chapters provide a foundation for the empirical data on teacher-communication styles presented in Chapters 3 through 7. The first chapter introduces the systems perspective as the unifying framework by which we analyze teacher behavior. It explains the rationale for studying the communicative interchanges between students and teacher in class. Chapter 2 describes our adaptation of the Leary (1957) model of interpersonal behavior to educational settings. It relates how we developed the Questionnaire on Teacher Interaction (QTI) to gather students' and teachers' perceptions of teacher-communication style. Subsequent chapters describe how the instrument was employed to investigate students' and teachers' perceptions of interpersonal teacher behavior (Chapter 3), develop a typology of teacher communication styles (4), study the relationship between student achievement and teacher communication style (5), and compare students' and teachers' perceptions of actual and desired teacher behavior (6). Chapter 7 describes changes in behavior throughout a teacher's professional career.

The next segment of the book is devoted to the study of school climate and teacher education. Two studies of school environment are initially presented. Chapter 8 discusses the relationships between the quality of the school environment and teacher communication styles in class. Next comes an analysis of teachers' and principals' perceptions of principal communication style using an adaptation of the QTI called the Questionnaire on Principal Interaction (QPI). Chapter 9 discusses the use of the QPI to compare principal communication style and teachers' satisfaction.

Chapters 10 through 12 describe research in teacher education settings. The first (10) discusses how another adaptation of the QTI (QSI, or the Questionnaire on Supervisor Interaction) is used to analyze the communication style of co-operating teachers. Chapter 11 compares interpersonal relations in classes of student and cooperating teachers. The last chapter summarizes some previous research results and presents recommendations for teacher education programs.

The book is intended for various audiences. While statistical tables and terms appear, we tried to make them user-friendly by avoiding overly-technical language and using appendices for more complex explanations and tables. As a result, we did not always include F-values or degrees of freedom and some researchers may find less statistical detail than desired. We will be happy to furnish this information on request.

Theo Wubbels, Utrecht University Utrecht, The Netherlands
Jack Levy, George Masons University, Fairfax, Virginia USA.
October 1992.

Chapter 1

A Systems Perspective on Classroom Communication

Hans Créton, Theo Wubbels and Herman Hooymayers

In order to understand interpersonal communication it is important to examine the ecological or contextual system in which it occurs. In educational terms, the immediate context for teachers is the classroom. Their natural communication partners are, of course, students. This thinking led us to evaluate and adopt general systems theory as a basis to analyze classroom communication. Systems concepts have been usefully employed in family therapy (Watzlawick, Beavin and Jackson, 1967; Haley, 1963). Wubbels, Créton and Holvast (1988) demonstrated some of these ideas can be productively used in describing classroom situations.

By interpreting the class as a communication system this chapter illustrates a number of characteristics of teacher–student communication. Among these are cause and effect, which are the 'dead-ends' of the communication process; report and command, which describe the 'what' and 'how' of communication and are of great importance; not being able to 'not communicate'; symmetrical and complementary interaction, which refer to similar and dissimilar behaviors of teachers and students and the problems they embody; blindness, which is a characteristic of many beginning teachers; paradoxical injunctions, in which teachers undermine their intentions; and metacommunication, which is a way out of problematic communication.

Before we discuss the characteristics, however, we must introduce two concepts which help frame the entire discussion. Circularity and change refer to the interdependent relationship of all aspects in a communication system. This idea leads to the second concept, which is the focus on teacher behavior as the most pragmatic point by which to analyze — and change — the learning environment.

Circularity and Change

The concepts of circularity and change are central to an understanding of systems theory and help describe all other characteristics. Circularity implies that all aspects of a system are intertwined. Changes in one will not only affect the others, but will then return like ripples of water moving between river banks. Thus, circular communication processes develop which not only *consist* of behavior but which *determine* behavior as well. The nature of any system, then, is greatly affected by its response — and in some cases, resistance — to change.

Classes are characterized by stability, resistance to change and circular processes. Teachers seek stability to provide sound instruction, as can be seen in the use of words like 'routines' and 'rituals' (Yinger, 1980; Au and Kawakami, 1984). These can be quite desirable, in that they help to protect the class from interruption, increase predictability and reduce ambiguity (Yinger, 1980; Shavelson, 1983). They can also be undesirable and not supportive of student achievement. Once stability has been established (whether positive or negative) both teachers and students seem hesitant to change (Blumenfeld and Meece, 1985; Doyle, 1983). The first day of school seems to set the trend for the rest of the year, and once the pattern is set it is difficult to modify (Brooks, 1985).

The presence of circularity can be inferred from Doyle's (1983) analysis of teacher–student communication as a process of negotiation. He proposes that teacher behavior in classrooms is probably produced by teacher–student interaction and is shaped by the demands of securing student cooperation. Since teacher behavior also *influences* teacher–student interactions the process is circular. Circularity continues over the life of the communication. People who are communicating continually exchange messages in response to earlier messages, even if there is an interruption of minutes, hours or days. If we haven't seen each other in some time, we simply 'pick up where we left off'. This makes it impossible to assign a beginning to the communication, unless we consider its entire history. Since communication consists of series of consecutive messages, therefore, the teacher's behavior is not only *caused* by students' actions, but also *confirms* them.

Focus on Teacher Behavior

A unique feature of the systems perspective is its refusal to seek out individual motives in problem situations. As will be discussed below, the notion of circularity and continual communication makes it difficult to identify beginning and end in teacher–student interaction. While we may be able to figure out who started what, the information is generally useless for the solution. The systems' perspective doesn't attempt to figure out why, either, since it doesn't place much importance on the individual motives of participants. Teacher–student relationships are not deduced from psychosocial backgrounds, but are seen as outcomes of a classroom system in which both teacher and students take part.

This behavioral orientation allows the systems perspective to deal with problems in the most pragmatic fashion, one which causes the system the least trauma. In terms of classroom problems, therefore, it leads to a focus on the teacher's behavior rather than the students', since it is easier to change one person instead of twenty-five. Campbell (1974) demonstrated the importance of teacher behavior to class character by analyzing classes which stayed together but had different teachers for each subject. The students were described as varying from 'a pack of hungry half-starved wolves with the math and English teachers, to docile lambs with their science teacher'.

Who's to Blame?

In general, researchers have only recently begun to reflect on teacher behaviors with regard to problems in the learning environment. Much of the research on undesirable classroom situations views misbehavior as a student characteristic or the result of poor management techniques (Doyle, 1986). Teachers usually think that students are to blame for most class disturbances, and cite various psychosocial reasons (Brophy and Rohrkemper, 1981; Metz, 1978; Sanford and Evertson, 1981; Sieber, 1979; Tikunoff and Ward, 1978, all in Doyle, 1986).

As we've implied, it's unreasonable to single out students for blame, since class-communication problems are the result of both students' and teachers' behavior. Wubbels, Créton and Holvast (1988) analyzed classes in which problem students were either absent or had permanently left. They found that often after an initial period of relief (for the teacher), someone else became the 'trouble maker'. In fact, the new problem student frequently displayed the same behaviors as the original. They concluded that misbehavior can't be attributed to a particular student. Communication situations seem to have an identity, or life of their own. If the basic behaviors of participants don't change (i.e., the character of the stability remains the same) and someone leaves, another will take his or her place. This explains why a new trouble maker appears just when the teacher believes his or her problems are over. The Wubbels, *et al.* finding corroborates similar results from family therapy research (Haley, 1971).

The phenomenon of 'blaming the other guy' is not uncommon, and can be explained in terms of 'punctuation'. When people punctuate communication sequences they figuratively provide 'full stops' (beginnings-ends) and 'commas' (pauses) regarding their own ideas and imagine similar punctuations in their partner's messages (Watzlawick, Beavin and Jackson, 1967, p. 54). People interpret punctuations differently and this naturally leads to differing opinions about which behavior is cause and which is effect. People in these situations — in our case teachers and students — may experience 'punctuation problems'. An example would be the teacher whose classroom is noted for its aggressive atmosphere. She feels the students aren't performing well because of their misbehavior, and as a result grades them harshly. Students, on the other hand, feel that their inattention and subsequent low grades come as a result of her confusing presentations.

When punctuation problems occur, teachers and students do not differ as to whether or how certain events took place. They tend to disagree about cause, effect and blame. Most believe it's the other's fault (since he/she/they started it), which is usually an unproductive line of reasoning.

Report and Command Aspects

Every form of communication has a *report* and a *command* aspect (Watzlawick, Beavin and Jackson, 1967). The report can be understood as the *what*, and the command as the *how* of communication. The report conveys the content, information, or description; the command carries instructions about how to interpret the report (Ruesch and Bateson, 1968 in LaFrance and Mayo, 1978). In a class, teacher and students relate in ways which are outside the subject matter (report) and often exist through non-verbal means (Woolfolk and Brooks, 1983; Blumenfeld and Meece, 1985; Stubbs, 1976).

Both the report and command aspects of the communication are closely interwoven. If a teacher is enthusiastic and captivating, or if he or she grades harshly, this will influence the teacher–student relationship. Likewise, students' curiosity about subject matter is aroused when teachers are willing to assist and encourage them (Deci, Nezlek and Sheinman, 1981). Clearly, the manner in which a teacher deals with each student influences motivation (de Bruyn, 1979). In addition, the same report message can affect students differently depending on the accompanying command aspect. For example, Marshall and Weinstein (1986) demonstrate that a behavior such as pointing out student mistakes can carry different underlying messages about student ability. One command interpretation might be 'I want to help you to learn'. A quite different translation, however, is also possible: 'You are too stupid to learn.'

Because the command-level communication is often ambiguous, it's important to analyze the nature of messages. Besides spoken words, the teacher–student relationship manifests itself non-verbally through bearing, gesture, facial expression, intonation, sound level, articulation and context, among other indicators. When a teacher doesn't consciously think about the report and command aspects of his or her message, students might react in a way that is different from the teacher's intentions, as in the following example:

A teacher was trying to restrain a student disturbance. With a cracking voice and flushed face he yelled: 'Anyone who says another damn thing has to copy twenty-five pages from the book and will report to the principal.' One student responded with: 'I thought you weren't allowed to curse', which was followed by an outburst of laughing from the other students.

At the report level the teacher indicated that the students ought to be afraid of him because of his power to punish them. At the command level, however, students probably interpreted his cracking voice as a sign of impotence. The content of the message was powerful and terror-inspiring. The command aspect, however, communicated the opposite: that the teacher was in danger of losing his grip on the situation. The student's reaction was therefore understandable. Though the teacher wanted to define the students' interpretation by the content of his message, he was not able to do so.

The command aspect of students' communications can also be ambiguous. Occasionally students will be full of questions about a particular subject. Their behavior might indicate a genuine interest in the subject, or something quite different — a desire to divert the teacher's attention from something else, like homework or a quiz. In analyzing problematic communication patterns it is almost always more profitable to concentrate on the command aspects of the interaction rather than the report.

The following example once again shows how the command aspect can be communicated subconsciously.

While the teacher makes a presentation, two students in the back quietly talk about something which has nothing to do with the subject. The teacher sees the students but continues his explanation. A few minutes later two other students start to converse. The teacher tells them to shut up, whereupon the irritated students call his attention to this inconsistency.

Here the teacher initially continues with the lesson. The report aspect of his message concerns the subject, but at the command level the students interpret his initial inaction as tacit acceptance of their non-participation. Other students, then, may have even interpreted this as an invitation to start talking. In any case, the subconscious transmission of an unintended message has created a conflict.

Teachers who have difficulty with class management often send mixed messages which deliver conflicting impressions at the report and command levels. An example would be a teacher who continually contradicts what he or she has just said by repeatedly warning students 'for the last time' while pronouncing the most terrible threats. Or, the teacher who indignantly says to a student: 'You just do as you like. I don't care whether you pay attention or not. You're only hurting yourself'. Here, the verbal message says 'I grant you permission' while the non-verbal says 'absolutely not!' Such conflicting communication usually has a negative effect on the person addressed (Waxler and Mishler, 1970; Haley, 1973).

The need to distinguish between the report and command levels is especially important in beginning relationships. This is for example true for first-year teachers, who are often confronted by students 'trying them out' (Brooks, 1985). The students basically want to know what the teacher will and will not permit. This process chiefly takes place at the command level, below the surface of their communication about the subject taught. This can be seen in the following example.

The teacher comes in. It is very noisy. She stands in front of the first desk in the middle row and looks at the class. Nobody reacts. She hesitates. Finally, she says: 'Take out your books, please. Exercise six.' Most students ignore her and continue talking. The teacher approaches two students in the front by the window. They are obviously doing something they should not do. After talking with them for a moment she resumes her original position: 'Exercise six, page fifty-seven' she says, raising her voice. Nobody reacts, but she continues unperturbed. 'Okay, the first sentence? Jim, you take the first sentence'. 'The first sentence?' he asks, as if she's said something very odd. 'Exercise six, page fifty-seven' whisper the students around him. Laughing, he reads the first paragraph. It is about a father who does not want his son to be treated by different doctors. The paragraph tries to create an analogy between medical specialists treating a patient and garage mechanics treating engines. When different mechanics would put different kinds of oil in the father's engine it would invariably break down.

'What is your conclusion?', the teacher asks. 'They must be using the wrong oil.' Great hilarity. 'No, they should have put more oil in him', says another. A few more of these remarks follow, but the teacher does not respond. Outwardly unconcerned, she looks at the class. She does not share their amusement, but neither does she resist it. 'Bart, what have you got?' she says to one of the students who is the noisiest laugher.

'Lemme look for my answer.' Of course, he can't find it. The question is directed to somebody else and the teacher finally gets a serious answer.

This pattern continues — teacher asks question, students joke around, teacher tries to ignore it until she finds a student willing to cooperate.

The command aspect predominates in nearly every student response. It seems as if they are continually telling each other and the teacher that 'I don't take this exercise seriously; I'll just ignore the teacher'. The answers not only indicate how students see their relationship with the teacher, but also act as an element in defining their own relationship. They derive their status from the competition to see who is the funniest. The teacher ignores messages from students at command level and only reacts to the content of the sentences. Because both sides stress a different communication level and thus talk at cross-purposes, they can also associate with each other in a relatively peaceful way and avoid confrontation. To properly assess the meaning of students' answers, teachers should focus on such non-verbal behaviors as voice, facial expression and bearing. This is usually more informative than the content aspect of students' responses if the communication is problematic.

Healthy relationships between people are characterized by communication which is more report than command-based (Watzlawick, Beavin and Jackson, 1967). When things aren't going that well, however, there is a constant struggle over the meaning of command-level messages, and the content aspect becomes less important (p. 52). Generally, this implies the predominance of non-verbal behaviors over verbal. Thus, when educational research is conducted in laboratories the verbal part of teacher behavior appears to explain more variance in student reactions than the non-verbal. In more natural settings, however, the non-verbal channel prevails. This may be due to the nature of the lab settings, where the relationship is generally pronounced and healthy.

We normally think of the command aspect of teacher communication being delivered with a gesture or other immediate non-verbal behavior. The way it is received actually depends on the history of the relationship, or the accumulation of all student and teacher molecular behaviors. This can include things which are below the surface, such as the choice of textbooks or the development of tests. When the curriculum is not presented clearly or instructional activities are difficult, students may begin to think they lack ability. In this way the command aspect also provides information about how communicators see themselves and each other.

Attempting the Impossible — Not Communicating

The teacher in the last example, like so many beginning teachers, tried to communicate solely on the basis of the subject matter. This attempt to avoid command-level interaction is doomed to failure, since it is present in all human communication (Woolfolk and Brooks, 1983). Not communicating at the command level would amount to not behaving (which, if two or more people are present, amounts to not breathing). As Watzlawick and his associates said '. . . one cannot NOT communicate' (p. 51). Thus, sending messages at the command level cannot be avoided. Further, every command-level behavior influences the recipient, even though its meaning isn't explained by the sender. An attempt by the teacher not to communicate may be interpreted by students as the teacher showing a one-sided interest in his or her subject and a corresponding lack of interest in them. Or, it may also be interpreted as evidence of the inability to talk to students, which was probably the case in the last example.

Doyle (1984) reported that successful junior high-school teachers tended to push on through the curriculum and did not let misbehavior become a central focus. This often meant that some rules were not enforced and the level of inappropriate behavior was occasionally high. Interventions to correct disruptive behavior are inherently risky because they call attention to potentially disruptive behavior. The teacher, in effect, risks sending the message that 'if you want to get attention you must misbehave' (Doyle, 1986). One should not deduce from this, however, that it is preferable to ignore undesirable behavior. Non-intervention is also risky because it transmits a message to students that misbehavior is acceptable. Thus, teachers continually face a dilemma. Those who are successful resolve it through effective management. They assure order and learning by clarifying goals and objectives, choosing motivational activities, anticipating potential misbehavior and catching it early (Kounin, 1970; Emmer, Evertson and Anderson, 1980; Evertson and Emmer, 1982).

Symmetrical and Complementary Interaction

Watzlawick, Beavin and Jackson characterize communication as either symmetrical or complementary (1967, p. 70). Symmetry implies that the behavior of one person is followed by the same kind of behavior in his or her partner. Complementary means that the two are behaving differently, in a more contrary manner. Both are part of life in a normal classroom. Sometimes a teacher will discipline a student who breaks a rule. Both would then be engaged in the same oppositional behavior. On the other hand, students and teacher might cooperate in the teaching–learning enterprise, showing both friendly and supportive behavior.

Classrooms are mostly characterized by complementary communication (example: active teacher, passive students). This is basically due to the different power positions of teacher and students in the school system. The teacher is the expert, the adult, the one who is responsible; the student is still learning, and only has a limited amount of responsibility. The teacher teaches, assesses and punishes; the student is taught, is assessed and is punished.

Both the symmetry and complementary aspects may lead to difficulties. Symmetrical communication may induce escalation and complementary can result in intensification and rigidity. An example of a symmetrical communication was the above description in which the 'cursing' teacher's anger was met with equal defiance from students. The behaviors on both sides seemed to escalate, with no resolution in sight. Beginning teachers frequently become involved in these types of communication patterns. They get caught in a vicious cycle with students in which both sides symmetrically intensify each other's behavior. Searching for culprits doesn't help. Only by changing our own behavior can we affect the behavior of the other person and thus break the destructive spiral. Sometimes the aggressive behaviors are identical, as when both the teacher and student grab the same book. The teacher thinks that he or she has the right and duty to confiscate the book because the student is constantly drawing pictures in it. The student in turn takes the view that the teacher should not touch his or her property. This identical behavior then escalates as aggression is met by aggression.

When the teacher's and students' positions are complementary there is the possibility that they can intensify each other. If, for example, the teacher and students have not formed a stable relationship the teacher will probably act in a dominant manner. This, more than likely, will result in student passivity and dependence. The teacher may not be satisfied with the passive student behavior, and become even more actively dominant. This would lead to even greater student submission. The teacher's dominant behavior can then be seen as both cause and result of students' dependent behavior. The more the teacher dominates the less students participate. An example of this complementary intensified communication can be seen in the case of the teacher who asks a question, doesn't wait long enough, and then answers it himself or herself. Whether they eventually arrive at an acceptable equilibrium depends on teachers' flexibility as classroom leaders and motivators. If they are not flexible enough the situation can evolve into rigidity. Teachers must be able to balance the level of their domination and student submission. If the balance doesn't include enough dominant behavior they can lose their job.

We have observed teachers who, having been involved with students in an extended complementary communication pattern, have changed in style from supportive to corrective and rigid. Such a teacher is John.

> John was very clear about what he expected of students and what they should expect from him. Students knew where they stood with him, what rules and what norms they had to comply with in his lessons, to what misbehaviors he reacted and how he reacted to them. Students weren't mischievous in class. John's students were relatively cooperative, but mostly submissive and passive, and he came to expect students to behave in this way. For some reason, over time he became less tolerant towards the exceptional student who misbehaved. In addition (or as an indication of his reduced tolerance) his understanding of what is 'usual' for students shifted. He began to disproportionately judge minor student misbehavior as major, and reacted more severely to these indiscretions. The passive behavior of the students that had first exemplified a desirable complementary relationship consequently helped the teacher become more severe. The teacher's increasingly dominant behavior required, in turn, more passive and dependent behavior from students, so that John became more harsh and students more frightened and passive. John might flare up when a student didn't take out his book at the beginning of the lesson. He also disregarded the bell and took a lot of time to finish the class and assign homework. A student who began to get his books together after the bell had the teacher reprimand him because of this 'impertinence'.

Harper, Scorceby and Boyce (1977) and Lederer and Jackson (1968) have shown how important it is to develop flexible behavior patterns in families. The analogy to classrooms is clear — teacher and students should develop varied interaction patterns and try not to get tangled in unproductive complementary or symmetrical behaviors. Teachers must be especially sensitive to the effects of their communication strategies on student behaviors. If things don't work it's time to try something else, even if it seems to run counter to common sense and will radically break the communication pattern. These changes can only emerge, however, as a result of the teacher's realization of the futility of continuing with the initial strategy.

An example is Helen, a beginning teacher who graded students more on their misbehavior than achievement and was overly severe in discipline. She was caught in an escalating situation where her students responded to her negativity with increasing non-participation and aggression. Finally, Helen realizes that punishment doesn't work, and she decides she has to try something else. She starts giving better grades whenever possible. This breaks the pattern and things begin to improve. She begins to make concessions in situations of little importance, like a student asking to be excused. Her flexibility saves the day.

Blindness

Classroom visitors are occasionally astonished to observe lessons in which teachers (frequently in their first year) seem to be completely unaware of what's going on. The following example describes a situation in which the teacher seems to be 'blind'.

Fred often loses himself in the content of the lesson. He lectures most of the time, although his students also talk a lot. He can often be observed yelling above the din, turned toward the blackboard, oblivious to what is happening behind him. As Fred gets louder, his students realize they can't hear themselves, and so they speak louder too. This leads to louder and faster teacher talk, less eye contact and greater confusion. It thus becomes more and more difficult for students who do want to listen, to understand the teacher. Ultimately, only a few students in front succeed in paying attention and the teacher becomes the only one left interested in the subject.

In this situation it seems as if the whole class is passing the teacher by. He manages to isolate himself and pretend to be blind and deaf. Such a situation may also occur when students are working individually. Teachers can avoid the rest of the class by intensively occupying themselves with one student. The greater the disorder, the closer they sit to the student, the louder and longer they talk with him or her and the more they turn their backs to the other students.

Blindness can escalate. The more the teacher turns a blind eye to the disorder, the greater that disorder becomes. Amazingly, the teacher reacts to the increasing disorder by increasing his blindness. Frequent blindness in a teacher can be dangerous, since a fundamental requirement of instruction is to maintain order. Good managers are 'withit' — they know nearly everything that goes on in the room. Blindness can be a fatal threat to this crucial skill (Kounin, 1970; Doyle, 1984; Smith and Geoffrey, 1968; Emmer, Evertson and Anderson, 1980; Evertson and Emmer, 1982).

When teachers who demonstrate blindness are confronted with this behavior by supervisors they are often astonished. Not only are they blind to what is happening, but they also think that they have nothing to do with it. 'It just happens', they often say.

Why do some teachers behave this way? What benefit can be gained? Blindness allows them to avoid a confrontation with the disorder and with corresponding feelings of helplessness. The confrontation would force them to face a situation they cannot cope with nor escape from. Every now and then, however, the confrontation cannot be avoided, as in the case of Helen. The disorder in her class frequently escalated to a point where she exploded at students. She then punished them severely for relatively unimportant misbehavior. She exhibited what we call the 'tea-kettle effect'. Thus, the primary gain from blindness is fear reduction. There is, however another benefit (Kanfer and Saslow, 1965; Liberman, 1970). Often a stable equilibrium eventually occurs, in which both parties allow each other to have their own way. The teacher is occupied with subject matter and allows most of the students to do something else. Their behavior, however, does not provoke the teacher and thus a livable, stable situation is created. Unfortunately, it may not be productive.

Paradoxical Injunction

Paradoxical injunctions come from the 'be spontaneous' contradiction. For example, one spouse tells the other 'You never buy me presents'. The statement essentially communicates a desire for the spouse to buy presents *spontaneously*. Naturally, he or she cannot comply, since the spontaneity has been ruined by the statement. Thus faced with a non-response to his or her request, the original spouse becomes even more unhappy.

In a paradoxical injunction, the first party demands behavior (or makes an injunction) which he or she believes the second should do spontaneously. When the second party does not (and cannot) respond spontaneously, the first party reacts negatively. The second party then reacts in a docile, non-spontaneous manner — exactly the opposite of the original intention. Paradoxical injunctions have extremely negative effects in relationships marked by unequal power. They can paralyze the person on the bottom, since he or she can neither obey the injunction nor step outside its framework (Watzlawick, Beavin and Jackson, 1967, p. 194).

It is not uncommon, for example, for teachers to blame students for not admiring what the teacher admires: literature, art, etc. The teacher might enforce his or her demands to admire literature, for example, by taking the students' attitudes toward literature into account in grades. The more the teacher demands, the less the students can respond spontaneously. Ironically, the demands actually prevent the gratification. The teacher's authority ensures that students cannot withdraw from the situation nor discuss their problem with him or her (which might be perceived as 'impudence'). Further, if students try to escape by falling in love with literature, for example, there's a chance the teacher won't trust them because of the history.

Students can also create paradoxical injunctions. For example, they can criticize the teacher for allowing disruptions and urge him or her to be more strict. When the teacher complies it's difficult for him or her to be effective because the students don't take it seriously, since they made the assignment. They often remind the teacher why he or she is behaving in a more dominant manner.

Metacommunication

An indication of a teacher's flexibility is a willingness to engage in metacommunication, or a discussion with one's partner about the status of their communication. A teacher may realize that the communication patterns aren't productive and decide to talk it over with students. Again, Helen provides us with an example:

> In order to improve her relationship with difficult students, Helen begins to see them after class. At first they continue fighting, and everyone engages in a lot of finger-pointing. In time, the conversations become more positive. In one such conversation Helen and one of the students talk about the situation at the girl's home. Helen offers to help with her problems in English. She relates the following:

> 'When the others had left, I asked her what she thought of her own behavior in class. Whether that was normal. No, she didn't think it was normal. I had quite a talk with her. She told me that she hated English and often did not understand it. At home her parents were very strict. Her father actually teaches English and he checks everything. I said: "When you have problems at home you should tell me, otherwise I'll never know. Tell me and we can review the part you don't understand." Things got better right away.'

Criteria for Healthy Relationships

From the foregoing examples a number of criteria for healthy classroom relationships have emerged. People who are communicating in a healthy manner:

1 Send consistent report and command messages.
2 Communicate more in a report than command-based manner.
3 Are flexible; they're open to change their communication patterns.
4 Behave according to what the situation calls for, rather than force a change in the context.
5 Do not exhibit pathological extremes — they seem moderate in their communication style.
6 Agree with their partners about punctuations (beginnings, ends, pauses).
7 Understand how they are being perceived by their partners.
8 Are able to change their communication style through metacommunication.

Conclusion

This chapter has tried to apply the systems-communication perspective to teacher–student communication. In addressing class situations the approach transfers the point of impact from an individual student (who is often considered to be the source of problems) to the teacher. It is primarily interested in analyzing the manner in which certain communication patterns cause particular student reactions, either positive or negative. The question 'why does this student behave this way?' thus changes to 'why does he or she behave this way in my class?', before finally becoming 'which feature of my teaching behavior contributes to the student behaving this way?' Through this reformulation student behavior (especially problem student behavior) becomes more teacher-oriented and thus easier to cope with.

In its emphasis on report and command-level messages, the systems' perspective strongly invites us to analyze subliminal, non-verbal teacher behaviors, or the 'style' over the 'substance'. This isn't normal for teachers, who are mostly trained to emphasize the content-level, or verbal, communication. This is why beginning teachers are able to communicate at the report level more effectively than at command level.

Prolonged research is needed to fully understand classroom communication from the systems perspective. To be successful, it is essential to isolate and analyze patterns which extend over a number of lessons. Considering the importance of context for the interpretation of behavior (Woolfolk and Brooks, 1983; Cazden, 1986), this type of research has to take place in real class situations. Thus, data would need to be collected in the form of participants' perspectives, observation narratives or running accounts of classroom events and processes.

In the introduction we provided a rationale for analyzing students' and teachers' perceptions of the learning environment. We believe this is an economical way to gather data on classroom communication patterns and this approach is used in the remaining chapters. We will first describe the development of a questionnaire and then report on its implementation. In some of the studies this data will be augmented by participant interviews and observations to broaden the research perspective.

Chapter 2

The Model for Interpersonal Teacher Behavior

Theo Wubbels, Hans Créton, Jack Levy and Herman Hooymayers

The Leary Model

Once our interest in the interpersonal aspect of teacher behavior was established, we needed a model to frame our analysis. It had to conform to a number of criteria:

1   Enable educators to observe and analyze interpersonal teacher behavior.
2   Provide a basis for instrument development to gather data on inter-personal behavior.
3   Provide a 'language' to describe the relationship between students and teachers.
4   Help educators become aware of the systems communication perspective in the classroom, described in the previous chapter. This would enable us to understand the effects which teachers and students have on each other's behavior.
5   Facilitate teacher development based on both teaching competencies and personality.
6   Explain the relationship between short-term 'molecular' teacher behavior and long-term communication style.

Our initial search through the education literature was unsuccessful, however, since most instruments on teacher behavior focus on instructional-methodological aspects (Simon and Boyer, 1974). They describe teaching behaviors such as planning, class management, evaluation, and the like. Others, such as the Tuckman Teacher Feedback Form (Tuckman and Yates, 1980) are not firmly rooted in a theory on interpersonal behavior.

Clinical psychology, however, offered several possible avenues (Bales, 1970). We eventually adopted a model developed by Leary (1957) which describes and measures specific interpersonal behaviors. We were gratified to note that Leary's work in this field has been repeatedly corroborated throughout the world (Lonner, 1980).

A product of extended, empirical research in clinical psychology, the Leary model places personality at the heart of interpersonal behavior. Leary believes that the way humans communicate is indicative of their personality. Along with other psychologists, he feels that the most important forces driving human behavior are the reduction of fear and corresponding maintenance of self-esteem. When people communicate they therefore consciously or unconsciously choose behaviors which avoid anxiety and allow them to feel good about themselves. These, of course, differ for each person and depend upon the personality of the communicating partner. One individual might choose an authoritarian style, whereas another prefers dependency to achieve the same end. Or, one might act friendly while the other seems unhappy. If successful in avoiding anxiety, people will perform similar behaviors to prolong the effect, thus developing certain patterns of communication. These patterns depend on the personalities of everyone who is interacting. Leary believed that people with the smallest behavioral repertoire — often those who were hospitalized for mental reasons — have the greatest control of the communication. Thus, a man who seems continually angry will cultivate anger in most people he talks with.

Leary constructed a model that made it possible to measure both normal and abnormal behavior on the same scale, and he was therefore able to apply it both inside and outside the clinic. As a result, his instrument has been used not only as a diagnostic tool in psychotherapy but also in the analysis of management behavior and other settings.

Leary and his co-workers analyzed hundreds of patient–therapist dialogues and group discussions in clinical and other situations. They then divided the discourse into short statements representing different kinds of interpersonal behavior. These were then coded and arranged into sixteen categories which, over time, were reduced to eight. These eight can be presented in a two-dimensional plane (see Figure 2.1). We've labelled the two dimensions Proximity (Cooperation–Opposition) and Influence (Dominance–Submission). The Proximity dimension designates the degree of cooperation or closeness between those who are communicating. Leary called this continuum the 'Affection–Hostility' axis. The Influence dimension indicates who is directing or controlling the communication, and how often. Leary also used the term Dominance–Submission to describe the continuum of behaviors in the Influence dimension.

As mentioned, the Leary model has held up well under testing in psychological research settings (e.g., Foa, 1961). While the Proximity and Influence dimensions have occasionally been called other names — Brown (1985), used Status and Solidarity, and Dunkin and Biddle (1974), used Warmth and Directivity — they have generally been accepted as universal descriptors of human interaction. The two dimensions have also transferred easily to education. Slater (1962) used them to effectively describe pedagogical relationships, and Dunkin and Biddle (1974) demonstrated their importance in teachers' efforts to influence classroom events.

Occasionally researchers have found additional dimensions. They have been described in a variety of ways, such as level of activation, intensity, dedication, independence, activity and inferiority (Carson, 1969; Bales, 1970; Lonner, 1980; Brown, 1965; Briar and Bieri, 1963). After a prolonged search for this additional element we concluded that its appearance can actually be caused by measurement error. Brekelmans (1989) and Wubbels, Créton, Brekelmans and Hooymayers (1987) found that factor analyses performed on data with a very small measurement

Figure 2.1: The Coordinate System of the Leary Model

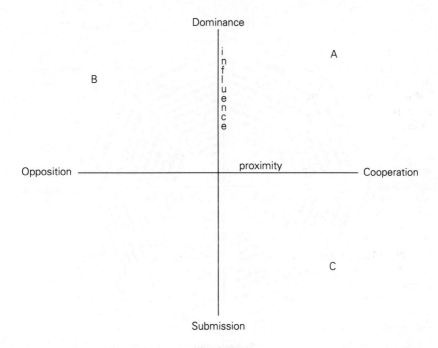

error (i.e., collected from a large number of students) yielded two dimensions, whereas three emerged when fewer students and larger errors were present.

Adaptation of the Leary Model

The Leary model allows for a graphic representation of all human interaction. The behavior of both (or all) parties in a discussion can be recorded on the chart according to how cooperative they are, who is controlling the discussion and to what degree. Let's imagine a dialogue between a parent and a child on the subject of crossing the street. As the parent explains the process she is engaging in Dominant behavior, since she is controlling the communication. If her explanation is presented in a patient, comfortable manner her behavior would also be highly Cooperative. Thus, she would be displaying high Dominant — high Co-operative behavior. This is indicated by an 'A' in Figure 2.1. If, however, the child has just nearly been run over by a bus the parent is likely to be agitated and possibly angry. She might even scream at the child to be more careful. Her communication in this case would still be Dominant but also highly Oppositional, as indicated by a 'B' in Fig. 2.1.

The child's behavior can also be graphed. In the first instance, if he is patiently listening he would be High Submissive/High Cooperative on the chart, or 'C'. If he believes that the bus was at fault in the second example and presents a strenuous defense against the parent's outburst, he would also be engaging in Oppositional behavior. If an argument ensues, the two would probably exchange turns dominating the communication. This is one of the keys to the Leary model

Figure 2.2: The Model for Interpersonal Teacher Behavior

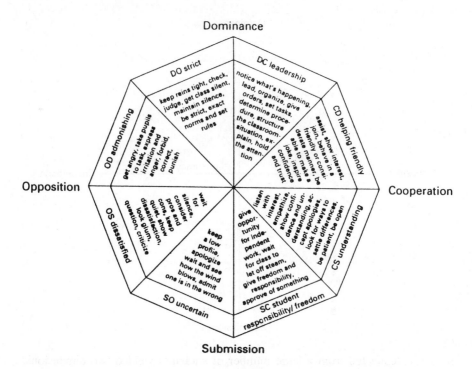

— communication *behaviors* continually change. Communication *styles* emerge only after a great many behaviors have occurred and been observed.

Another example may help to explain the concept of graphing human inter-action. We, the authors, are currently communicating (we hope) with you, the reader. We are controlling the communication by presenting information to you. Our behavior is therefore highly Dominant; since we want you to understand the Leary model we are trying to be highly Cooperative as well. You, on the other hand, must remain silent (for now). Your behavior can then be termed highly submissive. If you decide that you must speak with us and call on the phone, you become more Dominant with each suggestion you provide. If you tell us you love the model you are being Cooperative; if you think we've made a dreadful mistake you become more Oppositional.

In Figure 2.2 we begin to see how the model translates to the classroom. The figure provides examples of the different types of interpersonal behaviors dis-played by teachers. The eight equal sectors are labelled DC, CD, etc. according to their position in the coordinate system (much like the directions on a com-pass). For example, the two sectors DC and CD are both characterized by Domin-ance and Cooperation. In the DC sector, however the Dominance aspect prevails over the Cooperation aspect. Thus, a teacher displaying DC behavior might be explaining something to the class, organizing groups, making assignments, and the like. The adjacent CD sector includes behaviors of a more cooperative and less dominant character, and the teacher might be seen assisting students, or

Figure 2.3: The Model for Interpersonal Student Behavior

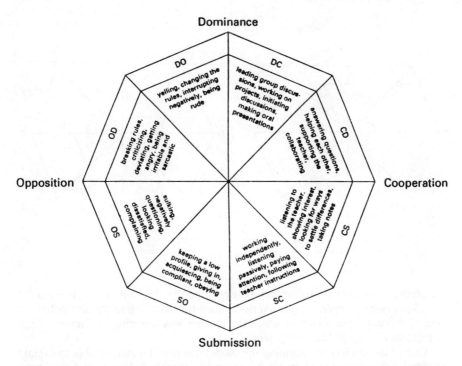

acting friendly or considerate. The sections of the model describe eight different behavior aspects: Leadership (DC), Helpful/Friendly (CD), Understanding (CS), Student Responsibility/Freedom (SC), Uncertain (SO), Dissatisfied (OS), Admonishing (OD) and Strict (DO).

The model can also be used to map the behavior of students, as can be seen in Figure 2.3.

Classroom Observations

The Leary model presented in Figure 2.2 can be used as the basis for an observation instrument to describe a teacher's classroom behavior. This mirrors one of Leary's own techniques in collecting data. It can be done in several ways:

1 The model can be transformed into a checklist. During a lesson, every time a teacher changes his or her behavior from one sector to another a check can be recorded.

2 The checklist can be employed on a time sampling basis, with the observer recording a behavior after a consistent interval, e.g., thirty seconds, one minute, etc.

3 The lesson can be recorded on audio or videotape. Each of the teacher's sentences can be coded and recorded according to the eight sectors.

For 2 and 3 the number of sentences can be added to get a sector score. These sums can then be represented in a profile.

Figure 2.4: Observational Data: Teacher's and Students' Behavior for a Lesson in Which the Teacher Is Lecturing

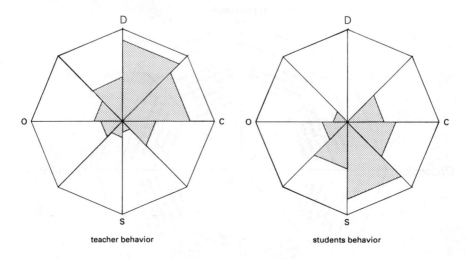

teacher behavior   students behavior

Student behavioral profiles can be developed in the same ways. Figures 2.4 and 2.5 provide examples of observational data for teacher and student behavior. Figure 2.4 describes a lesson in which the teacher was lecturing; in Figure 2.5 the students were engaged in group work.

One of the criteria for adopting the model was that it would be able to explain the relationship between short-term 'molecular' teacher behavior and long-term communication style. 'Molecular' behaviors are the descriptive, isolated behaviors which last only a few seconds or minutes, such as explaining a term, calling on a student to answer, and the like. As mentioned, people's communication behaviors continually change according to the situation and personalities of those involved. An observation of a lesson using the Leary model would therefore not describe a teacher's interpersonal style. This could only be established after an observational period which was long enough to discern repetitions, or patterns, of molecular behaviors. Once the observations are repeated frequently over time, the 'molecular' evolves into the 'molar', or extended behaviors which comprise communication style. Thus, we would begin to understand how a teacher facilitates student responses or establishes rapport.

The Questionnaire on Teacher Interaction

While the overall model seemed to fit classroom situations, we needed an instrument which could provide reliable data on interpersonal teacher behavior. Leary's own instrument, the Interpersonal Adjective Checklist (ICL, Laforge and Suczek, 1955) proved to be unwieldy for use with teachers and students. As a result, the Questionnaire on Teacher Interaction (QTI) evolved in the early 1980s from the ICL (Créton and Wubbels, 1984; Wubbels, Créton and Hooymayers, 1985; Brekelmans, 1989). Appendix 2.1 describes the evolution of the QTI from Leary's

Figure 2.5: *Observational Data: Teacher's and Students' Behavior for a Lesson in Which Students Are Engaged in Group Work*

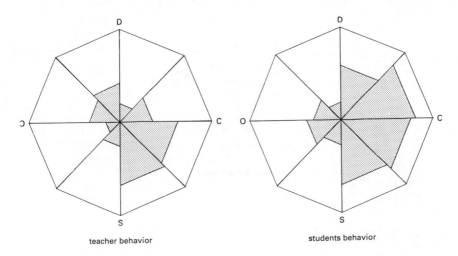

teacher behavior   students behavior

Interpersonal Adjective Checklist. An American version was developed in the late 1980s (Wubbels and Levy, 1991).

The Dutch version of the QTI was completed after four trial runs. It was tested and revised on the basis of focus groups with students and teachers, oral responses to sample items and corresponding statistical analyses. Each statement was correlated with all the scales of the questionnaire. Items were chosen or reworded to correlate highest with their own scale and lowest (highest negative) with the opposite scale in the model. Figure 2.6 presents the correlations for a CD (Helpful/Friendly) item which was ultimately included in the QTI. The figure also includes the correlations of an SC (Student Responsibility/Freedom) item which had to be reworded. In the first pilot it correlated highest with the CS (Understanding) scale instead of SC. We then changed the wording from 'S/he gives you freedom' to 'You have freedom in his/her class', and the correlation pattern improved considerably.

The QTI is divided into eight scales which conform to the eight sectors of the model. In the Dutch version each sector scale consists of about ten items (seventy-seven in total) which are answered on a five-point Likert scale. The American version has sixty-four items and a similar response scale (see Appendix 2.2). Table 2.1 presents a typical item for each sector scale and the number of items in each sector.

Reliability and Validity of the QTI

Several studies have been conducted on the reliability and validity of the QTI. They have included Dutch (e.g., Créton and Wubbels, 1984; Wubbels, Créton and Hooymayers 1985; Wubbels, Brekelmans and Hermans, 1987; Brekelmans, Wubbels and Créton, 1990; Brekelmans, 1989), American (Wubbels and Levy, 1991) and Australian (Fisher, Fraser and Wubbels, 1992) samples.

Figure 2.6: Examples of Item–Scale Correlations for a CD-Item and for a Pilot and Revised Version of an SC-Item

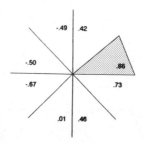

this teacher is friendly

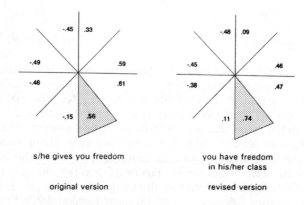

| s/he gives you freedom | you have freedom in his/her class |
| original version | revised version |

Table 2.1: Number of Items of the Dutch and American Version and a Typical Item for the QTI-Scales

Scale	Number of items Dutch American		Typical item
DC Leadership	10	7	S/he is a good leader
CD Helpful/friendly	10	8	S/he is someone we can depend on
CS Understanding	10	8	If we have something to say s/he will listen
SC Student responsibility/ freedom	9	8	S/he gives us a lot of free time in class
SO Uncertain	9	7	S/he seems uncertain
OS Dissatisfied	11	9	S/he is suspicious
OD Admonishing	9	8	S/he gets angry
DO Strict	9	9	S/he is strict

An important consideration in questionnaire development is that each item in a scale measures the same aspect of behavior for any teacher. For example, do the items on the Leadership (DC) scale refer to a common concept? If so, they can be described as 'homogeneous' or having internal consistency. Appendix 2.3 presents an overview of the eight QTI-Scales' internal consistencies. At the student level they are greater than 0.70 and at the class level generally above 0.80. While the scores indicate scale homogeneity at both levels, we generally limit usage of the QTI to the class level to insure credibility. Teachers can therefore receive reliable feedback about their interpersonal behavior on the basis of QTI class means.

We also needed to ascertain the degree of student agreement about the behavior of individual teachers. We considered students' answers in one class as repeated measures of the same variable (which in this case was teacher behavior). Using Cronbach's α (with the students treated as items) Brekelmans (1989) computed a mean of 0.92 for 206 classes. This is considerably higher than the standard often used for inter-observer reliability of 0.80.

It was important to analyze the consistency of student responses over time, or test–retest reliability. The test–retest coefficients presented in Appendix 2.4 are all above 0.65, the acceptable level for research purposes.

Brekelmans (1989) also conducted a generalizability study (Shavelson, Webb and Burstein, 1986) to determine the optimal conditions for providing feedback to teachers. She concluded that the QTI should be administered to at least ten students in a class for the data to be reliable. The QTI does not need to be administered more than once per year, since interpersonal teacher behavior remains relatively stable apart from the first few weeks. A minimum of two classes should complete the questionnaire for each teacher to achieve a reliable measure of overall style. In its ability to provide reliable generalized data, the QTI compares favorably with other classroom measurement instruments. Bertrand and LeClerc (1985) concluded that for many classroom process variables no measurement procedure could be constructed with an acceptable generalizability.

Intra-class correlations and structural analyses were conducted in order to verify the QTI's validity. Horst's (1949) general coefficient was calculated to ascertain intra-class correlation; this coefficient is large if the difference between classes is larger than the difference between students from one class. The intra-class correlations for the QTI were basically above 0.80 for every scale (e.g., Wubbels, Créton, Brekelmans and Hooymayers, 1987), leading us to conclude that differences between student perceptions were more a result of class differences than students'.

Structural analyses were conducted on correlations between scales. The Leary model requires the eight scales to be arranged in a circular order in the two-dimensional coordinate system, or graph. In terms of correlations between scales, this means that each scale should correlate highest with the scale next to it. As you move away from a scale the correlations should become lower until they reach the lowest point (highest negative) with the opposite scale. Apart from minor irregularities this requirement was met throughout several studies (Créton and Wubbels, 1984). Appendix 2.5 provides an example of the correlations between the scales found in one study.

To effectively use the QTI we had to be certain that it represented the two dimensions. Factor analyses on class means and confirmatory factor analyses using

Figure 2.7: *Expected Arrangement of QTI-Scales*

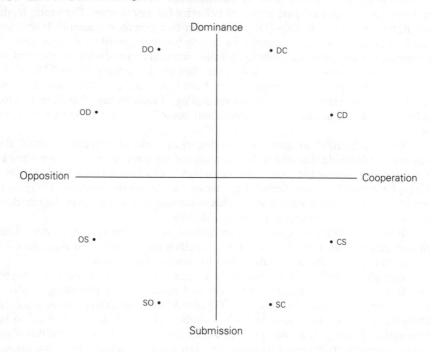

the LISREL program (Wubbels, Créton, Brekelmans and Hooymayers, 1987; Brekelmans, 1989) determined that the two-factor structure did indeed support the eight scales. Brekelmans' (1989) demonstrated that both factors explain 80 per cent of the variance on all the scales of the Dutch QTI. Similar results were obtained for the American version (Wubbels and Levy, 1991). Figures 2.7 and 2.8 present the theoretically expected arrangement of scales and the factor analyses' results for Dutch and American data. These were carried out for two orthogonal factors and the solution was rotated by hand. LISREL analyses further reinforced the presence of both dimensions. Analyses of the Australian data corroborated the Dutch and American results.

Profiles of Communication Styles

Each completed questionnaire yields a set of eight scale scores which are then combined into a profile (see Table 2.2). Scale scores equal the sum of all item scores and are reported in a range between zero and one. A scale score of 'one' indicates that all behaviors in a scale are always (or very much) displayed. A 'zero' is the opposite: the absence of scale behaviors.

The profile represents the teacher's communication style as perceived by the teacher or his or her students. It is usually depicted in a graph with scale scores represented by shading in each sector. For example, Figure 2.9 presents the average

Figure 2.8: Empirical Arrangement of QTI-Scales in Dutch and American Data

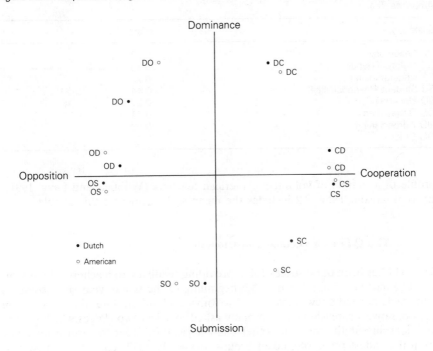

Figure 2.9: Mean Students' Perceptions of American Volunteer Teachers

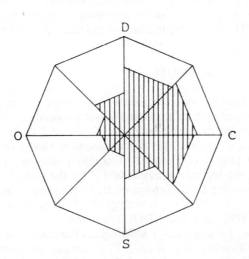

Table 2.2: *Mean Scale Scores for Student Perceptions of a Sample of Volunteer American Teachers*

Scale	score
DC Leadership	0.69
CD Helpful/Friendly	0.75
CS Understanding	0.71
SC Student Responsibility/Freedom	0.44
SO Uncertain	0.21
OS Dissatisfied	0.23
OD Admonishing	0.28
DO Strict	0.43

profile of a sample of volunteer American teachers (Wubbels and Levy, 1991). By comparison, Table 2.2 includes the mean scale scores for this sample.

The QTI as a Feedback Instrument

The QTI has been quite successful in providing feedback to teachers. The instrument cannot be administered at the beginning of the school year since students and teachers need a few weeks to get to know each other. After this honeymoon period, however, teachers are normally asked to select two classes which vary in age, learning ability, or some other characteristic in order to receive feedback from the widest range of student groups. Ironically, QTI-scores from these two different types of classes do not generally vary much, verifying the relative stability of teacher behavior. We will come back to this issue in Chapter 3. As mentioned, the instrument only needs to be administered once per year in order to provide useful results. As will be seen in the upcoming chapters, teachers have taken advantage of the QTI to improve instruction and the overall learning environment.

Short Version of the QTI

In order to make the QTI more accessible to teachers, a short (forty-eight-item) version was developed with an easy hand-scoring procedure. The short QTI and scoring procedures are presented in Figures 2.10 and 2.11. It includes six items for each of the eight sectors. They are arranged in blocks of four to facilitate hand scoring. On page 1 of Figure 2.10, the first item in each block assesses *Leadership* (DC), the second *Understanding* (CS), the third *Uncertain* (SO) and the fourth *Admonishing* (OD) behaviors. Items on page 2 are also grouped in blocks of four to assess *Helpful/Friendly* (CD), *Student Responsibility/Freedom* (SC), *Dissatisfied* (OS) and *Strict* (DO) behaviors.

The total score for a particular scale equals the sum of the circled numbers for the six items belonging to that scale. For example, the Uncertain scale total is obtained by adding scores on items 3, 7, 11, 15, 19 and 23. Figure 2.11 shows how one page was scored to obtain a total of 19 for Leadership, 17 for Understanding, 4 for Uncertain and 7 for Admonishing. How these scores can be transformed to get a profile is demonstrated in Figure 2.12.

Figure 2.10: Short Version of the QTI

STUDENT QUESTIONNAIRE

This questionnaire asks you to describe the behavior of your teacher. This is NOT a test. Your opinion is what is wanted.

On the next few pages you'll find **48** sentences about the teacher. For each sentence circle the number corresponding to your responses. For example:

	Never			Always	
This teacher expresses himself clearly	0	1	2	3	4

If you think that your teacher always expresses himself/herself clearly, circle the 4. If you think your teacher never expresses himself/herself clearly, circle the 0. You also can choose the numbers 1, 2 and 3 which are in between. If you want to change your answer cross it out and circle a new number. Please use both sides of the questionnaire. Thank you for your cooperation.

Don't forget to write the name of the teacher and other details below.

Teacher's name_____   Class_____ School_____

	never				always	
1. This teacher talks enthusiastically about her/his subject.	0	1	2	3	4	(Lea)
2. This teacher trusts us.	0	1	2	3	4	(Und)
3. This teacher seems uncertain.	0	1	2	3	4	(Unc)
4. This teacher gets angry unexpectedly.	0	1	2	3	4	(Adm)
5. This teacher explains things clearly.	0	1	2	3	4	(Lea)
6. If we don't agree with this teacher we can talk about it.	0	1	2	3	4	(Und)
7. This teacher is hesitant.	0	1	2	3	4	(Unc)
8. This teacher gets angry quickly.	0	1	2	3	4	(Adm)
9. This teacher holds our attention.	0	1	2	3	4	(Lea)
10. This teacher is willing to explain things again.	0	1	2	3	4	(Und)
11. This teacher acts as if she/he does not know what to do.	0	1	2	3	4	(Unc)
12. This teacher is too quick to correct us when we break a rule.	0	1	2	3	4	(Adm
13. This teacher knows everything that goes on in the classroom.	0	1	2	3	4	(Lea)
14. If we have something to say this teacher will listen.	0	1	2	3	4	(Und)
15. This teacher lets us boss her/him around.	0	1	2	3	4	(Unc)
16. This teacher is impatient.	0	1	2	3	4	(Adm)
17. This teacher is a good leader.	0	1	2	3	4	(Lea)
18. This teacher realizes when we don't understand.	0	1	2	3	4	(Und)
19. This teacher is not sure what to do when we fool around.	0	1	2	3	4	(Unc)
20. It is easy to pick a fight with this teacher.	0	1	2	3	4	(Adm)
21. This teacher acts confidently.	0	1	2	3	4	(Lea)
22. This teacher is patient.	0	1	2	3	4	(Und)
23. It's easy to make a fool out of this teacher	0	1	2	3	4	(Unc)
24. This teacher is sarcastic.	0	1	2	3	4	(Adm)

Figure 2.10 (Continued)

		never				always		
25.	This teacher helps us with our work.	0	1	2	3	4	(HFr)
26.	We can decide some things in this teacher's class.	0	1	2	3	4	(SRe)
27.	This teacher thinks we cheat.	0	1	2	3	4	(Dis)
28.	This teacher is strict.	0	1	2	3	4	(Str)
29.	This teacher is friendly.	0	1	2	3	4	(HFr)
30.	We can influence this teacher.	0	1	2	3	4	(SRe)
31.	This teacher thinks we don't know anything.	0	1	2	3	4	(Dis)
32.	We have to be silent in this teacher's class.	0	1	2	3	4	(Str)
33.	This teacher is someone we can depend on.	0	1	2	3	4	(HFr)
34.	This teacher lets us fool around in class.	0	1	2	3	4	(SRe)
35.	This teacher puts us down.	0	1	2	3	4	(Dis)
36.	This teacher's tests are hard.	0	1	2	3	4	(Str)
37.	This teacher has a sense of humor.	0	1	2	3	4	(HFr)
38.	This teacher lets us get away with a lot in class.	0	1	2	3	4	(SRe)
39.	This teacher thinks we can't do things well.	0	1	2	3	4	(Dis)
40.	This teacher's standards are very high.	0	1	2	3	4	(Str)
41.	This teacher can take a joke.	0	1	2	3	4	(HFr)
42.	This teacher gives us a lot of free time in class.	0	1	2	3	4	(SRe)
43.	This teacher seems dissatisfied.	0	1	2	3	4	(Dis)
44.	This teacher is severe when marking papers.	0	1	2	3	4	(Str)
45.	This teacher's class is pleasant.	0	1	2	3	4	(HFr)
46.	This teacher is lenient.	0	1	2	3	4	(SRe)
47.	This teacher is suspicious.	0	1	2	3	4	(Dis)
48.	We are afraid of this teacher	0	1	2	3	4	(Str)

For Teacher's Use Only
Lea............. HFr............. Und............. SRe............. Unc............. Dis............. Adm............. Str.............

Figure 2.11: Example of Completed Half of the Short Version of the QTI

Teacher's name _Jack Leury_   Class _4 B_   School _Montessori_

		never				always	
1.	This teacher talks enthusiastically about her/his subject.	0	1	2	3	**④**	(Lea)
2.	This teacher trusts us.	0	1	2	**③**	4	(Und)
3.	This teacher seems uncertain.	0	**①**	2	3	4	(Unc)
4.	This teacher gets angry unexpectedly.	**⓪**	1	2	3	4	(Adm)
5.	This teacher explains things clearly.	0	1	2	**③**	4	(Lea)
6.	If we don't agree with this teacher we can talk about it.	0	1	**②**	3	4	(Und)
7.	This teacher is hesitant.	**⓪**	1	2	3	4	(Unc)
8.	This teacher gets angry quickly.	0	**①**	2	3	4	(Adm)
9.	This teacher holds our attention.	0	1	2	**③**	4	(Lea)
10.	This teacher is willing to explain things again.	0	1	**②**	3	4	(Und)
11.	This teacher acts as if she/he does not know what to do.	0	1	**②**	3	4	(Unc)
12.	This teacher is too quick to correct us when we break a rule.	0	1	**②**	3	4	(Adm)
13.	This teacher knows everything that goes on in the classroom.	0	1	**②**	3	4	(Lea)
14.	If we have something to say this teacher will listen.	0	1	2	**③**	4	(Und)
15.	This teacher lets us boss her/him around.	0	**①**	2	3	4	(Unc)
16.	This teacher is impatient.	0	**①**	2	3	4	(Adm)
17.	This teacher is a good leader.	0	1	2	**③**	4	(Lea)
18.	This teacher realizes when we don't understand.	0	1	2	3	**④**	(Und)
19.	This teacher is not sure what to do when we fool around.	**⓪**	1	2	3	4	(Unc)
20.	It is easy to pick a fight with this teacher.	0	1	**②**	3	4	(Adm)
21.	This teacher acts confidently.	0	1	2	3	**④**	(Lea)
22.	This teacher is patient.	0	1	2	**③**	4	(Und)
23.	It's easy to make a fool out of this teacher	**⓪**	1	2	3	4	(Unc)
24.	This teacher is sarcastic.	0	**①**	2	3	4	(Adm)

Figure 2.12: Example of Transformation of Results from Figure 2.11 into a Profile

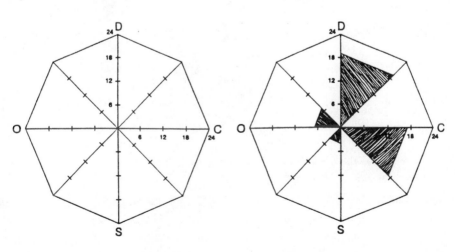

T. Wubbels, H. Créton, J. Levy and H. Hooymayers

Conclusion

In meeting all the necessary criteria, the Leary model provided us with an effective theoretical basis for our research. In Chapter 3 we will move from theory to reality, and use the model to describe the way teachers and students interact.

Chapter 3

Perceptions of Interpersonal Teacher Behavior

Jack Levy, Hans Créton and Theo Wubbels

During the last decade a rich pool of data has been developed about students' and teachers' perceptions of interpersonal teacher behavior. The data set formed as a result of QTI research in The Netherlands, Australia and the United States. In a number of studies the instrument was typically administered to secondary students in grades eight to twelve. The results, presented in this chapter, indicate broad agreement among students and teachers. Readers interested in the specific procedures used in the studies are referred to the research reports (Créton and Wubbels, 1984; Wubbels, Créton and Hooymayers, 1985; Brekelmans, 1989; Wubbels and Levy, 1991; Levy, Wubbels and Brekelmans, 1992; Fisher, Fraser and Wubbels, 1992).

The chapter will outline the students' and teachers' perceptions of both actual and ideal interpersonal teacher behavior. Several types of ideal, best and worst teachers are presented. Differences between classes of the same teacher are mentioned. Further relations between students' and teachers' characteristics and their perceptions will be described.

Average Perceptions

Volunteer and Random Samples

Figure 3.1 presents the average students' and teachers' perceptions from a volunteer sample (623 students) of twenty-two Dutch secondary-school teachers in different subjects and grade levels. Figure 3.2 shows the average of 463 students' perceptions for a random sample of 118 Dutch teachers (Créton and Wubbels, 1984). Data was also gathered from a volunteer American sample across disciplines, and from an Australian volunteer sample of science and mathematics teachers (Wubbels, 1993). This data is presented in Figure 3.3; the sector scores appear in Appendix 3.1.

The volunteer teachers' perceptions of their own behavior are similar across the three countries, as are the students'. The students and teachers see the teachers as high on Leadership, Strict, Helpful/Friendly and Understanding behavior. Uncertainty, Dissatisfaction and Admonishment are much less prominent. In terms

Figure 3.1: Average Students' and Teachers' Perceptions of Dutch Volunteer Teachers

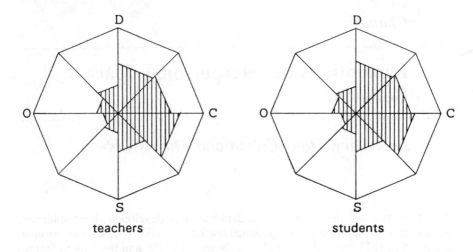

teachers   students

Figure 3.2: Average Students' Perceptions of Random Sample of Dutch Teachers

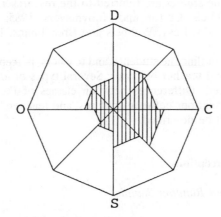

of social expectations, this pattern is desirable for most teaching situations and can be thought of as normal in classes with positive, supportive learning environments. This would be expected, since the teacher is an adult specialist in the subject and the student is young and has little experience. Further, it is normally advisable in a western countries (though perhaps not always appropriate, as will be explained in Chapter 5) for the teacher to act both dominantly and cooperatively. Later in this chapter we will discuss the extent to which teachers' ideals and students' perceptions of good teachers corroborate this idea of advisable teacher behavior.

Because exact scalar equivalence of the two versions of the QTI has not

Figure 3.3: *Average Students' Perceptions of Volunteer American Teachers (across disciplines) and Australian (science and mathematics) Teachers*

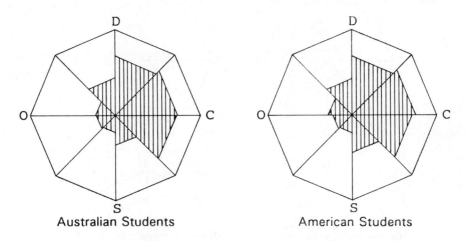

Australian Students   American Students

been demonstrated, differences between countries cannot be directly examined. Wubbels and Levy (1991) did not find any large differences between Dutch and American volunteer teachers' interpersonal teacher behavior. There was evidence, however, that American teachers place greater importance on strictness, whereas Dutch teachers, emphasize more student responsibility and freedom. This may reflect the greater amount of egalitarianism in The Netherlands than in the US.

There are some striking differences between students' perceptions of teachers who volunteered and those in the random sample (Créton and Wubbels, 1984). Volunteer teachers show slightly more Leadership, Helpful/Friendly and Understanding behavior than the teachers in the random sample and they are perceived by their students as less admonishing. These differences are important from a research standpoint. In light of our previous remarks on social expectations of good teaching, the differences may be due to the fact that the teachers volunteered for the research. By being willing to administer a questionnaire which gathers student feedback — as well as exhibiting Leadership and Helpful/Friendly behavior — they are conforming to the popular image of a good teacher. Thus, research on volunteer teachers may provide an overly-positive view of teachers in general.

There are some differences between the teachers' and students' perceptions of the teacher behavior. Teachers generally rank themselves higher in Leadership, Helpful/Friendly and Understanding behavior than their students. These differences will be described in greater detail in Chapter 6.

Students' Perceptions of a Teacher in Different Classes

Students' perceptions of experienced teachers' behavior do not differ much across classes. Figure 3.4 presents ratings of two teachers by four classes. While both teachers differ in their profiles, the classes for each teacher seemed to rate him or her consistently.

Figure 3.4: Students' Perceptions of Two Teachers in Four Different Classes (Dutch data)

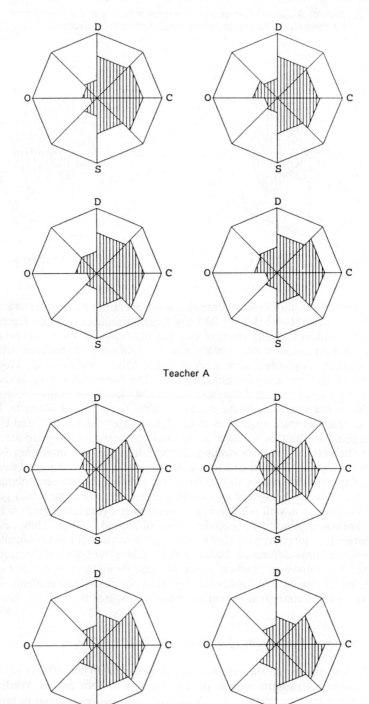

Teacher A

Teacher B

Figure 3.5: *Students' Perceptions of Three Classes of One Teacher (class at bottom — confrontation group, Dutch data)*

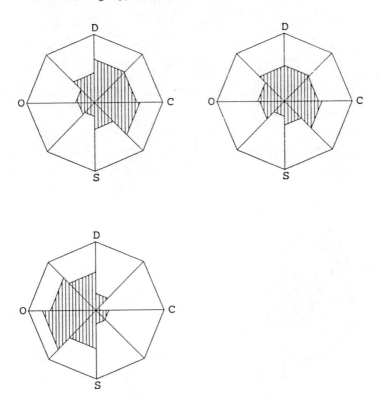

We did find some exceptional cases in which experienced teachers' classes differed greatly in their perceptions. In these instances the teacher often had a conflict with one class. The teacher who is profiled in Figure 3.5, for example, had a confrontation over the rules for a school party that he chaperoned. This resulted in a general deterioration of the teacher–student relationship with this group.

For beginning secondary teachers' differences between profiles in different classes are more prominent than for experienced teachers. Figure 3.6 shows a typical pattern for three classes of a first-year teacher. This teacher was selected because his combined profile fell on the midpoint between the profiles of beginning teachers with large and small variations across classes. First-year teachers seem to have difficulty in establishing and maintaining a consistent relationship with their students. Their behavioral repertoire is probably less developed than it will be later on. As a consequence, students have more influence on the nature of the evolving relationship.

Brekelmans (1989) found significant — though small — differences in students' perceptions of classes thought by the teacher to be either his or her best

Figure 3.6:   Students' Perceptions of Three Classes of a First-Year Teacher (Dutch data)

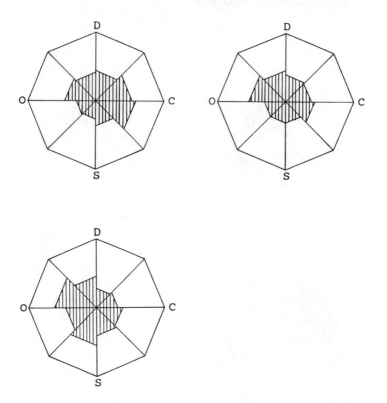

or worst. It appeared that students in the best class saw the teacher as more cooperative and less oppositional than those in the worst.

Students' and Teachers' Views of Good Teaching

Three types of data were gathered (in different studies) for this section. Students in The Netherlands, the United States and Australia were asked to rate their best teachers on the QTI. Also, teachers in the three countries provided self-perceptions about their ideal behavior. Finally, a smaller sample of American and Dutch students completed the QTI for a teacher they thought of as their worst. Figure 3.7 shows the average scores for these three groups in the United States. The results are similar for the other countries (see Appendix 3.2).

We compared the previous perceptions of teachers' behavior with the students' perceptions of their best teachers and the teachers' ideals. In general, the teachers neither reach their ideal nor match the behavior of the best teachers. Students

Figure 3.7: Average Teachers' Perceptions of Ideal Teacher Behavior and Average Students' Perceptions of Best and Worst Teachers in the United States

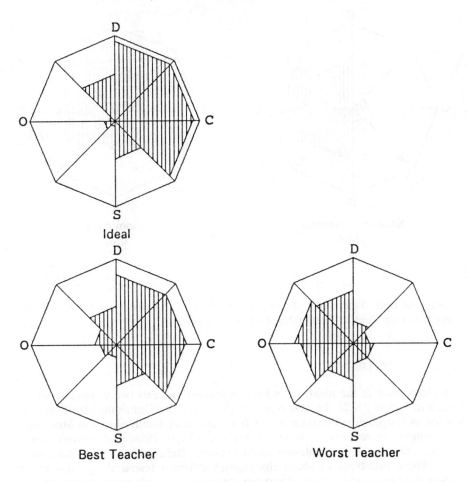

think that their best teachers are strong Leaders. They are more Friendly and Understanding, and less Uncertain, Dissatisfied and Admonishing. Best teachers also provide students with a little more Responsibility and Freedom. The ideal teacher as seen by teachers differs in the same way from the average teacher: they want to behave in a more Cooperative and less Oppositional manner. As might be expected, teachers' vision of ideal behaviors is more extreme than students' perceptions of their best teachers. For worst teachers a complementary picture emerges: they are perceived by students as being much more Oppositional and less Cooperative than average teachers.

In an analysis of the differences between the profiles of best and worst teachers Créton and Wubbels (1984) showed that quality of instruction in students' eyes is more closely related to the proximity (CO) than the influence (DS) dimension of the Leary model. While good teachers must clearly achieve high

Figure 3.8: Two Types of Teacher Ideals (Dutch data, teachers' perceptions)

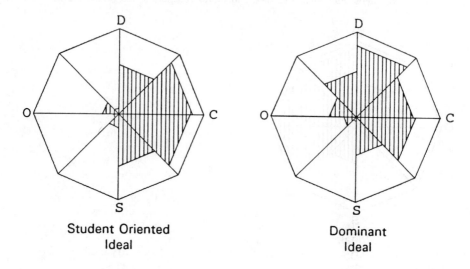

Student Oriented
Ideal

Dominant
Ideal

scores on both dimensions, students respond more to Friendly and Understanding behavior than to Leadership and Strictness.

Ideal Teachers

A closer look at the ideals of individual teachers reveals two distinct types, as seen in Figure 3.8. In the first type (which we call the Dominant Ideal) there is a lot of cooperative behavior and a fair amount of Leadership and Strictness. In addition to cooperative behavior, the second type (Student-Oriented Ideal), reflects the teacher's orientation toward student Responsibility and Freedom.

These two types of ideals characterize different teachers' opinions about the nature of an appropriate classroom atmosphere. Teachers often have distinct ideas about the best way to relate to students and they are markedly different across the profession. The Dominant Ideal teacher might say 'Students will not initiate learning activities if teachers don't control their work and demand a lot. Students are easily distracted, and allowing them too much freedom won't help them learn'. In contrast, the Student-Oriented Ideal teacher might then reply 'Students have to enjoy the class before they learn anything. If there is a pleasant, stimulating atmosphere they'll be motivated to study, which is an important pre-requisite for learning, and they'll consequently thrive. It's more important to reward students for their efforts and the things they do well than it is to correct their mistakes'.

This disagreement becomes significant when teachers are asked to describe the learning environment. Their perceptions often differ according to their ideals, which is one reason that we cannot rely solely on their self-reports (this will be examined in greater detail in Chapter 6). Further, the variation in ideals takes on

Figure 3.9: *Two Types of Best Teachers (Dutch data, students' perceptions)*

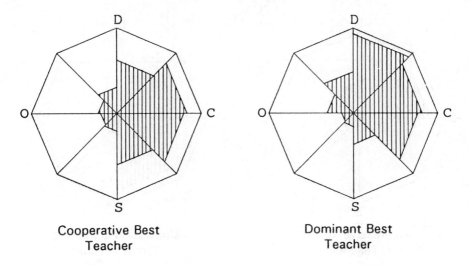

Cooperative Best
Teacher

Dominant Best
Teacher

added importance in light of the students' belief that a teacher's most important quality is not the level of dominance but proximity.

Best and Worst Teachers

Two types of best teachers and three types of worst teachers emerged from the samples. Among students' perceptions of best teachers the two types are similar to the two types of ideals (Figure 3.9). Apparently, some students prefer a stricter teacher whereas others would rather have a lot of responsibility and freedom. In The Netherlands younger students generally prefer stricter teachers while older students want more autonomy.

We also found three distinct types of worst teachers: Repressive, Uncertain–Tolerant and Uncertain–Aggressive (Figure 3.10). The Repressive type seemed to include only experienced teachers who are extremely oppositional, harsh and strict. John, the teacher in Chapter 1, belongs to the Repressive category. The two other types in the worst group were more frequently found among beginning teachers. Both types have classrooms known for their disorder and disruption. The Uncertain–Aggressive class is tense, and the Uncertain–Tolerant one is characterized by students who aren't required to (and don't) participate in lessons. The classroom atmosphere and teacher behavior in these classes will be described in more detail in Chapter 4.

Best and Worst Teacher in One Person

In three cases out of forty we found that the same person was chosen by some students as the best and by others as the worst teacher. In two cases the students

Figure 3.10 *Three Types of Worst Teachers (Dutch data, students' perceptions)*

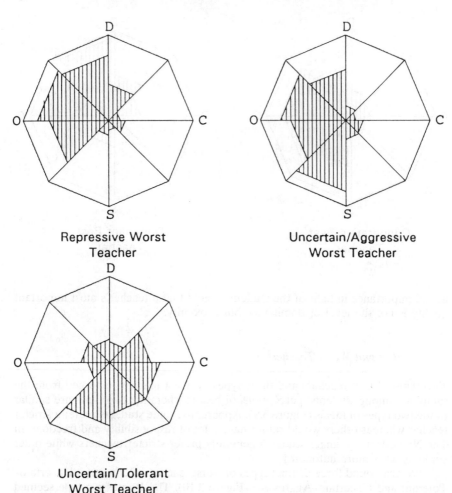

Repressive Worst
Teacher

Uncertain/Aggressive
Worst Teacher

Uncertain/Tolerant
Worst Teacher

who chose the teacher as the best saw him along the lines of the Dominant Best Teacher, while those who saw him as the worst classified him as Repressive (Figure 3.11). These cases are exceptional because students not only disagree about the quality of the teacher, but also about his behavior. In general, students consistently agree in their perceptions of teacher behavior, as has been described in Chapter 2.

In these exceptional cases students agree on the level of dominant behavior but disagree over the proximity dimension. Some believe the teacher is cooperative whereas others think he or she is oppositional. One reason for this might be that the teacher behaves differently towards different students. Another explanation is that students perceive the same teacher behavior differently.

Figure 3.11: Perceptions of Two Groups of Students in One Class that Chose Their Teacher as Best and Worst (Dutch data)

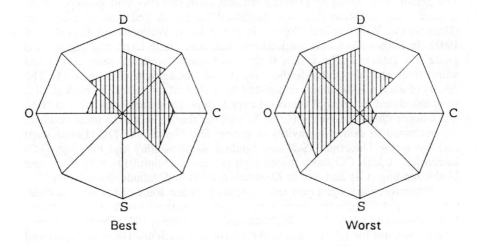

Best   **Worst**

Figure 3.12: Perceptions of Two Groups of Students in One Class that Chose Their Teacher as Best and Worst (Dutch data)

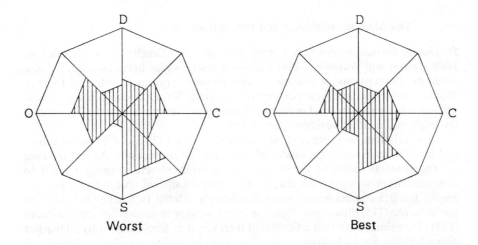

Worst   **Best**

In one case (Figure 3.12) the students' disagreement is much smaller than in the other two. The students describe the behavior in basically the same way. Their exceptionally high scores in Responsibility and Freedom signify the disagreement over quality. The teacher had a reputation for allowing the students great freedom in class, which was corroborated by student QTI-Scores. Apparently this communication style was controversial, since some students rated him as the best while others the worst.

Student Characteristics and Perceptions

The relationship between selected student characteristics and perceptions of teacher communication style was examined for Dutch and American samples (Brekelmans, Wubbels and Créton, in press; Levy, Wubbels and Brekelmans, 1992). In both studies data on students' sex, age, grade level, and report card grade was gathered. The Dutch study also included students' most recent test score, their attitudes towards the subject and the amount of homework. The results of each questionnaire completed by a student or teacher in both studies were calculated in terms of the two Leary factors: Dominance–Submission (DS) and Cooperation–Opposition (CO). The higher the DS score the more teachers are perceived to exhibit behaviors in sectors DO (Strict) and DC (Leadership) and less in the Uncertain (SO) and Student Responsibility and Freedom (SC) categories. A high CO score meant high ratings in Helpful/Friendly (CD) and Understanding (CS) and low in Dissatisfied (OS) and Admonishing (OD).

While there are significant relationships between some of the student characteristics and QTI-Factor scores they do not account for much of the variance. In the American study (Levy, Wubbels and Brekelmans, 1992) the total characteristics account for 1.2 per cent of the variance in students' DS perceptions and 1.8 per cent of their CO scores. Since a few more characteristics were examined in the Dutch study they accounted for a slightly higher percentage of the variance (about 2.5 per cent).[1,2]

Teacher Characteristics and Perceptions

Besides the two studies mentioned above, two additional Dutch studies (Brekelmans, 1989; Créton and Wubbels, 1984) examined relationships between teachers' and students' perceptions of teacher-communication style and selected teacher characteristics: sex, age, years of experience, grade level, the subject taught, self-esteem, job satisfaction and opinions of the teacher about educational goals and the preferred student–teacher relationship.

The relations were studied on the basis of mean DS and CO factor scores and for QTI scale scores for students' and teachers' perceptions. As was the case for the students, none of the teacher characteristics were strongly related to communication style, though there were some significant correlations. For example, teacher characteristics were significantly related to teacher behavior on the influence (DS) dimension. Relations were weaker in general for the proximity (CO) dimension. Maximum estimates of total variance accounted for by all teacher characteristics are as follows:

	influence DS	proximity CO
Students' Perceptions:	21 per cent	20 per cent
Teachers' Perceptions:	22 per cent	13 per cent

We also investigated the results for individual teacher characteristics. The relationship of age and teacher experience with communication style are closely connected to each other and will be discussed in Chapter 7. The remaining characteristics are covered below.

Figure 3.13: *Average Students' Perceptions of Male and Female American Volunteer Teachers*

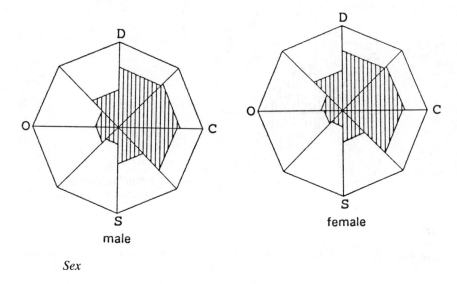

male

female

Sex

Figure 3.13 presents mean students' and teachers' perceptions for male and female teachers in the American study. Students and, to a lesser extent the teachers themselves, perceived male teachers as less dominant than their female colleagues. No significant relationships were found for the proximity dimension.

Grade Level

Grade level in the US was only related to the proximity dimension: teachers in the higher grades are perceived by their students as being more cooperative. This makes sense if one assumes that students in higher grades behave better and need less teacher discipline. In addition, Dutch teachers seem to allow students in the higher grades more responsibility and freedom than those at lower levels. It appears, therefore, the teachers adapt their behavior to student age.

Subject

Teachers of different subjects display different amounts of dominance. American social studies teachers were seen by both students and teachers as the least dominant, while foreign language and mathematics teachers were the most. Dutch foreign-language teachers were unique: they were perceived by students as more dominant and more oppositional than their colleagues. As can be seen from Figure 3.14, foreign-language teachers differed most in the amount of Strictness and Student Responsibility and Freedom. It is striking that these differences occurred in the most controversial categories in terms of teachers' views on quality (see the two types of teacher ideals).

Figure 3.14:   *Average Students' Perceptions of Dutch Teachers, Foreign Language vs. Other Subjects*

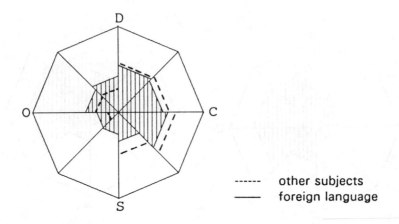

------ other subjects
—— foreign language

Figure 3.15:   *Example of Students' Perceptions of One Dutch Foreign-Language Teacher*

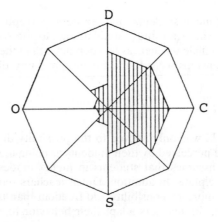

We want to emphasize that the general tendencies we've been describing about the behaviors of different categories of teachers are not strong. For the most part, differences between individual teachers are larger than between the means of different groups of teachers. If one selects two groups of teachers they will differ more within groups than across. For example, many individual American social studies teachers are more dominant than teachers of other subjects in our sample, although as a group they are less dominant than their colleagues in other subjects. Figure 3.15 provides an example in the case of Dutch foreign-language teachers.

We asked groups of foreign-language teachers in The Netherlands why they are perceived as more dominant and oppositional than other teachers. They offered a few hypotheses. First, they believed that foreign-language teachers are involved in whole-class instruction more than teachers of other subjects, since they don't want their students to practice much without guidance. This might result in greater enforcement of class rules, since whole-class teaching requires total cooperation from students. A second explanation can be seen from the nature of the subject itself. Students learning a foreign language are corrected more than in other classes. In addition to the frequency, the nature of the corrections can negatively influence the evolving relationship. Students who are corrected linguistically even though they express an understandable message can get frustrated.

Self-Esteem and Job Satisfaction

The higher a teacher's self-esteem the more the teacher was perceived as dominant by the students and the teacher. Job satisfaction of the teacher, however, appeared not to be related significantly to students' perceptions of the interpersonal teacher behavior. Teachers' perceptions of their own behavior were weakly related to job satisfaction. The less dominant a teacher was in his or her own eyes (as judged, for example, by how orderly the class was), the lower the teachers' job satisfaction and self-esteem appeared to be.

Teachers' Opinions

As might be expected, the teachers' views of their preferred relationship with students are related to the actual nature of the relationship. The connection is weak, however. First, the more teachers would rather act dominant the more they are perceived that way by students. The parallel is not true: when teachers want to act more cooperatively they aren't perceived as such by students. When teachers think about themselves, however, both their wish to be cooperative and dominant is reflected in the amount of cooperation and dominance they perceive. The relationship between teachers' opinions and perceptions of behavior are stronger for teachers than for students.

Two other aspects of teachers' opinions were related to perceptions of the teacher behavior (Brekelmans, 1989). The more teachers have an innovative attitude and the more they want to discuss school matters with their colleagues, the less they are perceived as dominant by their students. These attitudes may lead to greater disorder in their classrooms. Two explanations for this observation seem equally valid. First, the more disorder in the classroom, the more teachers will be dissatisfied with their performance and the more they might want to discuss this with their colleagues. On the other hand, if teachers spend a lot of time discussing teaching techniques and school matters they devote less attention to their students. Similar explanations will be offered in Chapter 8 about the relations between the teachers' perceptions of school and class-level environments.

There were many aspects of teachers' opinions, however, which were not related to the interpersonal relationships. Significant connections were not found between communication style and the level of emphasis teachers place on societal issues nor their thoughts on student-centered vs. subject-centered instruction.

Teacher Characteristics and Ideals

Levy, Wubbels and Brekelmans (1992) examined the relationships between teachers' ideals of communication style and selected teacher characteristics: sex, age, years of experience, grade level and the subject taught. Most teacher characteristics only play a small role in the way teachers envision their ideal communication behavior. The amount of variance accounted for by teacher characteristics in their ideal perceptions is 18 per cent for DS and 15 per cent for CO. This may be an indication of a universal, culturally-based view of 'good' teaching. The results about age and experience will be presented in Chapter 7.

Subject area was the only characteristic which was significantly related to ideal teacher-communication style, and this only with DS behavior. Consistent with our group discussions, foreign-language teachers wanted to be more dominant and social-studies teachers less dominant than their colleagues in other subject areas.

Conclusion

This chapter presented an overview of students' and teachers' perceptions of interpersonal teacher behavior. It is noteworthy that students' and teachers' characteristics are hardly related to the type of teacher behavior. Further, we found it significant that differences between classes of the same teacher are usually far smaller than between different teachers teaching the same group of students. This indicates that the teacher plays an important role in establishing the learning environment.

Now that we have described several profiles of best and worst teachers, we will present a typology of 'regular' teachers in the next chapter.

Notes

1   While low, there nevertheless were some differences according to various characteristics. This might be interpreted in the same two ways as in the discussion above on the same teacher being identified as best and worst. One possibility is that the results reflect different teacher behavior towards different students. The other is that teachers behave the same way toward different students but the students perceive the behavior differently. From the wording of the QTI-Items we think that the latter explanation is more valid. Items don't specifically refer to individual students, but to students in general (ex: 'This teacher helps us with our work'.) An interesting new line of inquiry would be to direct items to the individual respondent rather than the class ('This teacher helps me with my work'.) (see also Fraser, Giddings and McRobbie, 1992).
2   Even though the amount of variance is low — and students' characteristics in general do not appear to be important in their perception of teacher behavior — it may be instructive to analyze some of the results. Four variables account for most of the variance in the DS scores: sex, grade level, recent test scores (Dutch only) and attitudes toward subject (Dutch only). Girls, students in higher grade levels, those with higher recent test scores and those with more positive attitudes

all saw their teachers as more dominant than their counterparts. Five variables: sex, grade level, report card grade, recent test score and attitude towards the subject show separate significant relationships for the CO scores. Girls, students in higher grades, those with high recent test scores and grades, and those with positive attitudes toward the subject all saw their teachers as more cooperative.

Chapter 4

A Typology of Teacher Communication Style

Mieke Brekelmans, Jack Levy and Rely Rodriguez

In the last chapter we began to look at the data on teacher–student interaction in terms of communication patterns: teachers' views of their ideal, students' perceptions of the best and worst teachers. Having analyzed extreme behavior patterns we began to examine the more common profiles and grouped them in a typology. It gradually became clear that the typology would add to the growing body of research connecting student learning and teaching behaviors, teaching styles and students' perceptions of the learning environment (Brophy and Good, 1986; Fraser, 1986; Bennett, 1976). This chapter will describe the typology's origins, its attributes in terms of the model and the relationship between communication styles and class and teacher characteristics. In Chapter 5 we will turn to the research which brings together these communication patterns and student outcomes.

Background

There is only one typology to describe learning environments, and it was produced by Moos' (1978) Classroom Environment Scale (Fraser, 1986). It features five clusters which describe the following learning-environment orientations: control, innovation, affiliation, task completion and competition. While research on learning-environment typologies is scarce, there are many typologies of teaching styles (Bennett, 1976; Flanders, 1970; Good, 1979). The most familiar makes the distinction between directive and non-directive approaches to teaching. Briefly, open, non-directive teachers emphasize support, innovative instructional procedures and flexible rules. Directive teachers stress centralized control and seek to develop competitive, task-oriented classes (Schultz, 1982). A number of different substyles have been identified between these two extremes, however (Ramsay and Ransley, 1986).

Development

The data for this chapter came from several studies. The typology was initially developed in an analysis of students' perceptions of the communication style of nearly all the teachers (94 per cent) in a large Dutch urban secondary school (Brekelmans, 1989 primarily; also Wubbels, Brekelmans, Créton, and Hooymayers, 1990). Teachers selected their 'best' and 'worst' classes and each completed the QTI. Chi-square tests showed that the sample was representative in terms of the teacher's sex and subject matter.

Class means were computed for each teacher, and were then grouped using cluster analysis (Wishart, 1978; Everitt, 1980). A variety of control analyses were performed using different clustering procedures and similarity measures. The result was a reliable and stable typology which contained eight communication-style profiles (Brekelmans, 1989). The mean profiles for the eight categories in the typology are presented in Figure 4.1.

The results of Figure 4.1 can be understood in terms of the main point of each profile. The main point is calculated by converting the eight scale scores of a profile into vectors which can be totaled to produce one point on the model for interpersonal teacher behavior (Figure 4.2).

In Chapter 3 we observed that many teacher profiles are characterized by high scores on the Leadership (DC), Helpful/Friendly (CD) and Understanding (CS) QTI-Scales. To support this view we can see that three of the main points of the typology fall in the CD quadrant: the Directive, Authoritative and the Tolerant/Authoritative types. Two other types are also very close to this quadrant: the Drudging teacher's main point is exactly on the influence dimension and the Tolerant teacher's is just below the proximity axis in the CS quadrant. The hypothesis expressed in Chapter 3 has now become more specific in terms of present educational reality: most teachers are perceived by students as both dominant and cooperative.

The three types of teachers in the CD quadrant all show about the same amount of influence. While each one is fairly dominant, they differ in the amount of proximity. The Directive teacher is least cooperative and the Tolerant/Authoritative teacher most. The Directive teacher's relatively low proximity results from low scores on the cooperation scales and a high score in strictness. The Drudging teacher is a little less dominant and much less cooperative than the other three types. The Tolerant teacher is about as cooperative as the Authoritative teacher though far less dominant.

The main points of the Uncertain/Aggressive and Uncertain/Tolerant profiles are best noted by their low scores on the influence dimension. Both are seen as far more submissive than the other types. They differ strikingly from each other on the proximity dimension. The Uncertain/Tolerant teacher resembles the Directive teacher in cooperation, whereas the Uncertain/Aggressive teacher compares to the Repressive teacher in being highly oppositional. Finally, the Repressive teacher is the highest of all on the influence dimension. He or she combines pronounced dominance with extremely oppositional behavior.

Three other studies contributed to the development of the typology. Wubbels, Brekelmans and Hermans (1987) provided additional descriptive data from a sample of sixty-six physics classes. Two studies were conducted in the United States. Wubbels and Levy (1991) gathered QTI data from sixty-six classes and Levy, Rodriguez, and Wubbels (1992) collected QTI and observation information from twenty-eight classes. From this data set we distilled the teacher/student behaviors and learning environment characteristics which appear below. Every Dutch, American and Australian profile fits into one of the following types.[1]

Figure 4.1: Mean Profiles of the Eight Types of the Teacher Communication Style Typology

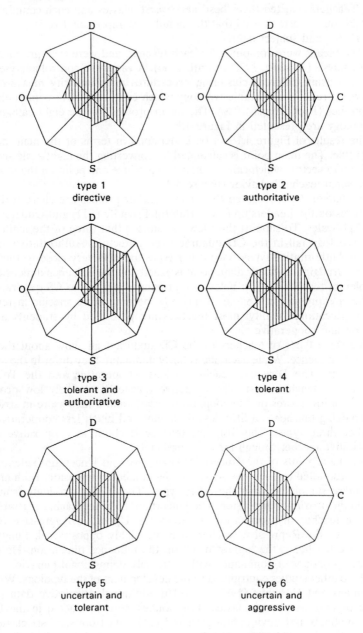

type 1
directive

type 2
authoritative

type 3
tolerant and
authoritative

type 4
tolerant

type 5
uncertain and
tolerant

type 6
uncertain and
aggressive

Figure 4.1: (Continued)

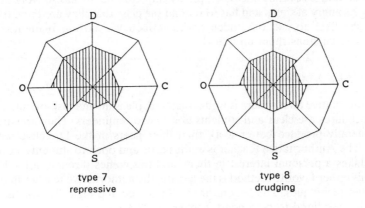

type 7
repressive

type 8
drudging

Figure 4.2   Main Point of the Eight Types of the Teacher Communication Style Typology

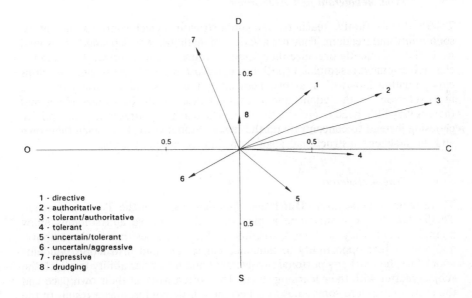

1 - directive
2 - authoritative
3 - tolerant/authoritative
4 - tolerant
5 - uncertain/tolerant
6 - uncertain/aggressive
7 - repressive
8 - drudging

The Typology

Type 1: Directive

This learning environment is well-structured and task-oriented. The Directive teacher is organized efficiently and normally completes all lessons on time. He or she dominates class discussion, but generally holds students' interest. Normally the teacher isn't very close to the students, though he or she is occasionally

49

friendly and understanding. He or she has high standards and is seen as demanding. While things seem businesslike, the teacher continually has to work at it. He or she gets angry at times and has to remind the class that they are there to work. He or she likes to call on students who misbehave and are inattentive. This normally straightens them up quickly.

Type 2: Authoritative

The Authoritative atmosphere is well-structured, pleasant and task-oriented. Rules and procedures are clear and students don't need reminders. They are attentive, and generally produce better work than their peers in the Directive teacher's classes. The Authoritative teacher is enthusiastic and open to students' needs. He or she takes a personal interest in them, and this comes through in the lessons. While his or her favorite method is the lecture, the authoritative teacher frequently uses other techniques. The lessons are well planned and logically structured. He or she is considered to be a good teacher by students.

Type 3: Tolerant and Authoritative

Tolerant/Authoritative teachers maintain a structure which supports student responsibility and freedom. They use a variety of methods, to which students respond well. They frequently organize their lessons around small group work. While the class environment resembles Type 2, the Tolerant/Authoritative teacher develops closer relationships with students. They enjoy the class and are highly involved in most lessons. Both students and teacher can occasionally be seen laughing, and there is very little need to enforce the rules. The teacher ignores minor disruptions, choosing instead to concentrate on the lesson. Students work to reach their own and the teacher's instructional goals with little or no complaints.

Type 4: Tolerant

There seem to be separate Dutch and American views of the Tolerant teacher. To the Dutch, the atmosphere is pleasant and supportive and students enjoy attending class. They have more freedom in Type 4 classes than in those above, and have a real opportunity to influence curriculum and instruction. Students appreciate the teacher's personal involvement and his or her ability to match the subject matter with their learning styles. They often work at their own pace and the class atmosphere sometimes may become a little confused as a result. In the US, however, the Tolerant teacher is seen to be disorganized. His or her lessons are not prepared well and they don't challenge students. The teacher often begins the lesson with an explanation and then sends the students off to individually complete an assignment. While the teacher is interested in their personal lives, his or her academic expectations for students aren't evident.

The differences in these two interpretations are in agreement with the results of the study which established the validity and reliability of the American QTI (Wubbels and Levy, 1991). This research showed that American teachers preferred to be more dominant, while their Dutch counterparts wanted to provide students with greater responsibility and freedom.

Type 5: Uncertain/Tolerant

Uncertain/Tolerant teachers are highly cooperative but don't show much leadership in class. Their lessons are poorly structured, are not introduced completely and don't have much follow-through. They generally tolerate disorder, and students are not task-oriented. Uncertain/Tolerant teachers display the classic 'Blindness' behavior described in Chapter 1.

The Uncertain/Tolerant teacher is quite concerned about the class, and is willing to explain things repeatedly to students who haven't been listening. The atmosphere is so unstructured, however, that only the students in front are attentive while the others play games, do homework, and the like. They are not provocative, however, and the teacher manages to ignore them while loudly and quickly covering the subject.

The Uncertain/Tolerant teacher's rules of behavior are arbitrary, and students don't know what to expect when infractions occur. The teacher's few efforts to stop the misbehavior are delivered without emphasis and have little effect on the class. Sometimes the teacher reacts quickly, and at other times completely ignores inattentiveness. His or her expectations of class performance are minimal and mostly immediate rather than long-range. The overall effect is of an unproductive equilibrium in which teacher and students seem to go their own way.

Type 6: Uncertain/Aggressive

These classes are characterized by an aggressive kind of disorder. Teacher and students regard each other as opponents and spend almost all their time in symmetrically escalating conflict. Students seize nearly every opportunity to be disruptive, and continually provoke the teacher by jumping up, laughing and shouting out. This generally brings a panicked over-reaction from the teacher which is met by even greater student misbehavior. An observer in this class might see the teacher and student fighting over a book which the student has been reading. The teacher grabs the book in an effort to force the student to pay attention. The student resists because he or she thinks the teacher has no right to his or her property. Since neither one backs down, the situation often escalates out of control.

In the middle of the confusion the Uncertain/Aggressive teacher may suddenly try to discipline a few students, but often manages to miss the real culprits. Because of the teacher's unpredictable and unbalanced behavior, the students feel that he or she is to blame. Rules of behavior aren't communicated or explained properly. The teacher spends most of his or her time trying to manage the class, yet seems unwilling to experiment with different instructional techniques. He or she prefers to think 'first, they'll have to behave'. Unfortunately, learning is the least important aspect of the class.

Type 7: Repressive

Students in the Repressive teacher's class are uninvolved and extremely docile. They follow the rules and are afraid of the teacher's angry outbursts. He or she seems to overreact to small transgressions, frequently making sarcastic remarks or giving failing grades. The Repressive teacher is the epitome of complementary rigidity.

The Repressive teacher's lessons are structured but not well-organized. While directions and background information are provided, few questions are allowed or encouraged. Occasionally, students will work on individual assignments, but will receive precious little help from the teacher. The atmosphere is guarded and unpleasant, and the students are apprehensive and fearful. Since the Repressive teacher's expectations are competition-oriented and inflated, students worry a lot about their exams. The teacher seems to repress student initiative, preferring to lecture while the students sit still. They perceive the teacher as unhappy and impatient and their silence seems like the calm before the storm.

Type 8: Drudging

The atmosphere in a Drudging teacher's class varies between Types 5 and 6 disorder. One thing is constant, however: the teacher continually struggles to manage the class. He or she usually succeeds (unlike Types 5 and 6), but not before expending a great deal of energy. Students pay attention as long as the teacher actively tries to motivate them. When they do get involved, the atmosphere is oriented toward the subject matter and the teacher doesn't generate much warmth. He or she generally follows a routine in which he or she does most of the talking and avoids experimenting with new methods. The Drudging teacher always seems to be going downhill and the class is neither enthusiastic nor supportive nor competitive. Unfortunately, because of the continual concern with class management the teacher sometimes looks as though he or she is on the verge of burnout.

Class and Teacher Characteristics

One of the studies which validated the typology (Wubbels, Brekelmans and Hermans, 1987) gathered additional student and teacher information from sixty-six physics classes. Student perceptions of other (non-QTI) aspects of the learning environment were measured by a Dutch instrument based on Rentoul and Fraser's (1979) Individualized Classroom Environment Questionnaire. The instrument has three scales: activity learning, reality learning and participation learning. The sixty-six physics classes which completed the instrument had also completed the QTI. Because the sample size was small (n = 45), a significance level of 10 per cent was adopted. Comparative results are presented in Table 4.1.

A significant amount (20–36 per cent) of the variance in the students' perceptions of the learning environment is accounted for by the teacher behavior style. Their views of the learning environment are in general agreement with expectations based on QTI-Scores. For example, participation learning is most closely associated with teachers who demonstrate highly cooperative communication styles. This result agrees with previous research which found that open, nondirective teachers emphasize innovative procedures (Schultz, 1982).

The study also gathered data on teacher characteristics: job satisfaction,

Table 4.1: *Mean Learning Environment by Communication Style and Results of Analyses of Variance*

type	reality learning	activity learning	participation learning
1 Directive	.45	.39	.33
2 Authoritative	.48	.33	.36
3 Authoritative and Tolerant	—	—	—
4 Tolerant	.49	.44	.30
5 Uncertain/Tolerant	.32	.25	.21
6 Uncertain/Aggressive	.35	.38	.26
7 Repressive	.42	.30	.24
8 Drudging	.40	.35	.26
F	4.48**	1.95*	1.91*

* $p < 0.10$ ** $P < 0.05$
— missing because of too few cases in the sample

experience, age, self-esteem, attitudes toward innovations, the type of interaction they prefer to have with students and their class goals. From this additional data we were able to expand the relationships discussed in Chapter 3 between QTI scale scores and teacher characteristics. Table 4.2 presents the expanded analysis, expressed in terms of QTI communication type (from the typology) and teacher characteristics. No relations were found for class size, mean student ability in a class, and teacher opinions about educational goals. As a result, they aren't included in Table 4.2.

Both experience and age seem to be important to teacher communication type. Older, experienced teachers are represented more frequently among the Directive (Type 1) and Repressive (7) types. Younger, less experienced teachers appear more frequently in the Drudging (8), Authoritative (2) and Tolerant (4) categories.

As can be seen for Types 5, 6 and 8 (those noted for disorder) class disruption is not limited to beginning teachers. Experienced teachers' classes can also be full of confusion and misbehavior. Beginning teachers, in fact, are well represented in the style categories which describe a pleasant class atmosphere. This finding speaks critically to the educational research practice of choosing 'expert' teachers on the basis of experience alone. We will elaborate further on this in Chapter 7.

There was a significant relationship between the way teachers would like to relate to students and the students' view of their communication style, especially in terms of dominance. Drudging (Type 8) teachers prefer to be least dominant and highly cooperative. Unfortunately, they never achieve this goal, and have great difficulty in building a productive class atmosphere.

Directive (Type 1) and Repressive (Type 4) teachers prefer to be most dominant toward students, and only want to show average cooperation. Both realize their dominance goals, but Repressive teachers hardly show any coopera-tion at all. They seem to mistake aggression for dominance, which is one of the reasons their classes are tense. Being able to separate dominance from aggression is, in our opinion, one of the most crucial teacher competencies. Teachers who are seen to be high-dominant/low-opposition (Types 1–3) have much more pro-ductive learning environments.

Table 4.2: Mean Teacher and Class Characteristics by Communication Style and Results of Analyses of Variance

type	job satisfaction	years of experience	age	attitude towards innovation	self esteem	wish to be dominant	wish to be cooperative	percentage boys
1 Directive	0.66	15	43	0.40	0.71	0.62	0.69	62
2 Authoritative	0.67	8	34	0.49	0.67	0.47	0.77	59
3 Authoritative/Tolerant	—	—	—	—	—	—	—	—
4 Tolerant	0.58	10	35	0.53	0.68	0.47	0.73	43
5 Uncertain/Tolerant	0.61	12	37	0.51	0.64	0.48	0.61	52
6 Uncertain/Aggressive	0.51	12	38	0.47	0.54	0.52	0.64	44
7 Repressive	0.52	17	45	0.35	0.62	0.59	0.68	41
8 Drudging	0.50	9	35	0.57	0.51	0.42	0.76	55
F	1.71	1.93*	3.80**	2.03*	2.14*	3.01**	0.77	2.60**

* $p < 0.10$ ** $p < 0.05$
—: missing because of too few cases in the sample

Interestingly, Drudging (8) teachers seem to be the most open to innovation. In fact, they may put too much energy into innovation and not enough into performance. The Repressive (7) teacher is the least inclined to innovate. They seem separated from their students by significant differences in age, values or interests, and it sours their behavior and attitudes. These are the teachers who are often heard to complain 'When I was their age....'. They don't invest much time in their work, and frequently seem close to burnout.

The Wubbels, Brekelmans and Hermans (1987) study also reported additional results concerning teacher characteristics. They found that job satisfaction is not significantly related to teacher-behavior styles, though there are differences between categories. Actually, the latter result is more in keeping with earlier research (Nials, 1981). Another outcome was that self-esteem is highest in teachers known for their positive classroom atmospheres and lowest for the Uncertain/Aggressive and Drudging types.

Finally, it seems that the proportion of boys in class is related to the typology categories. This was striking, since class size and average student ability are not related to teacher communication style. Directive (1), Authoritative (2) and Tolerant/Authoritative (3) teachers seemed to have a relatively high percentage of boys in class. More girls were found in Tolerant (4), Uncertain/Aggressive (6) and Repressive (7) teachers' classes. We realized that these results were obtained for physics classes, and that most of the teachers were male. Further, research has shown that girls like physics lessons less than boys. The result, then, might have been affected by the nature of the sample.

Note

1 Profiles belong to one of the types on the basis of the similarity of the profile with every type. The profile belongs to the type with which it has the highest similarity, provided that the profile has a higher similarity with this type than the mean of all the similarities between profiles in the sample.

Chapter 5

Student Performance, Attitudes, Instructional Strategies and Teacher-Communication Style

Mieke Brekelmans, Theo Wubbels and Jack Levy

This chapter will discuss the results of two related studies. The first (Brekelmans, 1989) used the QTI in the Dutch option of the Second International Science Study to investigate the relationship between students' perceptions of interpersonal teacher behavior and student achievement and attitudes. It also analyzed a number of other variables such as learning environment characteristics, teachers' opinions, teachers' perceptions of the communication style and different curricula. The results raised some questions about the extent to which teacher interpersonal behavior and teacher instructional behavior can be distinguished from each other. This led to a second study (Levy, Rodriguez and Wubbels, 1992) which will also be discussed.

Student Achievement and Teacher Communication Style

Data was gathered in sixty-six ninth-grade physics classes which included 1,105 students of about 15 years of age. The sample included twenty-one classes in which an experimental curriculum was used. The other forty-five classes were drawn from all Dutch grade-nine classes using a random sampling plan stratified for the type of school. The Netherlands has three types of secondary schools: MAVO (general secondary education, intermediate level), HAVO (general secondary education, higher level) and VWO (secondary education as preparation for studying at university). These school types represent a hierarchy of student ability, with MAVO at the low end.

Achievement was measured with a standardized and internationally developed physics test. The twenty-three-item test was one of the instruments used in the main part of the Second International Science Study. Attitudes were measured by a questionnaire on students' experience with, and motivation toward, physics. The instrument has five scales: appreciation of lessons, instructiveness, easiness, structuredness of lessons and subject matter, and motivation for physics. Brekelmans (1989) demonstrated that one factor underlies all five scales.[1]

Strength of Relationships

The data was analyzed in several ways. Brekelmans (1989) used a number of student and teacher variables in a multilevel model (Goldstein, 1987) as predictors of student achievement. Mean class scores for the students' perceptions of interpersonal teacher behavior were computed and the teacher profiles were grouped according to the typology presented in Chapter 4.

From this analysis it appears that 20 per cent of the variance in student achievement is accounted for by school class membership. Three quarters of this variance (15 per cent of total) is accounted for by student ability level. The remaining quarter (5 per cent) is the range in which teachers can make a difference. This means that student characteristics account for the larger part of student achievement. This is consistent with the great body of research which has shown that student characteristics such as Socio-Economic Status (SES) and previous achievement account for 50–80 per cent of their future achievement (e.g., Fraser, Walberg, Welch and Hattie, 1987). These student characteristics cannot be influenced in any significant way by the teacher. School and teacher factors therefore play a minor role when compared with SES and previous achievement.

Even though school class membership might only affect 20 per cent of the variance in student achievement, it is still an important factor. The effect size is such that a positive, supportive climate might make the difference between a student going to university or not. We were therefore interested in seeing if and how students' perceptions of interpersonal teacher behavior are related to their learning. We compared the relationship between these perceptions and achievement with the relationship between achievement and other factors in the learning environment which can be influenced by the teacher. From this perspective, students' perceptions of teacher interpersonal behavior or communication style appear to be quite important. Interpersonal teacher behavior accounts for 3.5 per cent of the 5 per cent of variance which can be influenced by the teacher. In other words, teacher communication style accounts for a majority of the variance in the cognitive student outcomes which are open to teacher influence.

Compared to other factors measured in this study interpersonal teacher behavior appeared to be strongly related to achievement. Student outcomes were not related at all to texbooks, nor to teachers' opinions about educational goals and teacher–student relationships. In addition, no significant relationship was detected between the teachers' own perceptions of communication style and student achievement. Other factors in the learning environment (activity learning, participation learning) were significantly related with student achievement and together accounted for half of the amount of variance that interpersonal teacher behavior accounted for. (Because there is overlap between interpersonal teacher behavior and learning environment characteristics the two percentages cannot be added).

A similar analysis was performed for attitudes, with the scores on the factor underlying the five attitude scales used as the dependent variable. It appeared that school class membership accounts for only 13 per cent of the variance in attitude scores. Students' perceptions of interpersonal teacher behavior account for about 70 per cent of this variance. Compared with the other factors measured in this study, students' perceptions were once again the most important factor.

Students' perceptions of teacher communication style are a much better

Table 5.1: Achievement and Attitudes by Communication Type

Type	achievement measure	attitude measure
1 Directive	0.81	0.62
2 Authoritative	0.71	0.79
3 Authoritative/Tolerant	missing*	missing*
4 Tolerant	0.87	0.53
5 Uncertain/Tolerant	0.47	0.51
6 Uncertain/Aggressive	0.49	0.20
7 Repressive	1.04	0.38
8 Drudging	0.64	0.00

* Too few cases to include in the analyses

predictor of student achievement than teachers' own perceptions. This makes sense, since students' views mediate the influence of the learning environment on student achievement (Walberg, 1976). On the basis of these results we concluded that students' perceptions of interpersonal teacher behavior are a better measure of the quality of instruction than teachers'.

Nature of the Relationships

What kind of interpersonal teacher behavior is most favorable for student achievement and student attitudes? This question was addressed in several ways: correlational analyses (Wubbels, Brekelmans and Hermans, 1987), analysis of the relationship between student achievement and teacher profiles from the typology (Wubbels, Brekelmans, Créton and Hooymayers, 1990), and a multilevel regression model which examined the differences between outcomes for different types of the typology (Brekelmans, 1989). These different analyses are consistent in identifying the teacher behavior styles which are most favorable to student achievement.

Achievement

Table 5.1 presents the achievement scores for the eight types of the typology after correction for all other influences. Remarkably, the Repressive teacher has the highest achievement outcomes. Teachers with disorderly classrooms (Types 5, 6, 8) reflect relatively low student achievement, whereas Directive, Authoritative and Tolerant teachers have relatively high outcomes. From these numbers it is difficult to determine the effect size. An example might help illustrate the result. The difference in outcome scores between Repressive teachers' students and those of the Uncertain/Tolerant and Uncertain/Aggressive teacher are about the same in magnitude as the difference between mean student achievement on the pre-university level (VWO) and on the general secondary higher level (HAVO). This difference is also the same as the difference between outcomes of students on the general secondary intermediate level (MAVO) and the higher level (HAVO). We therefore believe that interpersonal teacher behavior can influence student achievement to an extent roughly equal in size to one step in the hierarchy of student ability levels in the Dutch educational system. In

Figure 5.1: Teacher Behavior Profiles of Teachers with Relatively High and Low Student Achievement

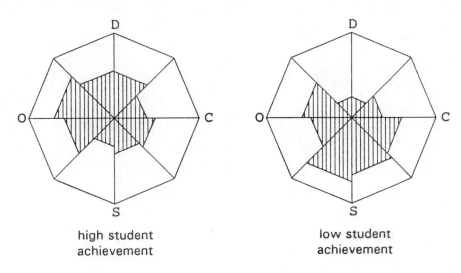

high student
achievement

low student
achievement

terms of an American 'tracking' system, this may mean the difference between membership in low, middle or high-ability groups, which will ultimately affect future admission to post-secondary education.

The relation between student achievement and communication style is due more to teacher behavior on the influence dimension than proximity. The more a teacher is perceived as dominant, the more his or her students achieve. Strict (DO), Leadership (DC) and Helpful/Friendly (CD) behaviors are positively related to student achievement, whereas Student Responsibility and Freedom (SC), Uncertain (SO) and Dissatisfied (OS) behaviors are negatively related. To clarify these results Figure 5.1 presents students' perceptions of the interpersonal behavior of two teachers with relatively high and relatively low achievement scores.

Attitudes

Table 5.1 also includes measures of the attitude scores after correction. The Authoritative and Directive teachers have the highest student attitude scores. Students of the Drudging, Uncertain/Aggressive and Repressive teachers have the worst attitudes. The relationship between student attitudes and teacher interpersonal behavior is connected much more intensely to the proximity dimension than influence.

The Cooperation scales of the model for interpersonal teacher behavior (Leadership, Helpful/Friendly, Understanding and Student Responsibility/ Freedom — DC, CD, CS and SC) are positively related to student attitudes. The more teachers behaved in these ways the more their students viewed the physics lessons positively. The Opposition scales (Strict, Admonishing, Dissatisfied and Uncertain — DO, OD, OS and SO) are all negatively related to student attitudes. This means that students with teachers whose tendency is to show above-average behavior on the right side of the D–S axis and below-average on the left side

Figure 5.2: Teacher Behavior Profiles of Teachers with Relatively High and Low Student Attitudes

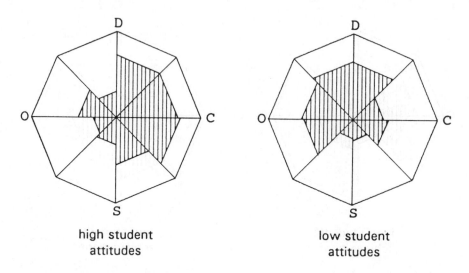

| high student | low student |
| attitudes | attitudes |

viewed their physics lessons more positively. The D–S axis therefore separates teacher behavior which is associated with positive and negative student attitudes.

As with Figure 5.1, Figure 5.2 presents students' perceptions of the communication style of two teachers with relatively and positive negative student attitudes.

Achievement and attitudes

The results for the relationship between communication style and student achievement and attitudes are not identical. The Repressive teacher has the highest student achievement scores, but is low in terms of student attitudes. Directive and Authoritative teachers are rather high in both outcome categories. The teachers with disorderly classrooms have students with negative attitudes and low achievement scores.

If teachers want students to be high-achieving and supportive they may find themselves in a quandary. This is due to the conflicting demands of the Strict (DO) and Student Responsibility/Freedom (SC) categories. To realize higher student achievement teachers have to be somewhat strict, while positive student attitudes require greater flexibility. The other six sectors of the model do not present such conflicting demands.

These results should be seen in light of Chapter 3's discussion of students' perceptions of best and worst teachers and of the teacher ideals. In general, teachers imagine their ideal classroom to be a positive environment with high-achieving students who have supportive attitudes. This is also true for students' perceptions of their best teachers. There is a slight difference in emphasis for the two types of teacher ideals and best teachers. The Dominant ideal and best teacher emphasize a learning environment which results in greater student achievement than their Student-Oriented counterparts, who focus on student attitudes.

Commentary

Due to the correlational nature of the study, the causal interpretations mentioned above should be made with reservation. Certain kinds of interpersonal teacher behavior may cause student outcomes. But a reciprocal causal interaction is possible, in which student achievement and motivation foster the interpersonal behavior of the teacher, which in turn improves student achievement and motivation. Helmke, Schneider and Weinert (1986) found indications of this kind of causal direction in their analysis of the relationship between cognitive and motivational student entry characteristics and instruction and management variables. The cross-situational and longitudinal stability of experienced teachers' communication styles (see Chapter 7) leads us to believe, however, that the causality proceeds from teacher to student and not vice versa. Causal inferences should be further tested through experimental research.

Interpersonal and Instructional Behavior

The results demonstrate that both the model and typology are well suited to describe the effect of different teacher behaviors on student outcomes. The direction of student outcome differences described above confirm Fraser's (1986) conclusions that students achieve more in classes they think have greater cohesiveness, satisfaction and goal-directedness and less disorganization and friction (Haertel, Walberg and Haertel, 1981). The results also seem to corroborate earlier findings about the effectiveness of direct instruction strategies (Brophy and Good, 1986). In one aspect of interpersonal teacher behavior the results extend prior research. Ramsay and Ransley (1986) found that open teaching styles were associated with the lowest outcomes. Our results emphasize however that disorder more than openness seems to be associated with low student outcomes.

It is well known that teaching behaviors and teaching styles are related to student learning (e.g., Brophy and Good, 1986; Bennett, 1976). These relationships are usually described in terms of teacher instructional strategies and management behavior. There also appears to be a connection between communication styles which are positively related to student performance and direct-instruction strategies. This raises the question of the extent of overlap between teacher interpersonal behavior and instructional strategies and management behavior. Levy, Rodriguez and Wubbels (1992) observed forty-six classes in an analysis of the relationship between interpersonal behavior, or communication style, and instructional behavior. They studied instructional behavior in terms of six aspects derived from the literature on effective teaching: organization, variation, monitoring, emphasis on student learning, management and student centeredness. In addition, students' and teachers' perceptions of teacher interpersonal behavior were gathered with the QTI.

Strength of Relationships

The amount of overlapping variance between the instructional and interpersonal behavior appeared to be 31 per cent. While the QTI therefore can be used as a partial measure of instructional behavior, the remaining 69 per cent indicates that instructional and interpersonal behaviors may address separate teaching characteristics. It seems that instructional and interpersonal teacher behavior occasionally overlap but are not completely synonymous.

Nature of Relationships

Relationships were expressed in terms of correlations between instructional characteristics and two measures of interpersonal behavior: the QTI factor scores (DS and CO) and the eight sector scores. Most correlations between instructional characteristics and students' perceptions of interpersonal behavior were not high — only three QTI scales overlapped to a small degree.

Significant relations were not found for students' perceptions of the proximity dimension and instructional behavior. The influence dimension appeared significantly related to the two instructional categories of Organization and Management. Thus, the more students perceive that teachers behave in dominant ways (Leadership and Strict behavior), the more the teachers displayed effective organizational and management techniques. On the sector level a negative relationship appeared between the instructional category of Organization and the QTI scales SC (Student Responsibility/Freedom), SO (Uncertain) and OD (Admonishing). Thus a teacher who, from students' perceptions, displayed uncertain behavior, or allowed students a lot of freedom in class, or often got angry, was not seen by observers to be clear in terms of directions, skill explanation or organization. In addition teachers who appeared more uncertain to students (SO) did not often display productive class management techniques.

Teachers' perceptions of interpersonal behavior were only significantly related for the proximity dimension and management techniques. When teachers thought they behaved in a Dissatisfied (OS) or Admonishing (OD) manner, observers felt they did not frequently use productive management techniques.

The results from both students' and teachers' perceptions support the contention that as teachers communicate uncertainty, anger, impatience and dissatisfaction, they display fewer instructional techniques associated with effectiveness. This research was conducted on a small sample with an instrument whose reliability will have to be re-tested. Thus, more research is needed on the topic.

Conclusion

The third chapter discussed students' perceptions of best teachers and teachers' perceptions of their ideal. These perceptions were understood as norms for good interpersonal relationships in the classroom. We concluded that students and teachers basically agree about good interpersonal teacher behavior, though there were some differences between individual students and teachers.

In this chapter we reinforced our description of appropriate interpersonal teacher behavior by supporting the norms on the basis of student achievement and attitudes. We can see that the profile of appropriate interpersonal teacher behavior according to outcomes matches the students' and teachers' perceptions in Chapter 3. Thus, teachers should behave in both a dominant and cooperative manner. We've also shown that disagreements over norms for positive inter-personal relationships depend on the emphasis placed on either student achieve-ment or attitudes. The more teachers want to be dominant the more they favor student achievement. These results provide some strong indications for the kind of interpersonal teacher behavior which should be encouraged through teacher education (see Chapter 12).

It also appears that the QTI can be somewhat helpful in evaluating instruc-tional effectiveness, since there is some overlap between interpersonal and in-structional behavior. The QTI can only provide limited guidance, however, and another mechanism is necessary to more completely measure and analyze in-structional effectiveness.

Note

1 Validity and reliability of the instruments was established. For more information about the nature of the study please refer to Brekelmans, Wubbels and Créton (1990).

Chapter 6

Comparison of Teachers' and Students' Perceptions of Interpersonal Teacher Behavior

Theo Wubbels, Mieke Brekelmans and Herman Hooymayers

At several points we've indicated that students' and teachers' perceptions of interpersonal teacher behavior differ. In the Introduction we mentioned that studies have shown students' perceptions of teacher behavior to be more consistent with observational data than teachers' perceptions. Chapter 3 discussed differences in mean students' and teachers' QTI-Scores and in Chapter 5 we noted that students' perceptions of interpersonal teacher behavior were more strongly related to student outcomes than teachers' own perceptions. This chapter will discuss the nature of these differences, beginning with a general description followed by an analysis of how teachers perceive their actual and ideal behaviors. We'll then present some explanations about the relationship between the real and ideal.

Agreement/Disagreement Between Teacher and Students

Wubbels, Brekelmans and Hermans (1987) computed correlations between a teacher's QTI-Scale scores in a class and the mean students' scale scores of that class. In general, teacher scales correlate highest with the corresponding student scales in the model (e.g., DC to DC, CD to CD, etc.). These correlations were only moderately high, however, and ranged between 0.18 and 0.53. Students and their teachers agreed most about the level of the teacher's Leadership and Strict behavior and least about Understanding and Friendly behavior.

In a number of studies absolute differences between a teacher's score and the corresponding students' score were computed for every QTI-Scale. The mean of the eight differences became the measure of each teacher's discrepancy between his or her own and students' perceptions. In one Dutch study the discrepancies and measurement error of students' and teachers' perceptions were compared for two classes each of 143 teachers (86 per cent of total) in two schools (Brekelmans, Wubbels and Hooymayers, 1988; Wubbels, Brekelmans and Hooymayers, 1992). The data was gathered at the start of a mandatory staff development program in

Table 6.1: *Discrepancies Between Teacher Ideal (I), Teacher Self-Perception (T) and Students' Perceptions of Behavior (S) and Measurement Errors in these Discrepancies (discrepancies are averaged over the eight sector scores)*

	I — S		I — T		T — S	
	discr.	meas.err.	discr.	meas.err.	discr.	meas.err.
best class	.16[a]	.06	.13	.07	.10	.07
worst class	.20	.06	.18	.07	.11	.07

a) Scores are mean absolute differences between two scales.
   Scores of a scale range from 0 to 1.

the schools. Department and school-based questionnaire results were used as an initial database to discuss teaching. Individual results were presented to each teacher only after all the data had been gathered. Teachers selected their best and worst classes to complete the QTI. The sample seemed representative of Dutch secondary-school teachers, as indicated by background characteristics compared through chi-square tests. Since teachers and students in the best classes might agree more than the worst classes about communication style, the results for both appear in Table 6.1.

The average of the discrepancy between students' and teachers' perceptions ranges from 0.09 to 0.14. This is much larger than the 0.01 difference between the perceptions provided by students after taking the QTI twice in a four-month interval. The same amount of discrepancies were also found in the American and Australian samples. There is, therefore, a considerable mismatch between the way a teacher and the class perceive the teacher's communication style.

The same study compared the students' and teacher's eight scale scores for each teacher. A sign test showed that a significant number of teachers had different scores than their students on five scales (Helpful/Friendly, Understanding, Uncertain, Dissatisfied and Admonishing — CD, CS, SO, OS, OD). The results demonstrated that the teachers had a more favorable judgment about the learning environment than did their students on scales that are positively related to student achievement and attitudes (e.g., Friendly behavior). About 70 per cent of the teachers' scores were higher than the students' scores. On scales which were negatively related (e.g., Uncertain behavior), 70 per cent of the teachers' scores were lower than their students' scores. A study by Brekelmans and Wubbels (1992), which employed a different methodology, corroborated these results.

An American study (Levy, Wubbels and Brekelmans, 1992) compared students' and teachers' perceptions across several categories of teachers. Throughout all the categories teachers saw themselves as significantly more dominant and cooperative than students did.

To illustrate the differences between teachers' and students' perceptions, Figure 6.1 presents the results from a sample of American volunteer teachers and Figure 6.2 presents results for volunteer first-year and experienced teachers in The Netherlands. We can see that, on average, the American and first-year Dutch teachers see the learning environment more favorably than their students. Paired t-tests show that most of the sector scores differ significantly for these two groups (Créton and Wubbels, 1984; Wubbels and Levy, 1991). The perceptions of the Dutch experienced volunteer teachers do not differ from those of their students.

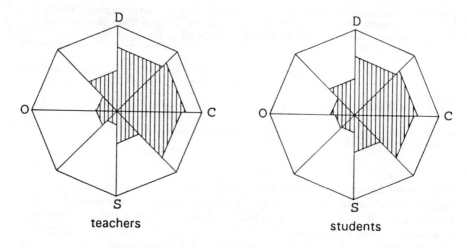

Figure 6.1: *Average Teachers' and Students' Perceptions of American Volunteer Teachers*

teachers

students

Figure 6.2: *Average Teachers' and Students' Perceptions of Beginning and Experienced Dutch Volunteer Teachers*

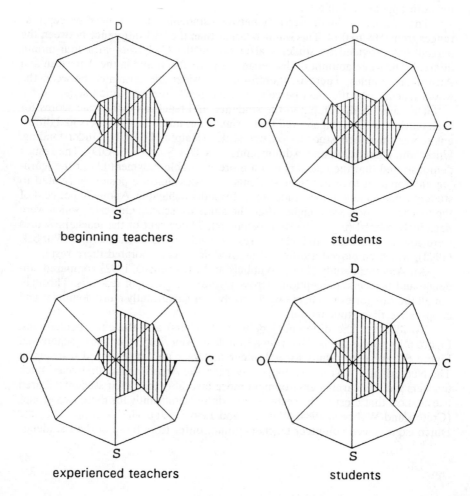

beginning teachers

students

experienced teachers

students

Figure 6.3: *Differences Between Teacher's and Students' Perceptions: the Teacher Sees the Communication More Positively than the Students*

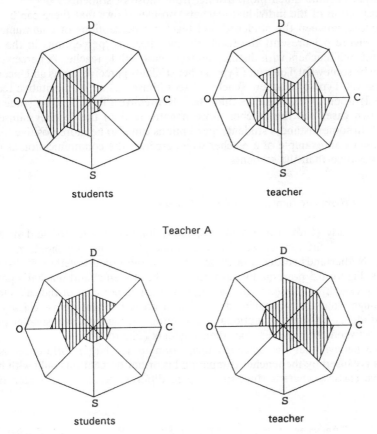

Teacher A

Teacher B

In general, we found larger differences between teachers' and students' perceptions among random samples of teachers than volunteers. In some studies they were also larger for beginning teachers than for those with more experience. This finding was not corroborated, however, by the Brekelmans and Wubbels' (1992) study.

Levy, Wubbels and Brekelmans (1992) and Brekelmans, Holvast and van Tartwijk (1992) analyzed students' and teachers' perceptions of interpersonal teacher behavior for different age and experience groups. They inferred that the discrepancies between students and teachers decrease during the first two years of teaching. They also found indications that as teachers become older the level of discrepancy increases. As American teachers grow older they see themselves as more dominant and cooperative. Their students clearly do not perceive this at all for the proximity dimension and only weakly for the influence dimension. The Dutch teachers' perceptions vary more in accordance with those of their students, although for the most experienced teachers their self-perceptions on the proximity dimension become much more distinct from those of students.

Inspection of the individual teachers' profiles shows that there can be huge differences between the students' and teacher's perceptions of communication styles. Figure 6.3 presents the teacher's and students' perceptions in the same class, for two teachers with distinct discrepancies. While teacher A perceives her class to be somewhat Tolerant (Type 4), her students perceive her as an Uncertain/Aggressive (Type 6) teacher. Teacher B sees himself as an Authoritative teacher (Type 2) whereas the students think he's Repressive (Type 7). The students in these two cases see the teacher more negatively than the teacher himself or herself. In some instances students' perceptions can also be more positive. Figure 6.4 presents an example of a teacher who perceives the communication as much more negative than the students.

Differences Between Different Classes

A Dutch study (Créton and Wubbels, 1984) compared teachers' and students' perceptions of different classes. To understand the results one should note that in The Netherlands students in these grades are grouped together for all their lessons. Figure 6.5 presents two examples of the students' and teacher's perceptions for two/three classes of the same teacher. In 75 per cent of the cases teachers thought that their behavior differed to a greater extent across classes than their students. In some exceptional cases, however, teachers saw smaller differences between their classes than their students (Figure 6.6).

We believe that the teacher's inclination to see larger differences across classes is caused by the teacher comparing his or her perceptions only with his or her own classes, whereas students compare different teachers with each other.

Figure 6.4: Differences Between Teacher's and Students' Perceptions: the Teacher Sees the Communication More Negatively than the Students

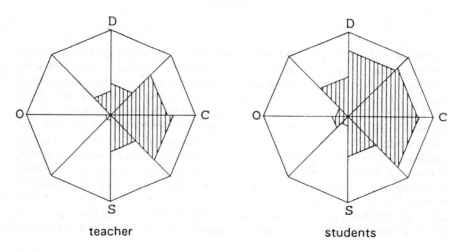

teacher   students

Figure 6.5: *Two Examples of Students' and Teacher's Perceptions in Different Classes of the Same Teacher: the Teacher Perceives Larger Differences than the Students*

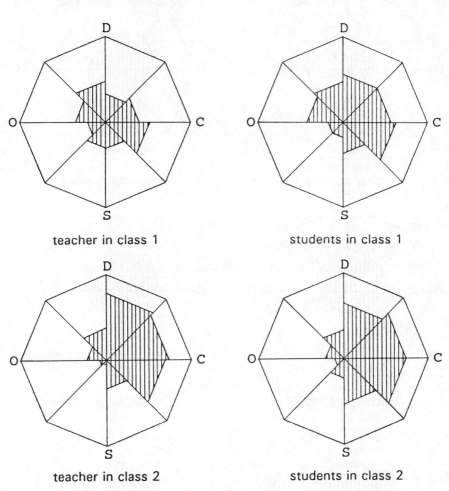

teacher in class 1

students in class 1

teacher in class 2

students in class 2

Teacher A

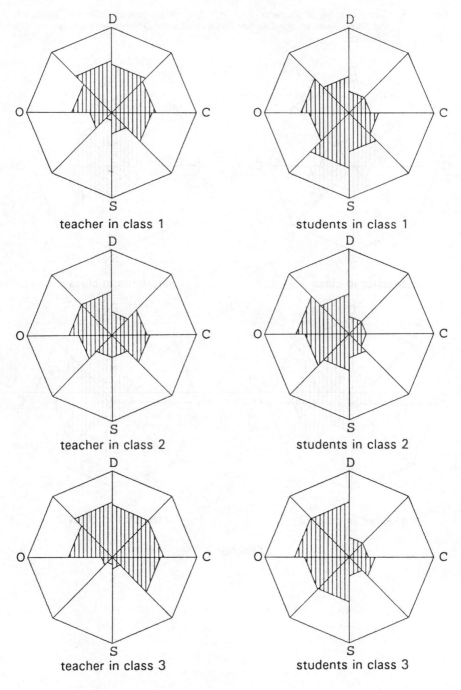

teacher in class 1

students in class 1

teacher in class 2

students in class 2

teacher in class 3

students in class 3

Teacher B

Figure 6.6: Two Examples of Students' and Teacher's Perceptions in Different Classes of the Same Teacher: the Teacher Perceives Smaller Differences than the Students

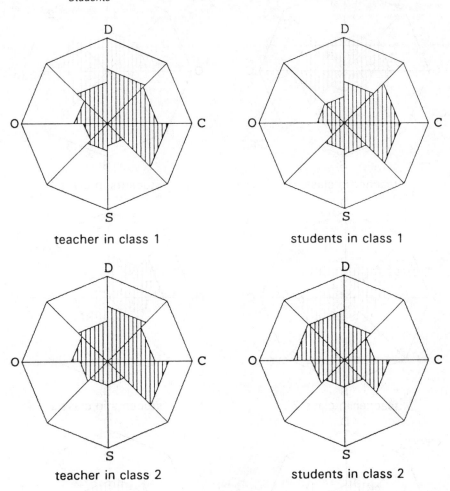

teacher in class 1   students in class 1

teacher in class 2   students in class 2

Teacher A

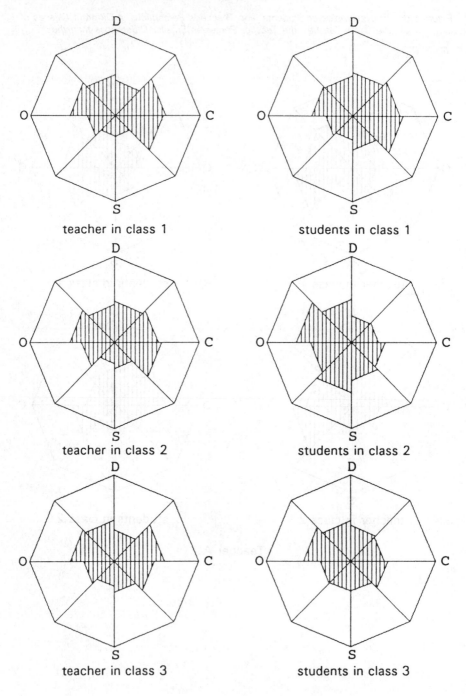

teacher in class 1

students in class 1

teacher in class 2

students in class 2

teacher in class 3

students in class 3

Teacher B

From Brekelmans' (1989) generalizability study it can be concluded that differences between students' perceptions of classes of different teachers are larger than differences between classes of one teacher. Teachers do not usually visit each other's classrooms and consequently are not familiar with other teachers' communication styles. They therefore only have a limited experience base to observe their own communication style, which is basically the way they behave in classes. They therefore tend to overestimate the differences between classes while students have a better perspective because they have many teachers.

Teachers, especially those at the beginning of their careers, often have distinct opinions about the differences between their classes. They frequently mention that they have a class where things are going very well and another that is a mess. They place the other classes in between these two extremes, and characterize them as 'usual'. They tend to be bitter about their problems in the difficult class and excited about their best one. Our results show that these perceptions may not be corroborated by the students' opinions.

Discrepancy and Perceived Behavior

We also investigated the relationship between the amount of discrepancy between the students' and teacher's perceptions and the character of a teacher's behavior in that class. Correlations were computed between every QTI-Scale of the students' perceptions and the discrepancy between the teacher's and students' perceptions (Wubbels, Brekelmans and Hooymayers, 1992). Brekelmans and Wubbels (1992) investigated if the categories of the typology are related to the amount of discrepancy in a sample of 1156 teacher-class combinations. Both analyses point in the same direction.

QTI-Scales that are positively related to student achievement and attitudes are negatively related to the discrepancy (see Table 6.2). The more a teacher and students disagree about the behavior displayed by the teacher, the less the teacher shows Leadership, Friendly and Understanding behavior. For the scales that are negatively related to student outcomes, the opposite relationship occurs. The more a teacher shows Uncertain, Dissatisfied and Admonishing behavior the larger the discrepancy between the teacher's self-report and the students' perception.

Brekelmans and Wubbels' (1992) analyses show that the discrepancies are greater for the proximity dimension than the influence dimension. Teacher types with relatively low student outcomes and/or attitudes (Uncertain/Aggressive, Uncertain/Tolerant, Repressive and Drudging) disagree most with their students about their behavior. They tend to see their behavior as more cooperative than their students, though they agree on the level of dominance.

In sum, the mismatch between self-reports and students' perceptions is larger for teachers who display little effective behavior than for those teachers who show a lot. Assuming students' perceptions are a valid measure of actual teacher behavior, we concluded that the more teachers behave in a manner which promotes student achievement, the more accurate they are in perceiving that behavior.

These results might help explain why beginning teachers disagree with their students more than their experienced peers do. In Chapter 4 we indicated that beginning teachers score higher on the Uncertain, Dissatisfied and Admonishing

Table 6.2: Correlations Between Students' Perceptions of Behavior and the Discrepancy Between Teacher Self-Report (T) and Students' Perceptions of Behavior (S)

	DC	CD	CS	SC	SO	OS	OD	DO
T–S	−.43	−.43	−.39	−.18	.39	.35	.32	.17

behavior scales (more elaborated data will be presented in Chapter 7). They therefore match the profiles of those teachers who disagree most with their students' perceptions. This might be caused by a difficulty in admitting that the quality of their relationship with students is not very high. Similarly, volunteer teachers have a more favorable communication style than teachers sampled at random (Chapter 3) and therefore see their behavior more in agreement with their students. We feel that the type of communication style is more responsible for the differences between teacher's and students' perceptions than individual teacher characteristics, such as experience.

Discrepancies — Teacher Ideal and Teacher's and Students' Perceptions

We investigated the discrepancies between teachers' ideal and students' perceptions for the sample from the two Dutch secondary schools. The analysis was conducted by computing absolute differences for every QTI-Scale. The mean of the eight differences for each teacher was used as the measure of discrepancy between his or her ideal and students' perceptions of the actual behavior. Discrepancies were also computed in the same way between teachers' self-perceptions and their ideals.

The differences between teachers' ideals and students' perceptions and between teachers' perceptions and their ideals appeared much larger than the measurement error for every teacher (Table 6.1). The students' view, therefore, was that no teacher in the sample attained his or her ideal. While the discrepancies are more distinct for the difference between ideal and students' perceptions than for the difference between ideal and teacher's self-perception, we can infer from the latter that teachers realize they are falling short of their goals. In general, however, the discrepancy between ideal and self-report is smaller than between ideal and students' perceptions.

We constructed a global measure for the eight QTI-Scales in order to simultaneously compare the position of teacher's self-reports to both students' perceptions and the teacher ideal. We based it on the relationships that have been described between QTI-Scores and student achievement. The scores on the three scales that are positively related to both student achievement and student attitudes (DC, CD and CS) were totaled, and the three negatively related scales (SO, OS and OD) were subtracted from them. We called this measure the *global QTI-Characteristic*.

When we compare the global QTI-Characteristic for the ideal, the teacher self-report and the students' perceptions, six possible arrangements emerge. Table 6.3 presents the percentage of teachers who demonstrate one of these arrangements. Because a teacher may be able to realize more aspects of his or

Table 6.3: Percentages of Teachers with a Particular Arrangement of Ideal (I), Self-Perception (T) and Students' Perceptions of Behavior (S) on the basis of global QTI-Characteristic

	best class	worst class
I > T > S	63	59
I > S > T	26	36
T > I > S	7	3
T > S > I	1	0
S > T > I	2	1
S > I > T	2	3
	101%	102%

her ideal in one class than another, we present the data for best and worst classes separately.

For most teachers the global QTI-Characteristic of their ideal is higher than the self-perception, which is also higher than the students'. The set of perceptions in Figure 6.7 is an example of this kind of arrangement. For these teachers the self-report falls in between their ideal and the students' perceptions of the actual behavior. They see their behavior more like their ideal than students, and this can be interpreted as wishful thinking. In effect, the teachers overestimate the quality of their performance.

There is also a group of teachers (about 30 per cent) whose students perceive them better than they themselves. Their self-report is lower than the students' perceptions of the actual behavior. The ideal is higher than both. An example of this arrangement appears in Figure 6.8. This group of teachers may view their behavior more negatively (in the light of their ideal) than their students, which could be interpreted as a protection against disappointment. These teachers underestimate the quality of their performance.

The literature on student and teacher perceptions of the learning environment generally reports that teacher perceptions are usually more favorable than students' (e.g., Fraser and O'Brien, 1985). Nisbett and Ross (1980) state that this seems to be a general human bias. Our results show that a great number of teachers do indeed see their own behavior more favorably then their students. It's important to note, however, that there is also a group of teachers who see their behavior in a more negative light.

Influence of Ideals on Self-Perceptions

We have seen that teachers' perceptions of their own behavior do not always match their ideal nor their students' perspective. Relations between teacher's ideals and students' perceptions are also weak. Holvast, Wubbels and Brekelmans (1988) reported, for example, low correlations (below 0.23) between student teachers' ideals and students' perceptions. Surprisingly they found a positive correlation between the ideal Strict and the students' perceptions of Uncertain behavior. The more students see the teacher as Uncertain, the more the teacher wants to be Strict.

Figure 6.7:   *Example of Teacher Self-Report and Ideal, and Students' Perceptions: the Self-Perception Is Closer to the Ideal than the Students' Perceptions*

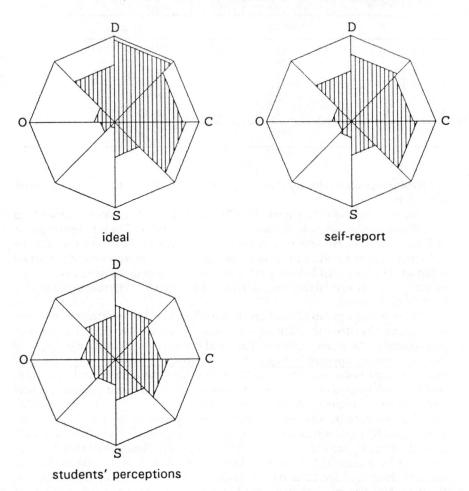

ideal

self-report

students' perceptions

We wondered about the cognitive processes which could produce the kind of relationships we found between teacher self-reports, students' perceptions and teacher ideals. The literature often describes the teacher as a rational professional who is engaged in information processing. We call this a rational-cognitive-action perspective on teacher action and thinking. Examples can be seen in the models of Shavelson and Stern (1981), Clark and Peterson (1986) and Hofer and Dobrick (1978, 1981). According to this view, cognition guides behavior. In terms of teacher–student communication, the teacher ideal is probably most important in this respect. Rational professionals will actively try to behave in keeping with their ideal. In actual practice, however, teachers are limited by their behavioral repertoire and the teaching context (Hamilton, 1983; Huber, 1982; Peters, 1984; Taylor, 1990). The rational-cognitive-action view assumes that teachers' self-

Figure 6.8: Example of Teacher Self-Report and Ideal, and Students' Perceptions: the Students' Perceptions Are Closer to the Ideal than the Self-Report

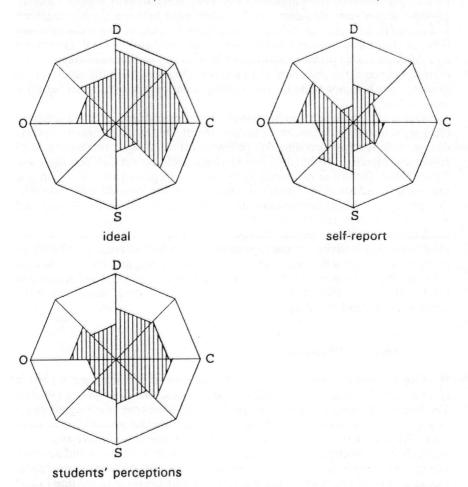

ideal   self-report

students' perceptions

reports are a result of their actual behavior. Teachers 'observe' their own behavior and perceive it accordingly. In sum, a strict rational-cognitive-action perspective implies that ideals might guide someone's practice but that someone's self-report is a result of the actual behavior alone.

Wubbels, Brekelmans and Hooymayers (1992) quantitatively tested the rational-cognitive-action perspective by examining whether the ideals that teachers hold are an important factor in the discrepancies between self-reports and students' perceptions. They used path analyses to investigate whether the self-report is related only to the students' perceptions or to ideals as well. The analyses were performed separately for best classes, worst classes and for the complete sample. They were performed both for the global QTI-Characteristic and every scale of the QTI separately. The analyses (see Appendix 6.1) show that teachers' self-perceptions are influenced by their ideal to a greater extent than students' perceptions influence the self-perception. They don't support a strict rational-cognitive-action view, therefore, on the relationship between teacher cognition and interpersonal behavior. When this perspective holds, we can reduce the gap between ideal and self-perception by changing either behavior or ideal. Tabachnick and Zeichner (1986) provide examples of how these two processes create closer correspondence between beliefs and behavior. One teacher in the study sought to change her behavior while the other changed her beliefs to bring her behavior more in line.

Our results show that another process might be involved, in that a teacher's ideal might directly influence his or her self-report. Due to the pressures of every-day teaching, teachers probably do not always act as rational professionals (e.g., Huber and Mandl, 1984; Mitchell and Marland, 1989; Weinert, 1978; Yinger and Villar, 1986). Distortion can occur in the process of perceiving a situation and processing its information. This distortion can be caused by such things as selective perception, causal attributions, or teacher beliefs and ideals (Nisbett and Ross, 1980; Huber and Mandl, 1984). This can be illustrated by one of the mechanisms to reduce cognitive dissonance (Festinger, 1957). When a teacher's ideal and actual behavior are not consistent, the teacher can align them better by changing his or her self-report. In this case, both the real and the ideal directly influence the self-report. As a result, the discrepancy between self-report and ideal will be smaller than the discrepancy between the students' perception of the actual behavior and the ideal.

Origins of Discrepancies

We have described the two most frequent arrangements of teacher self-reports in relation to their ideal and the students' perceptions. The descriptions (Wishful Thinking and Protection Against Disappointment) come from our interpretations and not from data about teacher's conscious or unconscious processes in explaining their perceptions. To investigate these ideas we interviewed university supervisors about the discrepancies between student teachers' self-reports and students' perceptions of their behavior. We collected perceptions for twenty-two student teachers, most of whom were teaching three or four classes, and discussed them with the university supervisors. These supervisors had been intensively involved in counseling the student teachers throughout their field experience. Supervisors and student teachers discussed the self-reports and observations in depth during approximately ten supervisory conferences.

From the comparisons of the student teachers' profiles it first appeared that the student teachers had different arrangements in different classes. Only seven of the twenty-two student teachers had consistent arrangements. Four repeatedly overestimated their performance: in every class their self-report fell between their ideal and students' perceptions. Three student teachers consistently saw their behavior as more negative than the students in all their classes. All the others had, according to their supervisors, various arrangements in different classes for their self-report, students' perceptions and ideal. The following are some possible explanations of the discrepancies on the basis of these interviews. These hypotheses must be tested in subsequent research.

Differences between student teachers' and students' perceptions, whether over- or underestimated, result in part from their inaccurate notions about the interpersonal effect of behaviors. Behavior considered strict by student teachers is often seen by students as aggressive. Further, students often rate a student teacher's behavior far less dominant than the student teachers themselves. Also, the student teachers tend to think their behavior varies more on the proximity dimension than students do. The student teachers are not used to performing in public. In a public situation such as a class larger variations in behavior and more expressive behaviors are necessary to have a noticeable impact on others than in a one-to-one relationship. In particular, student teachers often rate admonishing behaviors as more extreme than their students do. Finally, student teachers mistake uncertainty for student responsibility and freedom.

One reason why student teachers have various arrangements for different classes is that they do not have very differentiated perceptions of their performance. They tend not to be able to distinguish how their performance in specific lessons relates to a general perception of their communication style. They can, for example, be most impressed by a lesson which goes smoothly and has little disruption. This creates great satisfaction, and they consequently overestimate their performance for that class on all the QTI-Scales. If they aren't satisfied with the atmosphere in another lesson they might underestimate their performance.

A second example of this undifferentiated perception can be seen in teachers who let their self-perception be influenced by different aspects of their performance in different classes. The teacher might think that his or her communication style in class is excellent because of an effective technique. In another class, however, the technique might not have played that great a role, leading to the teacher's more realistic view of his or her communication style.

The supervisors believed that student teachers who underestimated their performance were easily confused by student behavior. They tended to be frightened by minor disturbances, unexpected student questions or remarks, and outside intrusions. They were highly sensitive to negative occurrences, and didn't seem to be aware of the strong points in their lessons. In the supervisory sessions they showed low self-esteem and appeared more helpless than other student teachers. They therefore impeded their own progress by focusing supervision on their difficult classes and overlooking the good ones. These student teachers were receptive to criticism about their teaching both in class and in supervision. Some also asked for and followed advice on how to improve. Others, however, only got depressed as a result of the criticism. They even managed to twist positive feedback into negative, further damaging their self-esteem.

Student teachers who consistently overestimated their performance were, according to their supervisors, highly confident and sometimes overly so. Their confidence can have two origins. It can develop as a consequence of their relatively good performance or it may be an (unconscious) act of protection. In the latter case the student teachers deny the existence of problems in order to protect themselves from the anxiety which would occur if they realized the truth. These teachers also seemed more casual about their lessons. They did not commit themselves strongly to student teaching or supervision. For the good student teachers this didn't present any great problem. The others, however, were displaying Blindness (Chapter 1): they were not aware of the things which went wrong in class. When confronted with these problems they denied them and seemed unwilling to face reality. Some, however, apparently knew within themselves that they weren't doing well — though they never admitted it openly — because they quit student teaching.

Finally, the consistent overestimation of one's own communication style seems to be related to external attribution of problems. According to the supervisors, student teachers who overestimated their behavior blamed students for their difficulties more often than themselves.

Conclusion

Teachers normally do not behave exactly according to their own ideals. Several reasons can be provided for this phenomenon. One reason might be the limits of the teacher's behavioral repertoire. In addition, the school context limits the possibilities of putting the ideal into practice. Finally, ideals might not be that important to teachers: they might not even think about the connection between their beliefs and their behavior. Since many beliefs are to some extent more implicit than explicit (Polanyi, 1966), teachers might therefore not be aware of the discrepancy between their ideal and their real behavior. Implications for teacher education of these kind of reasons for the discrepancies will be discussed in Chapter 12.

Our results show that since ideals partly shape self-reports, they can also distort them. A distortion can be directed two ways. The teachers' perceptions of their own behavior might be too optimistic when their self-perception is closer to the ideal than to the students' perception. Thus, cognitive dissonance can be reduced. This kind of arrangement also can be called an ego-enhancing or self-serving bias in the self-report (Nisbett and Ross, 1980). The teacher may try to prevent damage to his or her self-esteem in the same manner as when ego-enhancing attributions are employed (Ames, 1983; Peterson and Barger, 1985). Our results demonstrate that teachers may also be too pessimistic when they see their behavior more negatively than students. This strategy can protect them from disappointment when confronted with students' perceptions. Another interpretation holds that these teachers might see their behavior more negatively to stimulate themselves to improve their teaching. The reasons and interpretations presented are speculative and should be tested in subsequent research. Important variables would be the influences of internal emotional states, causal attributions, teacher expectancies and preconceptions about the self (Nisbett and Ross, 1980).

This study demonstrates that self-reports might be more a result of teacher ideals than actual behavior. This questions the validity of research which relies on teacher self-reports of the behavior in the learning environment (e.g., Schultz, 1982). This is especially important for evaluations of teacher preparation and staff development programs that often heavily depend on these types of self-analyses (Koehler, 1985). When such programs aim at changing teachers' beliefs they might actually change both beliefs and self-reports, while leaving real behavior unaffected. In these cases the evaluations generally result in an overly optimistic view of the program.

Chapter 7

Interpersonal Teacher Behavior Throughout the Career

Mieke Brekelmans and Hans Créton

Throughout their careers teachers often experience periods of growth and decline (e.g., Summers and Wolfe, 1977). These peaks and valleys may affect teacher-communication style. To adequately describe these changes, researchers would have to collect data from career beginning to end. This, of course, is clearly a daunting task. While we've begun the process — each year for the past four we've analyzed the interpersonal behavior of a group of teachers — a prolonged wait is not necessary for an impression of the communication-style changes teachers undergo as they gain experience. This chapter will analyze the interpersonal behavior of teachers in varying phases of their careers, They are:

— Teachers with four years of experience who have participated annually since they began,
— Two teachers with seven and nine years' experience, respectively, and
— Other groups of teachers with experience up to thirty years.

When combined, this data provides an illustration of teachers' behavior in different stages of their careers. The chapter starts with an explanation of the importance of tracking teacher-career changes. After discussing the results we then present some consequences for teacher education.

Rationale

A knowledge of teacher professional changes can help teacher educators understand the needs and abilities of teachers at different points in their careers. It can serve as the basis for customizing pre or in-service programs: planning interventions, arranging instructional content and sequence; and so on. Studies on the interpersonal aspect of changes in teacher behavior can lead to general improvement of the learning environment, including class management. As noted in Chapter 1, appropriate teacher interpersonal behavior is an important means for preventing discipline problems and fostering professional development (Rosenholtz, Bassler and Hoover-Dempsey, 1986).

While there is a lot of research on interpersonal teacher behavior in the classroom (e.g., Doyle, 1986; Brophy and Good, 1986), very little addresses change during the professional career. Research on teacher maturation often explores the effects of interventions rather than the natural changes which occur over the long term. One notable exception is a longitudinal study by Adams (1982), who used self-reports, classroom observations and students', peers' and supervisors' ratings to examine teacher behavior. He found a number of changes across experience levels. The largest occurred between the first and third year of teaching, in which there was a dramatic increase in the organized/systematic, affective, and stimulating behaviors of both elementary and secondary teachers. Elementary teachers also appeared to influence student behavior in a more positive way as they gained experience. While desirable student behavior also tended to increase for secondary teachers, this result was not statistically significant.

Several models of teacher career stages have been proposed. The most elaborate seems to be the 'Teacher Career Cycle Model', based on an extensive literature review (Christensen, Burke, Fessler and Hagstrom, 1983) and interviews and observations (Burke, Fessler and Christensen, 1984; Fessler, 1985). The model distinguishes eight components of a career cycle: pre-service, induction, competency building, enthusiastic and growing, career frustration, stable and stagnant, career wind-down and finally career exit. As might be expected, teachers differ in the amount of time they remain in various stages. According to Bloom and Jorde-Bloom (1988), some teachers can develop and maintain a high level of enthusiasm for long periods, up to and including their arrival at master-teacher status. These individuals will bypass the career frustration and stable and stagnant stages that others might experience. Allain (1985) and Bloom and Jorde-Bloom (1988) hypothesize that these teachers differ from the others because they derive strong intrinsic enjoyment from student contact. This is a further indication that strong interpersonal skills are vital for teacher professional development.

The Teacher Career

Design of the Study

To better understand teacher-behavior change we compared the communication styles of teachers with different amounts of experience. We analyzed data from 573 teachers and more than 25,000 students located in about 100 different secondary schools throughout The Netherlands. The teachers represent all different subject areas. We summarized the data by analyzing scores on the Influence (DS) and Proximity (CO) dimensions. The higher these scores are, the more dominant (DS) or cooperative (CO) the behavior of a teacher is perceived. As has been our practice throughout this research, we asked teachers to examine their actual and ideal behaviors and then compared these to the students' perceptions. Normally, two or more classes for each teacher participated. Teachers also indicated the number of years they had been in the classroom. To obtain students' and teachers' perceptions scores for each teacher we averaged across the different classes.

For the analyses we divided the teachers into the following six groups:

Figure 7.1:   Mean Influence (DS) Scores by Experience Level

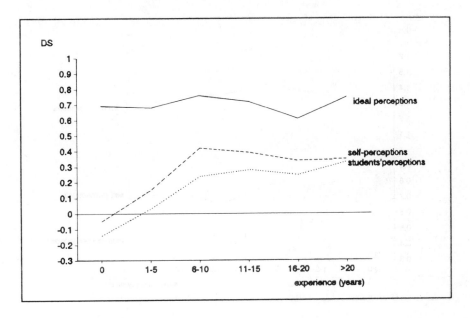

a   student teachers (217),
b   teachers with one–five years of experience (159),
c   six–ten years (53),
d   eleven–fifteen years (81),
e   sixteen–twenty years (42) and
f   more than twenty years (21).

The Influence Dimension

Figure 7.1 plots the means of the Influence (DS) scores for students' and teachers' ideal and self-perceptions of the six groups of teachers. As can be seen, teachers in different stages of their careers do not vary much in their perceptions of ideal dominant behavior. The results of an analysis of variance show that the mean scores of teachers' ideal perceptions are not significantly different (5 per cent level). Throughout their careers teachers apparently agree on the amount of dominant behavior desired in the classroom.

Students' and teachers' perceptions of actual behavior, however, noticeably vary for teachers across experience levels. Students' DS perceptions of student teachers and teachers with one–five years' experience differ significantly from the other groups. An increase in dominant behavior can be seen from the student-teacher period through six–ten years. After this point there is a relative constancy. We arrived at the same results for the teachers' self-perceptions, with the exception that there were no significant differences between one–five-year teachers, sixteen–twenty-year and more than twenty-year teachers.

Figure 7.2:   Mean Proximity (CO) Scores by Experience Level

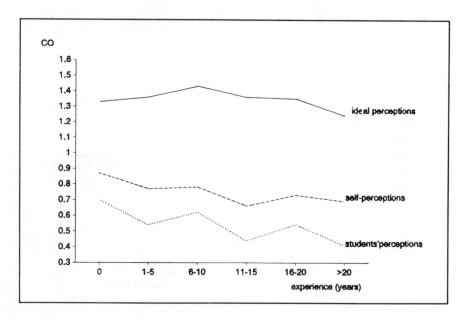

The Proximity Dimension

The results for the Proximity (CO) scores are reported in Figure 7.2. Once again, teachers' perceptions of ideal behavior (in this case cooperative) does not significantly change throughout their careers. Regardless of experience level, teachers basically agree on the amount of cooperative behavior they desire in the classroom.

Like the Influence domain, the mean Proximity-Scores for the students' and teachers' perceptions differ significantly across groups. The differences in the Proximity dimension, however, are much smaller than on the influence dimension and only a few are significant. According to students, student teachers behave more cooperatively than one–five and eleven–fifteen-year teachers. For teachers' self-perceptions, only the difference between student-teachers and teachers with eleven–fifteen years of experience are significant. This indicates a moderate decline in Proximity-Scores throughout the career.

Interpersonal Profiles

The mean ideal interpersonal profile of teachers in this sample can be designated as Tolerant/Authoritative. Three fourths (75 per cent) of the teachers preferred this profile, while 23 per cent preferred the Authoritative type.

Table 7.1 presents the number of profiles of different types by experience. To illustrate the differences at various stages in their teaching career, Figure 7.3 displays the mean students' perceptions of student teachers, six–ten and more than twenty-year teachers.

Table 7.1: Percentages of Profiles (students' perceptions) for Teachers with Different Experience Levels (in years)

exp.	type[a]1	type 2	type 3	type 4	type 5	type 6	type 7	type 8
0[b]	6	7	11	42	27	4	0	3
1–5	12	19	8	19	20	8	1	13
6–10	30	21	6	21	6	2	4	9
11–15	37	19	4	11	4	6	8	11
15–20	29	16	11	13	3	8	11	11
> 20	28	17	6	6	11	11	17	6

a) type 1 = directive; type 2 = authoritative; type 3 = tolerant and authoritative; type 4 = tolerant; type 5 = uncertain/tolerant; type 6 = uncertain/aggressive; type 7 = repressive; type 8 = drudging
b) student-teachers

Figure 7.3: Average Teacher Profiles for Different Experience Levels (students' perceptions)

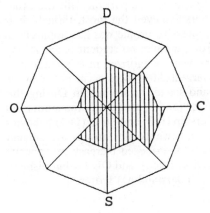

Student-teachers
Tolerant

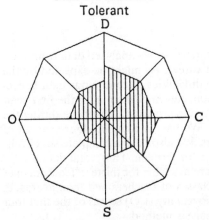

6-10 years of experience
Directive

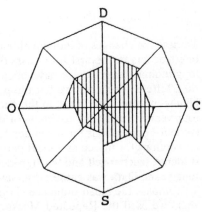

> 20 years of experience
Directive

According to their students, student teachers conform to the Tolerant type. They maintain a supportive atmosphere during their lessons and allow students the opportunity to influence class procedures and content. The teachers' tolerant behavior — which is sometimes interpreted by students in the Uncertain sector — occasionally produces slight disorder in the room. Of the student teachers in our sample 42 per cent had a Tolerant profile, while 27 per cent fit the Uncertain/Tolerant type. Uncertain/Tolerant teachers display a great deal of cooperative behavior and not much Leadership. In a study of physics teachers the Tolerant and Uncertain/Tolerant profiles reflected average affective outcomes (student attitudes). The Uncertain/Tolerant profile, had lower cognitive outcomes (student achievement) than almost all other interpersonal types (see Chapter 5).

Students see teachers with six–ten and more than twenty years' experience as Directive. Directive teachers are well-structured and task-oriented. 30 per cent of the six–ten year teachers and 28 per cent of the twenty-plus group fit this profile. Directive physics teachers' students achieve well and have more positive attitudes in comparison with the other teacher types. 17 per cent of the twenty-plus group were seen by students as Repressive. In comparison with the other types, students of Repressive physics teachers achieved the most, though their affective needs were left unsatisfied. The Repressive profile was less apparent in teachers with fewer years of experience. For example, no student teachers and only 4 per cent of the six–ten-year teachers were categorized in this manner.

From Figure 7.3 we can infer that the largest differences occur between the start of the career (as a student teacher) and six–ten years into it. During this period the amount of Uncertain (SO) behavior (and consequently the amount of disorder) decreases and the amount of Leadership (DC) and Strict (DO) behavior increases. Differences between the six–ten and twenty-plus groups are smaller than at the start of the career. They actually describe an increase in opposite behavior, as can be seen by the higher OS (Dissatisfied), and OD (Admonishing) and lower CD (Helping/Friendly) and CS (Understanding) scores.

The First Four Years

Design of the Study

To describe changes of individual teacher's behavior we analyzed data from fifty-one teachers in the first four years of their career. As might be expected by the longitudinal design, there have been some difficulties in continuous data collection. Fifteen teachers have left the profession, eleven of them after the first year. Nineteen were interrupted in the data-gathering process at least once during the four years, usually due to illness or exams. We have a complete four-year set of students' perceptions for seventeen teachers. We also have a complete set of self-perceptions for fifteen and ideal perceptions for thirteen. Thus, total data sets — students, teacher-self and teacher-ideal — are available for thirteen teachers over four years. Data was gathered in several classes of teachers and then averaged. To compare the mean Influence (DS) and Proximity (CO) scores of the first four years we used the Repeated Measures Analysis method.

Figure 7.4: Mean Influence (DS) Scores by Teaching Year

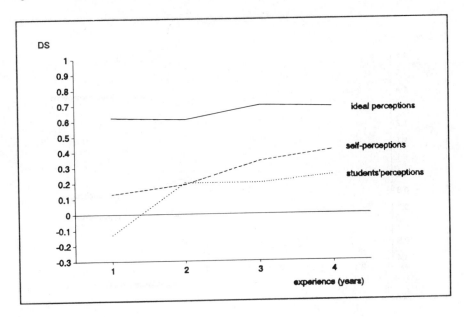

The Influence Dimension

Figure 7.4 presents a plot of the means of the Influence (DS) scores. As occurred in the cross-sectional analysis, there was an upward trend in teachers' self-perceptions and students' perceptions of dominant teacher behavior during the first year of their careers. Once again there was no significant shift in teachers' perceptions of ideal behavior. Repeated measures analyses show that for students' views and teachers' self-perceptions there is a significant relationship between the Influence (DS) scores and years of experience. The most prominent change in students' perceptions is in the second year. It is interesting to note that teachers see themselves as less dominant than students do in the first year, but the scores even out one year later.

The Proximity Dimension

Figure 7.5 presents a plot of the means of the Proximity (CO) scores. Once again in agreement with our cross-sectional analysis, there was no significant shift in teachers' perceptions of ideal cooperative behavior. In addition, there were no significant relationships found between both the teachers' and students' proximity perceptions and years of experience. According to both students and teachers, therefore, cooperative behavior does not significantly increase during the first four years of the teaching career.

Figure 7.5: Mean Proximity (CO) Scores by Teaching Year

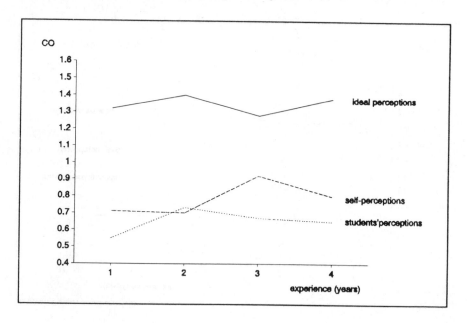

Two Teachers

The two data sets referred to above illustrate the variation between teachers with different experience levels as well as trends in the development of beginning teachers. Every teacher is unique, however, and their attitudes, interpersonal approaches and change experiences cannot be understood solely by group scores.

This section will therefore build on the previous reports with in-depth descriptions of some individual teachers. During the study we conducted open-ended, detailed interviews with several teachers about their relationships with students. Though not the central topic of the interviews, the teachers had received QTI-Profiles each year. We asked them about their experiences in different classes, relationship changes across the years, and motives for their behavior and ideals. The following are case descriptions of the two teachers who have participated the longest in the study: Hugh (nine years) and Tom (seven years).

We will first present some background information, then the profiles and finally excerpts and discussions from the interviews at the end of Hugh's ninth and Tom's seventh year. Both cases include some behavioral change patterns that can be considered average (for the teachers in our study), and others which greatly deviate from the norm.

Hugh

Hugh began to teach when he was thirty. He has a Ph.D in philosophy and is a fully qualified classical-languages teacher. We began working with Hugh in his second year, and have compiled data over the last eight. During this time Hugh

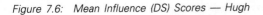

Figure 7.6: Mean Influence (DS) Scores — Hugh

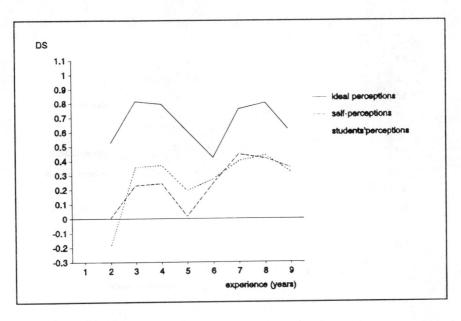

has taught at two secondary schools in different cities in The Netherlands. When we started gathering data in his second year, Hugh had a part-time tenured position in one of the two schools and was employed on a temporary basis in the other. In his fourth year both appointments became permanent. His assignment across the two schools grew from twenty-one classes/week in the second year to twenty-nine in the fourth. For most of his career Hugh has taught six different levels of classical languages. His students were in grades nine–twelve of pre-university education. From the second to the eighth year of his career Hugh also was an advisor to a group of students. Starting in his third year, Hugh had non-teaching assignments ranging from one to six periods per week, largely to do committee work. Hugh estimated that the time he spends on extra-curricular activities (school camps, sports, projects, study weeks, etc.) has varied from zero to 150 hours per year.

Data on Hugh's interpersonal behavior from his students and himself (ideal and self-perception) was gathered once every year in several classes (two–five).

Dimension scores

Figure 7.6 presents Hugh's Dominance (Influence) scores from years two–nine of his career. Figure 7.7 displays his Cooperative (Proximity) behavior during this period. Self-perceptions and students' perceptions were averaged over the different classes.

Students' perceptions of Hugh's dominant behavior at the beginning of his career reflect the same pattern of increase found for the beginning teachers in the longitudinal segment of this study. Hugh's students' saw his greatest change during the third year. Whereas at the end of the second year his students' thought he

Figure 7.7: Mean Proximity (CO) Scores — Hugh

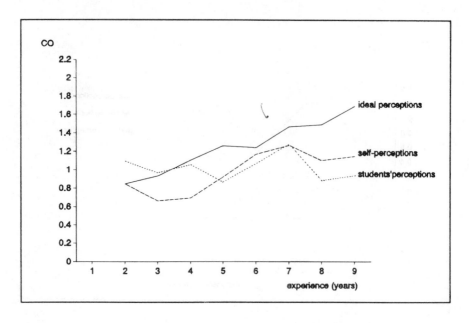

was less dominant than he himself believed, this order reversed one year later. In the longitudinal study we found the greatest change in dominant behavior in the second year. Since we do not have QTI data on Hugh's first year we cannot comment on whether he changed by the end of the second. Hugh thinks that his increase in dominant behavior at the beginning was more moderate than his students believe. In general there is not much difference between the students' views and Hugh's self-perception. His beliefs about ideal dominant behavior are in basic agreement with the other teachers in the study.

In years two–four Hugh's students perceived some fluctuations but no significant upward movement in his cooperative behavior (see Figure 7.7). This is in keeping with the patterns we discovered in both the cross-sectional and the longitudinal segments of our study.

Importantly, the pattern of Hugh's ideal perceptions of both dominant and cooperative behavior do not agree with the previous reports. The longitudinal study, for example, revealed that most teachers maintained a stable perception of ideal cooperative behavior during their first four years. In addition, teachers with different seniority did not vary significantly in their perceptions of ideal interpersonal behavior. In contrast, Hugh's ideal perceptions change in the direction of more cooperative behavior during his first nine years. At the start of his career Hugh preferred less cooperative behavior than most other teachers, whereas after nine years of experience he preferred more.

Hugh's perception of his actual cooperative behavior more closely conforms to his ideals than to his students' views. After the fourth year it shows the same increase we found with his ideal perception, although his self-perception stabilizes

Figure 7.8: *Average Profiles of Hugh in Different Years (students' perceptions)*

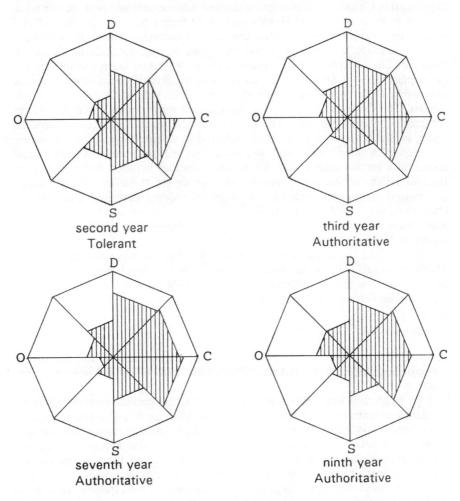

after the seventh year. As with his Dominance scores, Hugh saw less cooperative behavior than his students did at the start of his career. By the seventh year, however, this order had reversed.

Interpersonal profiles

Figure 7.8 presents Hugh's interpersonal profiles (averaged across classes) during his second year (four classes), third (three), seventh (three) and ninth (two) years. The students felt that Hugh matched the Tolerant type during his second year. His class atmosphere could be characterized as supportive and sometimes disorderly. By his third year, and also in his seventh and ninth, he has changed in students' eyes to an Authoritative teacher. His lessons were more structured and the atmosphere was directed toward achievement and task completion. This interpersonal profile is one of the most favorable (in terms of the physics teachers mentioned in Chapter 5) in promoting student achievement and positive attitudes.

An analysis of each of Hugh's eight QTI-Scales between the second and third years reveals the largest differences in the Leadership–Uncertain hourglass, with an increase in Leadership and an accompanying decrease in Uncertain behavior. The Strict-Student Responsibility and Freedom hourglass follows the same pattern, with Strictness increasing and Student Responsibility/Freedom decreasing. Differences from the third to the seventh year on the scales are much smaller. The Cooperative scales slightly increase during years three–seven, but contract between seven–nine. This agrees with the results of our cross-sectional study, in which experienced teachers behaved in a more Oppositional manner.

Figure 7.8 describes the average perceptions of Hugh's students from several classes in a certain school year. There are variations between different classes. Because Hugh decided which classes could participate, the differences cannot be generalized to all of his students. Variations in students' perceptions in different classes are larger for Cooperative behavior than for Dominant. To better understand these differences Figure 7.9 presents the interpersonal profiles from four classes in Hugh's fifth year.

By the time Hugh reached his fifth year the differences between classes were relatively large. The average students' perceptions of Hugh was Authoritative (two out of four classes), though one class thought he was Uncertain/Tolerant and another Tolerant/Authoritative.

In Hugh's words ...

In his ninth year we interviewed Hugh for a personal account of his professional life and relationships with students. This section summarizes and interprets that meeting.

To Hugh, it is important that secondary students become increasingly independent and learn to make their own choices. Allowing freedom and promoting responsibility in the classroom are effective ways to stimulate autonomy and creativity. Hugh believes a teacher has to build this kind of relationship with students. He opens each new class in a traditional manner: structured, teacher-directed lessons, careful monitoring of homework and centralized introduction of new content.

Hugh thinks this approach provides students with a solid framework to build confidence in their teacher. He will occasionally stray outside the scope of his lessons, temporarily untracked by personal contact, humor, or a serious conversation. As confidence increases, these momentary side trips help establish an atmosphere of freedom and responsibility.

By stimulating independence and creativity through structure, Hugh demonstrates substantial leadership behavior. For many teachers (as in the following case of Tom), allowing students responsibility and freedom is accompanied by less leadership and a great deal of uncertainty.

In Hugh's view one must be very clear and structured in explanations, use simple expressions and write all assignments on the board. The goal is to build an environment where students believe they will learn because of the teacher's careful attention to clarity and simplicity.

Hugh generally allows students more freedom in procedures and relationships rather than content, which he tightly controls through his leadership behavior.

Figure 7.9: *Profiles of Hugh in Four Classes in the Fifth Year (students' perceptions)*

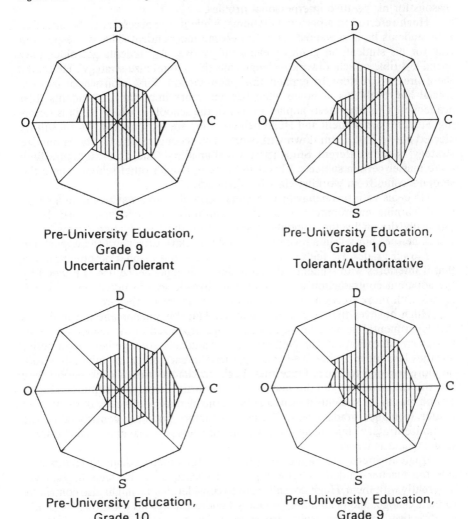

Pre-University Education,
Grade 9
Uncertain/Tolerant

Pre-University Education,
Grade 10
Tolerant/Authoritative

Pre-University Education,
Grade 10
Authoritative

Pre-University Education,
Grade 9
Authoritative

Hugh describes himself as enthusiastic about his profession. By now he doesn't need to prepare much for class, since he's conducted these lessons so many times. He is stimulated by the interaction with students, which allows for the spontaneous and enjoyable mini-diversions he could never have planned. Hugh feels it is possible to teach effectively by placing minimal energy on content and maximum on student involvement. He believes that it isn't necessary to be enthusiastic every lesson, and teachers who attempt this put themselves under needless pressure. Teachers need to be open-minded, remain in touch with students, and not become enslaved by the rules. Personal contact with students is more important than adherence to subject matter and the formal school rules.

Hugh's loyalty to this belief and his realistic goals are undoubtedly the main reasons for his positive interpersonal profiles.

Hugh referred to a personal dilemma: while it was necessary to be directive with students he also wanted them to become independent. This was especially true for his students in grades eleven and twelve. As students get older they spend less time on schoolwork — Hugh calls this a 'minimize-strategy'. He thinks there are two reasons to explain this phenomenon. First, non-school matters (social life, problems at home, etc.) become more important to students than academics. This hypothesis applies to one of the schools in which Hugh is teaching. Students are affluent and Hugh believes they are self-directed. As a result he elected not to load them down with work. The second reason for the 'minimize strategy' is quite different. Students may feel unable — and, as a result, unwilling — to master certain subjects. This is the case in Hugh's other school, where the students come from working-class backgrounds.

He deals with this behavior in a much more directive way, creating a structured learning environment in which he carefully monitors their work. He is especially driven by the students' need to pass their graduation exams. As a result, he sees himself in a much stricter role (a 'slave driver') in the upper than in the lower grades. He feels compelled to teach in this manner despite his belief that it interferes with students' development of independence. He is puzzled by the apparent contradiction in being able to provide some students in the lower grades with more freedom and responsibility than those who are older.

Hugh believes that two factors help explain this phenomenon. The first is the departmental manner in which classes are organized in the higher grades of secondary education (in The Netherlands). If students are together for an entire day they become more involved and supportive of each other and might therefore be more inclined to learn. Once they begin to change groups each period they lose this cohesiveness, and this may affect their achievement and attitudes. Hugh's second reason for students not succeeding is the increasing difficulty of the subject matter in higher grade levels. These two factors not only contribute to the 'minimize strategy', but are also responsible for a less personal interaction between students and teacher.

Hugh attributed the change of attitude of the older students to factors outside the teacher–student relationship. As a consequence, he feels he behaves differently with them. Hugh doesn't seem to consider that he might also contribute to their change, and in so doing probably underestimates his own role. He thinks his directive, controlling, 'slave driver' behavior is a result of students' inability and unwillingness to learn the subject matter. An alternative explanation is that Hugh feels the graduation-exam pressure and is less secure in allowing students freedom and promoting responsibility. In taking a more active teaching role he contributes to greater student passivity.

While the extent of his involvement with students in both lower and upper grades is the same, his behavior is quite different. In the lower grades Hugh acts in an extremely cooperative and occasionally submissive way. He identifies with students, helps them and is able to build their responsibility. In the upper grades, however, he believes he is more dominant in one of the two schools. His concern for the exams makes him feel that he must be strict. Hugh's students, however, do not vary across grades in their views of his strictness.

Hugh thinks he changed his behavior. He believes he is more assertive, but also more flexible and calm in his reactions to students. At the start of his career he was very occupied with content and less concerned with students. He felt that his formal preparation in methodology was inadequate. Hugh is calmer now, he says, because he has a thorough command of the subject matter. When he started teaching he was confronted with unexpected situations, and occasionally did not react well. He is now able to draw on his extensive experience in these predicaments and is rarely caught off guard.

Hugh believes he is more assertive, he says, because he is less hesitant. When he entered a classroom as a beginning teacher and students were noisy, he always hesitated. He now tries to be more active: 'What is happening?' He demonstrates empathy with students' concerns, but also stimulates them to get back to work. He only hesitates when he deliberately decides to do so. He feels it is important to see everything in the room before making the decision to react when things seem to be slipping out of control. Creating a disorder-free climate demands teacher subtlety and astute interpretations of student signals. A teacher must not unilaterally enforce compliance unless absolutely necessary.

From the self-perception in Figure 7.7 it appears that Hugh thinks he learned to be more cooperative and in touch with students. Students, on the other hand did not perceive this upward trend as strongly, since they saw Hugh basically cooperative all the time. He is capable of establishing clear rules without overly corrective behavior. In the first few years Hugh developed a repertoire of small disciplinary actions which he has learned to employ at appropriate moments. This contrasts greatly with the blind behavior and sudden outbursts we will see in the next case.

Hugh has a good insight into the effects of cooperation: the more cooperative the teacher, the more cooperative the student (a symmetrical relationship between student and teacher behavior). In terms of the Influence dimension, he is not sufficiently aware of how his dominant behavior induces students to be submissive (a complementary relationship between student and teacher behavior).

Tom

Tom completed a Masters degree in physics and is a fully qualified teacher in both physics and mathematics. He started his teaching career at twenty-six. With the exception of the fourth year, we collected data on Tom's interpersonal behavior throughout the first seven years of his career. Tom changed schools after the second year; after four years his appointment became permanent. Between his second and fifth years his teaching load increased from nineteen to twenty-eight classes weekly. During his sixth year Tom began to teach three classes at night. Tom's non-teaching periods have ranged from one to three since he began. He estimates his annual number of extracurricular hours (school camps, sports, projects, study weeks, etc.) has varied from fifty to about 250. In most years Tom taught nine different levels of physics and math. In addition he also began to teach computer science. His students were in grades eight–twelve of pre-university education and the higher level of general secondary education. From the second year of his career Tom also was an advisor of a group of students.

Data on Tom's interpersonal behavior, including students' perceptions and his own views of his actual and ideal behavior, were gathered once each year in two–seven classes.

Figure 7.10:   Mean Influence (DS) Scores — Tom

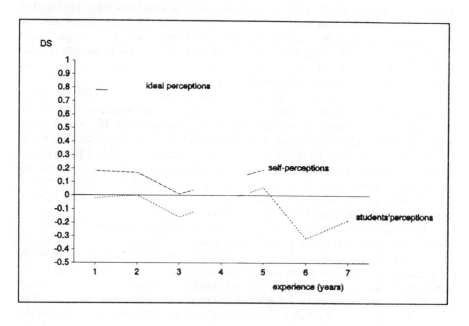

Dimension scores

Figures 7.10 and 7.11 describe Tom's Influence and Proximity-Scores in the first seven years of his teaching career (minus the fourths). Self-perceptions and students' perceptions scores were averaged over the different classes in which data was gathered.

In contrast with most teachers in our study, Tom's dominant behavior does not generally increase in his first seven years though there are fluctuations. After the decrease in the third year, there is a slight increase (according to both students and Tom himself), but then it goes down again. Students' perceptions of Tom's dominant behavior are lower than the average for a first-year teacher. In 67 per cent of the classes where we collected both students' and self-perceptions, Tom consistently overestimated — and never underestimated — his dominant behavior.

Unfortunately, we only have data on Tom's ideal perception in his first year. At that time he would rather have been more dominant than he and his students thought he was.

Tom's cooperative behavior (see Figure 7.11) follows the same pattern, in that there is no overall increase in the first seven years. This is in keeping with the results reported in the longitudinal and cross-sectional segments of this study. Tom is exceptional, however, in the sense that the discrepancy between his students' and his own perceptions is larger than the average normally found with either beginning or veteran teachers. Students are more negative about Tom's cooperative behavior than about other teachers. On the other hand, Tom's perceptions of his own cooperative behavior (and ideal behavior in the first year) are more positive than those of 'the average teacher' in our study. In 83 per cent of

Figure 7.11: Mean Proximity (CO) Scores — Tom

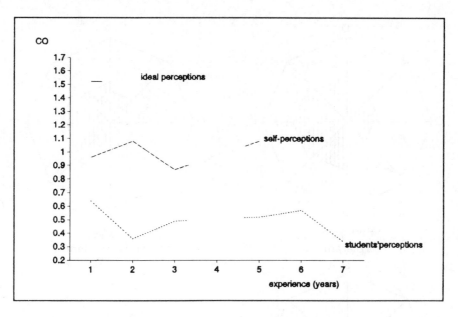

the classes which participated Tom overestimated his cooperative behavior. Once again, there were no underestimations.

Interpersonal profiles

The profiles in Figure 7.12 represent average students' perceptions in Tom's first, third and seventh years (seven classes each year). During his first year students saw Tom as Tolerant. As mentioned above, Tom's classes can be characterized as supportive and occasionally disorderly, a profile which is rather prevalent with beginning teachers. Hugh also had this type of profile at the start of his career though he displayed more Understanding and less Admonishing behavior. By the third year Tom is seen as an Uncertain/Tolerant type. The increase in dominant behavior (Leadership and Strictness) which characterized Hugh's career didn't occur for Tom. In the third year his Leadership decreases and Uncertain behavior increases. Worse, his Helpful/Friendly index also decreases, with an accompanying increase in Admonishing behavior. Students' profiles of Tom at this point indicate a less structured environment with greater disorder than in the first year. In his third year Tom transferred to a more traditional school. His Uncertain/Tolerant profile continued until the seventh year, when students experienced a further decrease in the Helpful/Friendly and Understanding sectors. This decrease in cooperative behavior resembles Hugh's changes between his seventh and ninth year. It is also in agreement with the cross-sectional study, which found that teachers with more years of experience become more Oppositional.

The profiles in Figure 7.12 present an average portrayal of students' perceptions from several of Tom's classes in three selected years. Students' perceptions vary, however, across classes. Since Tom, like Hugh, selected the classes which

Figure 7.12: Average Profiles of Tom in Different Years (students' perceptions)

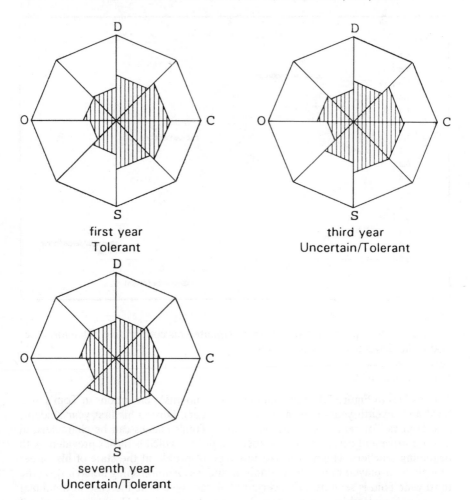

first year
Tolerant

third year
Uncertain/Tolerant

seventh year
Uncertain/Tolerant

participated the differences cannot be generalized to all of his students. As with Hugh, differences between classes are in greater evidence for cooperative behavior than dominant. To understand these differences, Figure 7.13 presents interpersonal profiles from Tom's seventh year of teaching. The three classes shown (out of seven in which data were collected) varied most in perceptions. While the divergence in the remaining four was not as large, it was still noticeable.

In comparing the three classes, the differences in the Leadership–Uncertain hourglass is most prominent. The Uncertain cone in the Uncertain/Aggressive profile (first row on left) is more than twice as large as the Leadership sector. The Uncertain/Tolerant profile (on right) has a fifty/fifty segmentation between the two scales, and the Tolerant profile clearly favors Leadership over Uncertain. It seems therefore that Tom hasn't yet reached stability between the two opposing

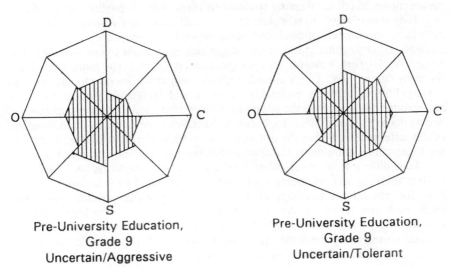

Figure 7.13: Profiles of Tom in Three Classes in the Seventh Year (students' perceptions)

Pre-University Education,
Grade 9
Uncertain/Aggressive

Pre-University Education,
Grade 9
Uncertain/Tolerant

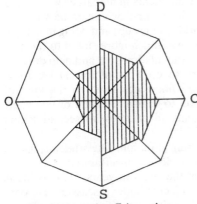

Pre-University Education,
Grade 11
Tolerant

behaviors — the balance between his Leadership and Uncertain scales is not consistent.

In Tom's words....

As with Hugh, we interviewed Tom for a first-hand account of his seven years in the profession. Once again, we summarize his narrative and offer some interpretations.

Tom's main motive in teaching is to develop a trusting relationship with his students. He rejects the role in which the teacher acts as an enforcer, preferring one in which he can use his expertise to help students understand difficult subject matter.

Tom's definition of 'developing trust' seems vague — we think he probably means 'being liked' or 'wanting students to learn through intrinsic motivation'.

Tom always wants to stimulate students and elicit their reactions. To do so, he asks them all kinds of questions, some of which are surprising. He wants his students' input to come ahead of his own, which contributes to commotion in his classroom. To Tom, however, this is logical and desirable: 'The more incentives, the more commotion'. Tom's attitude seems to jeopardize his developing consistent equilibrium between leadership behavior and facilitating student freedom and responsibility. He feels the latter is naturally connected to teacher uncertainty, and he doesn't see any difference between them. We believe that an understanding of this difference as well as the distinction between leadership and strict behavior are important requirements for appropriate teacher–student relationships.

Tom differs from many other teachers (such as Hugh) in his belief that student thinking and involvement can only be stimulated by submissive teacher behavior. He refuses to adopt what he calls 'a repressive position', but what might be better termed a 'dominant position'. He consequently forces himself into an interpersonal profile which overemphasizes Uncertain behavior. This attitude seems to be the most important reason for Tom's remarkable lack of change in dominant behavior in his first seven years.

In Tom's opinion, one of the most significant events in his career was changing schools in his third year. He relates that in his first two years he was in a school where students were accustomed to working in groups and doing individual activities. He thought his communication style was much more suited to this first school than the second. There, he could allow students freedom and help develop their responsibility, and it was not necessary to do a lot of formal lecturing. Students in his second school, however, were not accustomed to the kind of tolerant teaching style he preferred and he had to change. In spite of two years of experience, he therefore had more problems adapting to his second school than his first.

The change imprisoned Tom in a conflicting situation. The students, aware of his frustration, probably interpreted his behavior as uncertainty.

Tom believes his behavior has changed in the last four years. He now limits student sidetracks if he thinks an important subject is under discussion. He considers the consequences of his behavior and doesn't unconditionally support students' activity as he did in the beginning of his career. Tom is more sensitive to disruptions and takes time in September to explain his rules and methodology. He thinks he has become stricter in certain areas.

Tom's lessons are more structured and he has a clearer grasp of his goals and how to attain them. He feels that students appreciate his change in behavior and provided the following example to prove the point. When students start talking, Tom does not immediately stop them. He only puts an end to it when they become a nuisance — and even then he begins to 'grumble' rather than take direct action. Further, when the class is noisy he frequently joins in the fun rather than act to maintain order. Unfortunately, when things have gone too far and he loses control Tom expends a great deal of energy in getting everyone back on track. He says he doesn't enjoy doing this, since he wants to be liked.

This image of Tom trying to manage his class is worrisome because his behavior is inconsistent and inadequate. What is accepted for the first student is not tolerated for the tenth. Even when he intervenes — or 'grumbles' — to maintain order, he probably directs his attention to the wrong student. This 'wrong time–wrong place' behavior is seen by students as oppositional. On the other hand, when he behaves the same way at the right moment — to the right student — the same behavior may be perceived as cooperative.

As mentioned, Tom believes he has become more dominant and feels that students appreciate the change. His classes don't agree, according to the interpersonal profiles. Figure 7.10 does show an increase in Dominance between the third and fifth years, but it sharply falls off after that. Students' perceive Tom's cooperative behavior consistently for years three–six in Figure 7.11, but again there's a drop off in the seventh year. While not readily apparent in Figure 7.12, a close examination of the first and seventh years' profiles would show a decrease in Helpful/Friendly (CD) and Understanding (CS) behavior. Thus, the shift toward Dominance in Tom's eyes is viewed by students as a shift toward Opposition. One possible explanation can be found in Tom's inadequate concept of communication style and limited repertoire of Dominant behavior. Tom's unsatisfactory understanding of interpersonal behavior is reflected in his inability to differentiate between the Strict (DO) and Leadership (DC) and Freedom/Responsibility (SC) and Uncertain (SO) sectors. As a result, it seems that students interpret his actions in a different way than he intended. For example, if he tries to establish rules his students might see him as Admonishing; if he attempts to be Friendly, they might think he is Uncertain and lacks control.

Conclusion

As has been seen, students' and teachers' perceptions of both Influence and Proximity dimensions are generally lower than teachers' ideals. In the Dominance (DS) half of the model students' and teachers' self-perceptions progress toward the ideal at the beginning of a teacher's career. On the cooperation (CO) side, however, the discrepancy between the students' and teachers' views of actual behavior and the teachers' ideal seems to increase. While Tom is an exception, it appears that throughout their careers teachers try to demonstrate increasing Leadership and Strict behavior. In effect, they attempt to behave in accordance with their ideal. This shift does not occur for the Proximity dimension — teachers don't become more Friendly and Understanding in later stages of their careers.

There is a possible explanation for this difference between the Influence and Proximity changes. Most student-teachers are about twenty–twenty-five years old and have not — to any large degree — provided leadership to other people. While they develop dominance patterns through daily classroom practice, they often begin from 'ground zero'. Friendly, Helping and Understanding behavior, on the other hand, are more familiar to them. As a result, their cooperative repertoire is more established and they need less practice.

As their careers progress teachers become less cooperative and their enthusiasm seems to dwindle at the hands of routine and stress. They may gradually distance themselves from students, and their norms and values may change (Hermans, Créton and Hooymayers, 1987). They also can become increasingly tired, impatient, demanding and dissatisfied with students. A small change in a teacher's cooperative behavior can lead to negative communication spirals. We will discuss the consequences of this phenomenon for teacher education in Chapter 12.

As teachers mature they experience greater changes in the Influence dimension than the Proximity. One possible explanation is that the former reflects personal characteristics (with experience as one of the relevant factors), while the latter is a result of teacher–student interaction. Support for this rationale can be seen when comparing a teacher's different classes. Students' perceptions across classes are much more consistent for the Influence dimension than for the Proximity.

Development of cooperative behavior may require teacher-education procedures which differ from those for dominance. Skill training may be most effective in developing the influence dimension. For proximity behavior, however, pre and in-service programs might simply help teachers uncover skills which they already possess. Helping teachers understand the systems nature of classroom communication can further assist them to mine their interpersonal repertoire. This will also be discussed in Chapter 12.

In sum, the results indicate that both students and teachers believe that interpersonal behavior changes during the professional career. The changes are mainly found in Dominant behavior, which intensifies toward the teacher's ideal during the first ten years. After this point, Dominance stabilizes. Cooperative behavior, however, basically remains consistent throughout the entire teaching career and there is no shift toward the ideal. In our previous research with physics teachers (see Chapter 5) we noted that dominant behavior positively relates to student achievement. In a similar manner, cooperative behavior is also positively associated with affective outcomes. The results lead us to conclude that teachers with about ten years of experience have the best interpersonal relationships to promote student achievement and positive attitudes. Chapter 8 will expand our focus on teacher-communication styles from the classroom to the school.

Chapter 8

Interpersonal Teacher Behavior and School Environment

Darrell Fisher, Barry Fraser and Theo Wubbels

This chapter describes the results of a study which brings together for the first time research on school-level environment and teacher–student relationships in the classroom. The study was conducted in seven schools in Tasmania and Western Australia in which forty-six teachers provided perceptions of their school-level environments and 792 students on their classroom environments. In order to assess these perceptions two questionnaires were used, the School Level Environment Questionnaire (SLEQ) and the Questionnaire on Teacher Interaction (QTI). This chapter describes the first use of the QTI in Australia. It begins with comments on the distinction between school-level and classroom environment, and then describes assessment of school environment, the development, validation and use of the SLEQ, interpersonal behavior of teachers in the classroom and the use of the QTI. The chapter concludes with a discussion of some relationships between the scores on the two instruments.

School-Level and Classroom-Level Environment

A distinction needs to be drawn between school-level and classroom-level environment (Fraser and Rentoul, 1982; Genn, 1984). Whereas classroom climate normally refers to relationships between teachers and their students or among students, school climate pertains to a teacher's relationships with other teachers, senior staff and the school principal. Students' perceptions are frequently used to measure classroom environment. They are not often included in measurements of school climate, however, because some students might not be aware of important school-level characteristics. The school environment can also be considered more global than the classroom environment.

Classroom environment research has been based on different theoretical and conceptual foundations than research at the school level. The theoretical underpinnings of classroom research come from perceptual psychology, personality studies and field theory (e.g., Lewin, 1936; Murray, 1938; Pace and Stern, 1958) and are described in several reviews (e.g., Chavez, 1984; Fraser, 1986, 1989; Fraser and Walberg, 1991; Moos, 1979; Walberg, 1979). School-environment research has been associated with the field of educational administration and rests on the assumption that schools can be viewed as formal organizations (Anderson, 1982; Thomas, 1976).

For many years there has been an inference in educational literature that positive school environment is linked with student achievement. The suggestion is that if teachers have a healthy working environment then better student achievement will result. For example Hughes (1991, p. 62) asserted that every school has a pervasive climate which influences the behavior of staff and students to succeed in teaching and learning. Brookover, Schweitzer, Schneider, Beady, Flood and Wisenbaker (1978) stated that the quality of school climate may influence the behavior of all participants and especially students' academic performance. Furthermore, Purkey and Smith (1985) observed that the research is persuasive in suggesting that student academic performance is strongly affected by school culture. While other support can be found for the hypothesis that schools with favorable climates or cultures are academically more successful with students, some writers (e.g., Partland and Karineit, cited in Walberg, 1979) have argued that conclusions on these relationships are premature because the data on school environments and student outcomes have been confounded by several issues. The link between school and classroom environment continues to be of interest and is addressed in this chapter.

Assessment of School Environment and Teacher Interpersonal Behavior

In order to describe school atmosphere one must understand its relationship to other formal organizations. Through his work in a variety of environments, including school classrooms, hospitals, prisons and military bases, Moos (1974) developed three broad categories of dimensions which describe diverse psychosocial settings. They are: Relationship Dimensions (e.g., peer support, involvement) which identify the nature and intensity of personal relationships, and assess the extent to which people are involved in the environment and the degree to which they support and help each other; Personal Development Dimensions (e.g., autonomy, competition) which assess the basic directions along which personal growth and self-enhancement tend to occur; and System Maintenance and System Change Dimensions (e.g., innovation, clarity, work pressure) which involve the extent to which the environment is orderly, clear in expectations, maintains control and is responsive to change. This three-category framework was used to develop the School Level Environment Questionnaire (SLEQ).

Some examples of existing school-environment instruments are the College Characteristics Index (CCI; Pace and Stern, 1958) which measures students' or staff perceptions of thirty environment characteristics; the High School Characteristics Index (HSCI; Stern, 1970) which is an adaptation of the CCI; the widely used Organizational Climate Description Questionnaire (OCDQ; Halpin and Croft, 1963); and the Work Environment Scale (WES, Moos, 1981; Fisher and Fraser, 1983). More recently the School Level Environment Questionnaire (SLEQ) has been found to be a useful instrument for assessing teachers' perceptions of school-level environment. This instrument consists of fifty-six items across seven scales.

As mentioned, this chapter examines the relationship between school environments and interpersonal teacher behavior, or communication style. The Leary model and its accompanying Questionnaire on Teacher Interaction (QTI) was used to describe the interpersonal behavior of teachers in the classroom. Both the model and instrument were described in Chapter 2.

Methodology

Forty-six teachers in seven schools completed the School Level Environment Questionnaire (SLEQ), and a mean score was calculated for each SLEQ-Scale at each school. The QTI was administered to one class selected by each teacher. Mean scores were calculated for each of the eight scales per class. Each teacher also completed the QTI twice, once describing their actual relationship with that class and once describing what they believed an ideal classroom situation would be like.

Development and Validation of the SLEQ

The School Level Environment Questionnaire, which measures teachers' perceptions of the psychosocial dimensions of the school environment, grew out of previous work with the WES. A careful review of the potential strengths and problems associated with existing school environment instruments, including the WES, suggested that the SLEQ should satisfy the following six criteria (Rentoul and Fraser, 1983; Fisher and Fraser, 1990; Fisher and Fraser, 1991).

1 Its dimensions should reflect important aspects in the literature on school environment, such as relationships among teachers and between teachers and students and the organizational structure (e.g., decision-making).
2 It should cover Moos's three general categories of dimensions: Relationship, Personal Development and System Maintenance/System Change.
3 Its dimensions and individual items should address aspects of the school environment perceived to be salient by teachers.
4 It should only include material relevant to the school.
5 It should provide a measure of school-level environment which has minimal overlap with existing measures of classroom-level environment.
6 It should have a small number of reliable scales, each containing a fairly small number of items.

To satisfy the criteria, the SLEQ was developed. It featured seven scales, each of which belongs to one of Moos's three categories. They are listed below.

Student Support (Relationship)
Affiliation (Relationship)
Professional Interest (Personal Development)
Staff Freedom (System Maintenance/Change)
Participatory Decision Making (System Maintenance/Change)
Innovation (System Maintenance/Change)
Resource Adequacy (System Maintenance/Change)

Following initial uses of the SLEQ and discussions with teachers we concluded that it was weak in measuring how work pressure influenced teachers' perceptions of their environment. Moos's Work Environment Scale also indicated the value of a Work Pressure scale, and it was therefore added to the System Maintenance/Change category.

The SLEQ consists of fifty-six items (eight scales, seven items each). Each item is scored on a five-point Likert scale which runs from Strongly Agree to Strongly Disagree. Table 8.1 provides scale descriptions, sample items and Moos's categories as well as information on the scoring of the SLEQ-Items. The SLEQ has two forms: one which assesses perceptions of what a school work environment is actually like and a second for the preferred (or ideal) environment. The preferred form aims at goals and value orientations. Item wording is almost identical in the actual and preferred forms except that an item such as 'Teachers *are* encouraged to be innovative in this school' in the actual form would be changed to 'Teachers *would be* encouraged to be innovative in this school' in the preferred form.

Validation of SLEQ

Validation data are available for the SLEQ for four samples and include information about each scale's internal consistency (Cronbach alpha reliability) and discriminant validity (mean correlation of a scale with the other seven scales). The first sample in Table 8.2 consisted of eighty-three teachers from nineteen co-educational government schools (seven elementary and twelve secondary) in the Sydney metropolitan area. The second sample consisted of thirty-four secondary school teachers, each in a different government high school in New South Wales. Each of these teachers was teaching in his or her first year after completion of pre-service training. Approximately equal numbers of science and social-science teachers, males and females, and metropolitan and country schools made up the sample. The third group consisted of 109 teachers in ten elementary and secondary schools in Tasmania. These teachers are the only ones who responded to both the preferred as well as actual form of the SLEQ. It should be noted that the Work Pressure scale had not yet been added to the questionnaire. It was only used with the fourth sample, which consisted of forty-six teachers in the seven schools in Tasmania and Western Australia.

Table 8.2 shows that the alpha coefficient for different SLEQ-Scales ranged from 0.64 to 0.92. These values suggest that each SLEQ-Scale displays satisfactory internal consistency for a scale composed of only seven items. Previous calculations of the mean correlation of each scale with other SLEQ-Scales ranged from 0.05 to 0.42, which indicated satisfactory discriminant validity and suggested that the instrument measures distinct although somewhat overlapping aspects of school environment.

A school-environment instrument should be able to differentiate between the perceptions of teachers in different schools. The views of teachers within the same school should be relatively similar, while differing from perceptions of those in other schools. This characteristic was explored for each scale of the SLEQ's actual form for the sample of 109 teachers in ten schools described in Table 8.2. A one-way ANOVA was performed for each scale, with school membership as the main effect. It was found that each SLEQ-Scale differentiated significantly

Table 8.1: Description of Scales in SLEO and their Classification According to Moos's Scheme

Scale Name	Description of Scale	Sample Item	Moos's general category
Student Support	There is a good rapport between teachers and students and students behave in a responsible self-disciplined manner.	There are many difficult students in the school (–)	Relationship
Affiliation	Teachers can obtain assistance, advice and encouragement and are made to feel accepted by colleagues.	I feel that I could rely on my colleagues for help if I should need it (+).	Relationship
Professional Interest	Teachers discuss professional matters, show interest in their work and seek further professional development	Teachers frequently discuss teaching methods and strategies with each other (+).	Personal development
Staff Freedom	Teachers are free of set rules guidelines and procedures, and of supervision to ensure rule compliance.	I am often supervised to ensure that I follow directions correctly (–).	System maintenance and system change
Participatory Decision-Making	Teachers have the opportunity to participate in decision making.	Teachers are frequently asked to participate in decisions concerning administrative policies and procedures (+).	System maintenance and system change
Innovation	The school is in favor of planned change and experimentation, and fosters classroom openness and individualization.	Teachers are encouraged to be innovative in this school (+).	System maintenance and system change
Resource Adequacy	Support personnel, facilities, finance, equipment and resources are suitable and adequate.	The supply of equipment and resources is inadequate (–).	System maintenance and system change
Work Pressure	The extent to which work pressure dominates school environment.	Teachers have to work long hours to keep up with the workload (+).	System maintenance and system change

Items designated (+) are scored by allocating 5, 4, 3, 2, 1, respectively, for the responses Strongly Agree, Agree, Not Sure, Disagree, Strongly Disagree. Items designated (–) are scored in the reverse manner. Omitted or invalid responses are given a score of 3.

Table 8.2: *Internal Consistency (Alpha Reliability) for Each SLEQ-Scale for Four Samples*

Scale		Alpha reliability			
	Number of items	Sample 1	Sample 2	Sample 3	Sample 4
Student Support	7	0.70	0.79	0.85	0.92
Affiliation	7	0.87	0.85	0.84	0.85
Professional Interest	7	0.86	0.81	0.81	0.80
Staff freedom	7	0.73	0.68	0.64	0.65
Participatory decision-making	7	0.80	0.69	0.82	0.79
Innovation	7	0.84	0.78	0.81	0.66
Resource adequacy	7	0.81	0.80	0.65	0.76
Work Pressure	7				0.85
Sample size Teachers		83	34	109	46
Schools		19	34	10	7

(1 per cent level) between schools and that the eta^2 statistic (an estimate of the proportion of variance in SLEQ-Scores attributable to school membership) ranged from 16 to 40 per cent for different scales. We therefore concluded that the instrument does indeed differentiate between the perceptions of teachers in different schools.

The Questionnaire on Teacher Interaction (QTI)

Previous chapters (2–5) have described the development and validation of the QTI, its cross-cultural usefulness, the typology of interpersonal teacher-behavior profiles and the relationship of communication style to student achievement. This chapter describes the first use of the QTI in Australia. Reliability data of the QTI has already been presented in the second chapter. The reliabilities for the Australian sample appeared satisfactory (see Appendix 2.3).

Results and Interpretation

Differences Between Schools

Analyses were intended to determine whether there were any differences between the environments of the seven schools as detected by the SLEQ. In the following Table 8.3, one is low and five is high.

An analysis of variance was completed for every scale to see if there was a school effect on the SLEQ-Scores. Because of the small number of cases per school, the 10 per cent level of significance was adopted as reasonable. The results indicated that significant effects occurred on Student Support, with school five being highest, followed by school three; and on Staff Freedom, in which school five was especially low. It is interesting to note that school five is a new secondary college (grades eleven and twelve) and it is possible that staff perceive a reduced level of freedom while policies are being established.

Table 8.3: School Mean Scores on SLEQ-Scales

School	SS	AF	PE	SF	PDM	IN	RA	WP
1	1.7	1.8	2.2	2.4	2.7	2.9	2.5	1.9
2	1.7	1.6	2.5	2.2	2.6	2.7	2.1	2.0
3	2.4	1.6	2.3	2.3	2.4	2.9	2.8	1.4
4	2.0	2.1	2.3	2.3	2.5	2.7	2.4	1.8
5	3.2	2.3	2.5	2.0	2.6	2.5	2.8	2.4
6	1.8	2.1	2.6	2.7	2.9	3.0	2.3	2.3
7	1.8	1.7	2.1	2.6	2.2	2.3	2.0	1.7
F value	8.45*	1.44	0.51	2.11*	0.66	1.72	1.80	1.84

df between groups = 6, within groups = 39.   N = 46. * = p < .10

Table 8.4: Mean QTI-Scores for Seven Schools for Students' (st) and Teachers' (t)
Perceptions

School	DC		CD		CS		SC		SO		OS		OD		DO	
	st	t	st	t	st	t	st	t	st	t	st	t	st	t	st	t
1	.69	.72	.74	.86	.74	.84	.33	.34	.20	.21	.19	.18	.22	.22	.44	.44
2	.69	.73	.72	.82	.70	.79	.36	.32	.20	.13	.25	.24	.27	.23	.47	.49
3	.78	.83	.80	.93	.77	.86	.33	.31	.15	.05	.14	.11	.18	.13	.48	.48
4	.77	.79	.81	.89	.77	.85	.32	.32	.15	.14	.22	.22	.20	.20	.47	.49
5	.68	.66	.75	.77	.72	.74	.42	.39	.22	.18	.21	.21	.22	.23	.36	.38
6	.57	.70	.61	.78	.63	.78	.33	.29	.29	.27	.31	.28	.32	.25	.48	.54
7	.73	.73	.79	.87	.75	.84	.34	.30	.19	.10	.18	.16	.17	.16	.43	.47

Teacher Interaction

Table 8.4 presents QTI-Scores for both students' and teachers' perceptions in the seven schools. Teachers in school five and students in school six have less favorable perceptions than the others, i.e., they have lower scores on scales which relate positively to student achievement.

Analyses of variance were performed to determine whether there was a school effect on the QTI-Scores. The results of each questionnaire completed by a student or teacher were calculated in terms of the two Leary factors: Dominance–Submission (DS) and Cooperation–Opposition (CO). In Table 8.5 the higher the DS score the more teachers are perceived to exhibit behaviors in the DO (Strict) and DC (Leadership) sectors, and less in Uncertain (SO) or Student Responsibility and Freedom (SC). The higher the CO score the more teachers are thought to exhibit behaviors in the CD (Friendly) and CS (Understanding) sectors, and less in Dissatisfied (OS) and Admonishing (OD).

Analyses of variance indicate that there are significant school effects for teacher self-perception on the Cooperation–Opposition dimension, with School six the lowest and School three highest. In School six, therefore, the teachers don't believe they are as Helpful, Friendly and Understanding as those in other schools. They also think they are more Dissatisfied and Admonishing than their other-school peers. The opposite is true for School three. Students' perceptions

Table 8.5: Scores on QTI-Dimensions for Teacher's Ideal, Teacher's Self-Perception, Students' Perceptions and Results of Analyses of Variance

School		DS	CO
1	Teacher Ideal	0.89	1.90
	Teacher Self-Perception	0.59	1.34
	Student Perception	0.57	1.14
2	Teacher Ideal	1.04	1.76
	Teacher Self-Perception	0.72	1.22
	Student Perception	0.58	0.98
3	Teacher Ideal	1.16	2.00
	Teacher Self-Perception	0.91	1.67
	Student Perception	0.75	1.34
4	Teacher Ideal	0.93	1.99
	Teacher Self-Perception	0.75	1.41
	Student Perception	0.72	1.26
5	Teacher Ideal	0.74	1.68
	Teacher Self-Perception	0.45	1.17
	Student Perception	0.38	1.16
6	Teacher Ideal	0.90	1.62
	Teacher Self-Perception	0.61	1.01
	Student Perception	0.39	1.61
7	Teacher Ideal	0.90	2.02
	Teacher Self-Perception	0.76	1.46
	Student Perception	0.60	1.26
F-Values	Teacher Ideal	1.85	1.25
	Teacher Self-Perception	1.22	1.97*
	Student Perception	1.83	1.93*

df 6/39   N for students = 192, N for teachers = 46 * = P < 0.10

for these schools reinforce their teachers' perceptions. No differences between teacher ideals in different schools were detected.

Relationship Between School Environment and Teacher Communication Style

Correlation between QTI-Factor scores and SLEQ-Scores were calculated to see if teachers' perceptions of the school environment are a predictor of students' or teachers' perceptions of the classroom environment, or of teacher ideals (see Table 8.6). The school was used as the unit of analysis, taking the teachers' mean SLEQ-Scores in a school as the measure for the school-level environment. For five of the eight SLEQ-Scales there are no significant correlations with the QTI-Factor scores. This result indicates that the relationship between SLEQ and QTI-Scores is (for most scales) weak. There are significant relationships for three scales: Work Pressure, Participatory Decision-Making and Professional Interest.

If the 5 per cent level of significance is accepted then Work Pressure is a predictor of all the QTI-Scores with correlations ranging from −0.26 to −0.43. The

Table 8.6: Correlations Between DS and CO Dimensions with Professional Interest, Participatory Decision-Making and Work Pressure

		Professional Interest	Participatory Decision-Making	Work Pressure
Student	DS	−.33*	−.27*	−.43*
Perceptions	CO	−.37*	−.37*	−.26*
Teacher	DS	.19	−.22	−.36*
Perceptions	CO	−.41*	−.37*	−.43*
Teacher	DS	−.08	−.09	−.33*
Ideal	CO	−.38*	−.30*	−.36*

N = 46   * = P < .05

higher the Work Pressure, the lower are the teacher's Dominance and Cooperation in the classroom. This lower Dominance may mean that there is more disorder in the classroom. This is corroborated by the perception of lower Cooperation; that is, greater Work Pressure on teachers contributes to class disruption, which further contributes to more Admonishing behavior.

A second set of significant correlations was found with the Participatory Decision-Making scale (−0.27 to −0.37), indicating that the more teachers participate in making decisions at the school-level the less they are perceived by their students as dominant and cooperative in the classroom. There are two possible explanations for this result. Teachers who are highly involved in school-level activities may strongly believe in participatory management, and thereby allow students greater freedom in class decisions. On the other hand, teachers who spend a great deal of time and energy at the school level may not be able to pay as much attention to their classes. Students take greater control of the class and this contributes to disorder and resistance by the teacher.

A third set of significant correlations was found with the Professional Interest scale (−0.33 to −0.41). The more teachers are engaged in matters of Professional Interest the less dominant and cooperative they are perceived by their students and the less cooperative they perceive themselves. The above interpretations might also explain this result, but another possible explanation is that the disorder contributes to the teacher's interest in professional development. In any case, teachers who scored high in Professional Interest seemed to have disorderly classes.

Conclusion

This study has reinforced previous perceptions that the School Level Environment Questionnaire is a valid and reliable instrument and well worth using by teachers interested in data on their work environment. The results obtained can be used for targeted professional development. For example the teachers in School five of our sample may wish to discuss the issue of obtaining greater freedom in their school, while teachers in School three might want to look at student behavior and institute procedures to help both students and teachers.

The QTI has been established as a valid and reliable instrument for use in Australian schools and can provide teachers with insights about their relationships with students. Australian teachers have found this a valuable source of information, particularly the comparisons between their own and students' perceptions. The sample in the study was small, however, and caution needs to be used when making interpretations. Continued research with larger groups is needed in Australia. Some studies are currently underway to determine relationships between teacher personality types and QTI-Scales, and between perceptions of the classroom environment in science laboratories, QTI-Scales and student outcomes on cognitive and practical skills.

For the first time, an attempt has been made to examine the relationships between the perceptions of school-level environment and classroom environment as detected by the two instruments. While the data is preliminary, the weak relationship between the SLEQ and QTI-Scores nevertheless indicates that a teacher's behavior in class may have little to do with his or her perception of the school environment. As a result, it seems that teachers believe they have considerable freedom to shape their own classroom regardless of the school atmosphere. Further data is required in order to pursue this line of research.

Chapter 9

Principals' Interpersonal Behavior and Teachers' Satisfaction

Lya Kremer-Hayon and Theo Wubbels

The importance of the principals' leadership role in school effectiveness has been well documented in the literature. This chapter approaches the topic from the standpoint of interpersonal behavior, broadening previous analyses of the relationships between principals and their staffs. It describes how the QTI was adapted to become the Questionnaire on Principal Interaction (QPI), and then used in an exploratory study to test the instrument's utility. Teachers' perceptions of both actual and desired principal behavior were investigated and related to teachers' satisfaction with the school environment. The study population included ninety-six elementary teachers randomly selected from the Northern educational district of Israel.

Questionnaire on Principal Interaction (QPI)

Before the QTI could become the QPI it first had to be converted into Hebrew. Both the Dutch and American QTI's were translated and compared. The items that emerged differently in the two interpretations were revised by a third person, proficient in all three languages. This Hebrew revision was translated back into Dutch and English, and the latter two were compared with the original. Minor discrepancies were revised again until a fully satisfactory version was achieved. The translated items were then adapted to suit principals' interpersonal behavior. For example, the QTI-Item 'We need his or her permission before we speak' became in the QPI 'We need to get his or her permission for any irregular activity'. Some items had to be removed and others were added. The scale labels were also slightly adapted: Leadership (DC), Helpful/Friendly (CD), Understanding (CS), Teacher Responsibility and Freedom (SC), Uncertain (SO), Dissatisfied (OS), Objecting (OD), and Strict (DO).

A content validity analysis was conducted by a group of fifteen school principals (not included in the study sample), and two education professors. After several rounds of changes this process yielded an inter-rater agreement of 87 per cent, indicating that item and scale classifications were appropriate.

Table 9.1 presents sample items and the total number for each scale, and internal consistencies (alpha reliabilities) for the ninety-six teachers who answered

Table 9.1: Number of Items, Alpha Reliabilities and a Typical Item of QPI-Scales

Scales	Number of items	Typical item	Alpha
Leadership	7	S/he is a good leader	.69
Helpful/Friendly	7	S/he helps us with our teaching tasks	.81
Understanding	8	S/he is a good listener	.85
Teacher Responsibility/Freedom	9	S/he is permissive	.70
Uncertain	6	S/he is uncertain in school	.86
Dissatisfied	8	S/he is suspicious	.75
Objecting	8	S/he gets angry easily	.85
Strict	9	S/he expects us to obey	.70

Table 9.2: Factor Analysis of the QPI-Scales

Scales	Factor 1	Factor 2	Factor 3
Leadership	.71	.21	.60
Helpful/Friendly	.78	.38	.32
Understanding	.90	.25	.15
Teacher Responsibility/Freedom	.50	.70	−.24
Uncertain	−.47	.71	−.37
Dissatisfied	−.79	.35	.14
Objecting	−.67	.59	.12
Strict	−.54	.03	.78
Variance	47%	22%	16%

the QPI about their principal. The alphas indicate that the QPI has sufficient reliability for research purposes (Nunnally, 1967).

Table 9.2 presents the results of a factor analysis of the QPI's eight scales in which the factors were rotated by hand. The analysis points to three dimensions. Two of these resemble the Cooperation–Opposition dimension (factor 1) and the Dominance–Submission dimension (factor 3). The presence of two factors which are similar to Leary's is an initial indication of the QPI's validity. The existence of a third factor can be a contraindication, however. Nonetheless we believe the third factor probably resulted from measurement errors similar to those described for the QTI in Chapter 2. Future research which collects data on principals' interpersonal behavior from groups of teachers — as opposed to the present one:one dyad design — will allow us to further investigate the third factor.

The Questionnaire on Principal Interaction is presented in Appendix 9.1. Each item is answered on a five-point Likert scale from (one) never to (five) always.

Principal–Teacher Relationships

This study primarily tested the usefulness of the QPI. We did expect, however, to find significant relationships between QPI-Scores and teachers' satisfaction with the school environment. Prior to describing the study we will summarize relevant literature.

In their classic work on school climate, Halpin and Croft (1963) emphasized the importance of open-school climates and the need for genuine behaviors of teachers and principals. Since then, principals' importance in promoting school effectiveness, staff development, teacher motivation, student achievement, and positive school climate has been confirmed in a number of studies (e.g., Brookover and Lezotte, 1977; Ellet and Walberg, 1979; Sergiovanni, 1987; Heck, Larsen and Marcoulides, 1990; Fullan and Stiegelbauer, 1992). Moreover, principals consider their relationship with teachers to be the most prominent aspect of their roles (Lortie, 1987). It is not surprising, then, that a large segment of the educational administration literature is devoted to principals as instructional leaders. The research has resulted in many descriptions of leadership roles and corresponding attributes and skills for principals. Interpersonal communication is one of the most important skill areas, as will be seen in the following description of some elements that constitute effective leadership and their impact on school functions.

Principals' roles have been envisioned in a variety of ways. Stodgill (1974) developed three trait categories: Self-oriented (including intelligence), Task-related (including achievement and accountability) and Social Characteristics (including cooperativeness, prestige and social ability). Salley, McPherson and Baehr (1978) conceived of four role orientations: Administration, School Climate (including interpersonal relations), Program and Student Development.

Interpersonal relations play an especially important role in the four dimensional profiles developed by Leithwood and Montgomery (1986): Problem Solver, Problem Manager, Humanitarian, and Administrator. This is clearly true for the Humanitarian principals who primarily focus on the following areas:

— school climate and interpersonal relationships, including staff involvement in school activities,
— a positive attitude, demonstrated by cheerfulness and sincerity,
— encouraging and direct behavior with the school staff, and
— getting teachers to express personal goals.

Hall and Hord (1987) identified three different styles of leadership: Responsive, Managerial, and Initiative. The Responsive principal places trust in teachers' judgment, is ready to help, and attends to teachers' requests. In a study that included over 2,500 teachers and 1,200 principals, Smith and Andrews (1989) found that effective principals were rated higher than their less effective colleagues on interations with teachers.

As mentioned, these studies point to the interpersonal arena as a central element in the principal's role. It is extremely difficult to find a study in which these characteristics do not emerge as a salient factor in school climate, staff development and school effectiveness. Principal–teacher relationships are also an important component of most instruments which assess school organizational climate (see Chapter 8).

The knowledge base on this topic was initially developed outside of education. An early contributor was Carl Rogers, who introduced and emphasized the importance of helping relationships to educational practitioners. Following Rogerian theory, researchers developed inventories to measure interpersonal communications factors and found that positive interrelationships correlated more to indirect rather than direct leadership style (Barrett-Lenard, 1970; see also Blumberg and Greenfield, 1980).

Regarding the impact of principal–teacher relationships in schools, it appears that most studies conclude there is a positive correlation between a supportive leadership style and teacher involvement and dedication to school matters. Leithwood and Montgomery (1986), for example, found that teacher support and approval from their administrators were positively related to teachers' satisfaction. In a later study, Leithwood (1990) reported that the principal's support was highly correlated with teacher's professional development. Based on these findings, researchers recommend open communications between teachers and principals. They believe it provides opportunities for maturation, especially for teachers. When teachers and principals fully discuss problems and issues, the process helps teacher growth in professional expertise, and psychological and career development (Hopkins, 1990).

In summary, it is clear that the research highlights the considerable impact of principal–teacher relationships on various aspects of school effectiveness and teachers' satisfaction.

Design of the Study

Objective

The primary objective of this exploratory study was to test the QPI and use it to gain a more specific portrait of principals' communication styles and their relationships with teachers. We also wanted to investigate if teachers' perceptions of these relationships are related to their satisfaction with the school environment. Finally, we compared the difference between a teacher's perception of actual and desired principal behavior and his or her satisfaction. We selected this issue to understand if teachers' satisfaction is related more to actual principal behavior or to the difference between actual and desired behavior.

Instruments

Data was gathered from ninety-six elementary school teachers. Included were the teachers' perceptions of the actual and desired principal interpersonal behavior (QPI-Scores) and teachers' scores on the Teacher Satisfaction Questionnaire (TSQ). This questionnaire measures satisfaction with the school atmosphere in general, the principal's approach to professional development, and the role of the principal in causing school stress. In addition to these three categories, the TSQ includes items on teachers' desire to transfer schools, and stress caused by other factors in school. A high score on some items is interpreted as a low level of satisfaction.

Analyses

Profiles of actual and desired principal communication styles were computed for every teacher. Correlations were calculated between the teachers' perceptions

Table 9.3: *Teachers' Perceptions of Actual and Desired Principals' Profiles in the Typology*

Type	Actual	Desired
Directive	12	5
Authoritative	16	17
Tolerant and authoritative	21	47
Tolerant	10	5
Uncertain/tolerant	14	3
Uncertain/aggressive	10	10
Repressive	—	—
Drudging	10	7
Impossible to classify	3	—
Missing	—	2

of actual principal behavior and teachers' satisfaction. In a similar manner, the absolute difference of every scale between desired and actual behavior was correlated with teachers' satisfaction scores.

Results

Actual principal communication style

Data from the ninety-six teachers on the actual communication style of principals was compared with the profiles of the typology described in Chapter 4. Table 9.3 presents the distribution of the principal styles in the typology. It must be noted that the adaptation of the items to better describe principals' communication behaviors may have affected the interpretation of some of the categories in the typology.

The principal sample reflects all but one category in the typology. Most principals belong to the Tolerant/Authoritative, Authoritative and Uncertain/ Tolerant types, in which they often demonstrate Helpful/Friendly (CD) and Understanding (CS) behaviors. Some display more Leadership behavior (DC) and others allow more Teacher Responsibility and Freedom (SC). Compared to the distribution of teachers in the typology, more principals display a communication style characterized by low Dominance and high Submission scores.

No principals of the Repressive type were found. This is probably due to the unwillingness of teachers to allow principals to behave repressively. They differ from students, who fear repressive teachers, and have enough confidence to sucessfully challenge these types of principals.

Three principal profiles could not be classified because they did not resemble any one of the types to a sufficient degree (see note Chapter 4). These are characterized by extremely low scores on the Uncertain scale combined with a strong showing in Teacher Responsibility and Freedom, as seen in Figure 9.1a. This differs from the results obtained by using the QTI with secondary teachers and students. When teachers are perceived to be high in Student Responsibility and Freedom, they also generate high scores in Uncertain behavior. Allowing students responsibility and freedom in class is always perceived as showing some uncertainty (see Figure 9.2, the profiles of the Tolerant and of the Uncertain/

Figure 9.1: Examples of Principal Profiles that Could Not Be Classified According to the Typology

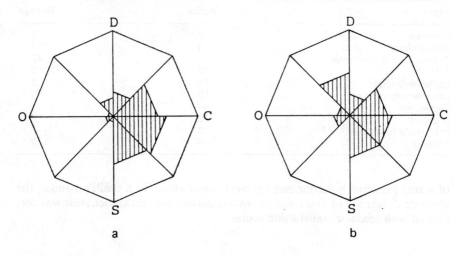

a   b

Figure 9.2: Profiles of the Tolerant and Uncertain/Tolerant Teacher (from Chapter 4)

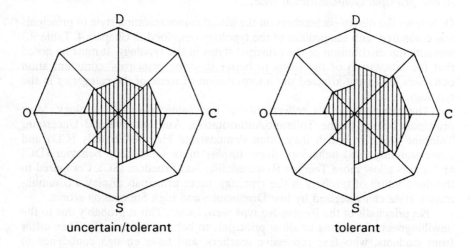

uncertain/tolerant   tolerant

Tolerant teacher). Apparently it is possible for principals to allow teachers responsibility and freedom without being perceived as uncertain. This is an important difference, since uncertain behavior is usually perceived as a weakness.

Profile 'b' in Figure 9.1 reflects high scores on both Teacher Responsibility/ Freedom and Strict behavior. This principal is extraordinary in that she is perceived as being Strict, yet she didn't score high on the Objecting or Leadership scales. In contrast, students perceive teachers who are very strict to either be strong leaders (the Directive teacher) or aggressive (the Repressive teacher), as seen from Figure 9.3.

Figure 9.3: Profiles of the Directive and Repressive Teacher (from Chapter 4)

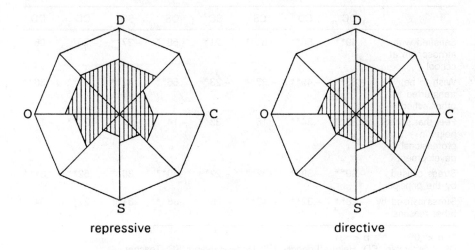

repressive   directive

Figure 9.4: Mean Teachers' Perceptions of Actual and Desired Principal Behavior

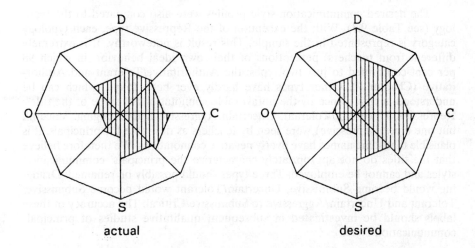

actual   desired

Desired principal communication style

The teachers also answered the QPI about the behavior they would like their principal to display. Figure 9.4 presents the mean profiles of actual and desired principal behavior in our sample.

In a statistically significant result, the teachers clearly want their principals to show more Leadership, Helpful/Friendly and Understanding behavior. They are satisfied with the principal's behavior in the Objecting and Dissatisfied scales. In the Uncertain, Strict, and Freedom/Responsibility categories the differences between actual and desired behavior are small.

Table 9.4: Correlations Between Teachers' Perceptions of Actual Principal Interpersonal Behavior and Teacher Satisfaction and Stress

	DC	CD	CS	SC	OS	SO	OD	DO
Satisfied with atmosphere at school	.49**	.56**	.50**	.21*	−.58**	−.37**	−.20*	−.06
Wish to be transferred to other school	−.33**	−.45**	−.37**	−.23*	.56**	.42**	.41**	.38**
Feel that school helps in professional development	.35**	.34**	.16	.33**	−.14	−.11	−.24**	−.11
Stress caused by the principal	−.30**	−.39**	−.32**	−.22*	.40**	.30**	.52**	.37**
Stress caused by other reasons	−.28**	−.32**	−.42**	−.09	.36**	.31**	.22*	.04

*: p < .05   **: p < .01
DC: Leadership; CD: Helpful/Friendly; CS: Understanding; SC: Teacher Responsibility/Freedom; SO: Uncertain; OS: Dissatisfied; OD: Objecting; DO: Strict

The desired communication-style profiles were also compared to the typology (see Table 9.3). With the exception of the Repressive type, each typology category is represented in the sample. This result is noteworthy. It is extremely different from teachers' perceptions of their own ideal behavior, in which 98 per cent conformed to just two types: the Authoritative/Tolerant and Authoritative (Chapter 7). Other types have hardly ever been found, which can be understood at first glance by the unfavorable connotations of some of the titles: Repressive, Uncertain/Tolerant, Uncertain/Aggressive and Drudging. Since all but one type (Repressive) were seen by teachers as desirable for principals, it is plausible that some names have overly negative connotations. We therefore believe that the titles do not appropriately characterize the principals' communication styles and cannot be employed. Three types should possibly be renamed: Drudging would become Submissive, Uncertain/Tolerant would become Submissive/Tolerant and Uncertain/Aggressive to Submissive/Critical. The accuracy of these labels should be investigated in subsequent qualitative studies of principal-communication style.

Perceptions of actual principal behavior and satisfaction

Table 9.4 presents correlations between the teachers' perceptions of the principal's behavior on the QPI-Scales and the TSQ-Items. The cooperation scales correlate positively and significantly to teacher's satisfaction with school environment and negatively to dissatisfaction. The pattern is mirrored for the opposition scales. We can therefore conclude that the more a principal's communication style is characterized by high levels of cooperation and low levels of opposition, the more teachers are satisfied with the school environment.

A notable result is the similarity of the correlations between QPI-Scales and 'stress caused by the principal' and 'stress caused by other causes'. Apparently,

Table 9.5: *Correlations of the Difference Between the Teacher's Perceptions of Actual and Desired Principal Interpersonal Behavior and Teacher Satisfaction and Stress*

	DC	CD	CS	SC	OS	SO	OD	DO
Satisfied with atmosphere at school	−.11	−.11	−.10	−.15	−.12	.07	−.01	−.07
Wish to be transferred to other school	−.25*	−.29**	−.30**	.04	.24*	.28**	.24*	−.04
Feel that school helps in professional development	−.15	−.21*	.17	.03	.21*	−.32**	.04	−.03
Stress caused by the principal	−.08	−.03	−.05	.05	−.15	−.04	.03	−.14
Stress caused by other reasons	−.14	−.11	−.02	−.04	.12	.18	.02	−.10

*: $p < .05$ **: $p < .01$
DC: Leadership; CD: Helpful/Friendly; CS: Understanding; SC: Teacher Responsibility/ Freedom; SO: Uncertain; OS: Dissatisfied; OD: Objecting; DO: Strict

the more a principal is seen as strict the more teachers perceive stress caused both by the principal and by other causes. It seems that a principal's communication style may induce stress itself and may also similarly strengthen other stress causes. This would mean that teachers' perceptions of stress are reinforced by a negative principal-communication style. This is also true in the reverse. Stress caused by other factors can influence stress caused by the principal.

Difference between actual and desired behavior and satisfaction

The difference between teachers' perceptions of actual and desired principal interpersonal behavior is not strongly related to teachers' satisfaction (see Table 9.5). Only two satisfaction items significantly correlated with several QPI-Scales. This implies that the teacher's perceptions of the actual principal behavior are more important to teacher's satisfaction than the difference between the actual and desired behavior.

Conclusion

This chapter described how the Questionnaire on Teacher Interaction (QTI) was successfully adapted to map principal interpersonal behavior. The potential usefulness of the Questionnaire on Principal Interaction (QPI) was demonstrated by its ability to detect meaningful relationships between perceptions of principal behavior and teachers' satisfaction.

The study raised doubts about the appropriateness of using some of the labels of the teacher-communication style typology with principals. It seemed that these titles needed to be changed in a way which implies less negative connotations. In addition, the QPI's validity has not yet been corroborated in a satisfactory manner. These results illustrate the need for more (qualitative) studies of principal-communication style in relation to the QPI.

The study confirmed earlier research on the positive relationship between cooperative principal behavior and teacher's satisfaction. The sample teachers' perceptions (both actual and desired) revealed two types of principals who behave in a manner that is negatively related to teachers' satisfaction: Submissive/ Critical (the possible alternate name for the Uncertain/Aggressive type) and Submissive (the Drudging type). It is striking that although these principals are less effective than many colleagues in promoting teachers' satisfaction they are considered by some teachers as desirable.

The comparison of actual and desired principal behavior showed that most principals do not live up to teachers' ideals. Teachers generally want principals to be better leaders and to help and understand them more appropriately. This result, as well as the one mentioned in the previous paragraph, indicates that improvement in principal–teacher relations is possible and training may be fruitful. It appears that principals may need to extend their behavioral repertoire, especially in the Cooperation side of the Leary model.

The reported relations between teachers' perceptions of principal behavior and teachers' satisfaction indicate that in the process of principals promoting teacher effectiveness the teacher's perception of the principal-communication style may mediate between the principal behavior and appropriate teaching behavior. It therefore seems important for future research in principal leadership to include teachers' perceptions. The QPI and the SLEQ (described in the previous chapter) are potentially useful instruments for this purpose.

Our results point to the need for feedback to principals on their interpersonal relationships with teachers. In order for principals to improve in this area it is important for them to understand how their behavior is perceived by the faculty. Subsequent research will investigate how the QPI can play a feedback role in the pre and in-service development of school principals.

Chapter 10

Supervisors' Interpersonal Behavior and Student Teachers' Satisfaction

---

Lya Kremer-Hayon and Theo Wubbels

This chapter demonstrates the versatility of the QTI and Leary Model with populations other than secondary teachers and students. Both were successfully adapted to describe the relations between cooperating and student teachers, and the results can be used to strengthen teacher education. The chapter begins with a description of how the QTI was adapted for use with these new groups and became the Questionnaire on Supervisor Interaction (QSI). It then reviews the literature on the relationship between cooperating and student teachers and describes a study in which the QSI was used to investigate supervisors' communication style and student teachers' satisfaction. The study sample consisted of 113 student teachers in their second and third years of study in a state teachers' college in the Northern part of Israel. Except for kibbutz colleges which have idiosyncratic features, the sample in this college is representative of the statewide student-teacher population.

Questionnaire on Supervisor Interaction (QSI)

Development

The Questionnaire on Supervisor Interaction (QSI) followed a similar development process as the QPI (Chapter 9). The items from the Hebrew version of the QTI were adapted to the interactions between student teachers and cooperating teachers. Some items had to be removed and others added. The scale labels were also slightly adapted: Leadership (DC), Helpful/Friendly (CD), Understanding (CS), Student Teacher Responsibility and Freedom (SC), Uncertain (SO), Dissatisfied (OS), Objecting (OD) and Strict (DO).

The adapted questionnaire was administered to fifty student teachers and tested for reliability with the Cronbach's alpha formula. After additional adaption a new version of sixty-one items was made. Table 10.1 shows the number of items of each scale, sample items and the internal consistency (alpha reliabilities) in the sample of 113 student teachers.

The internal consistencies indicate that the QSI has sufficient reliability for research purposes (Nunnally, 1967). Interestingly, the four scales which yielded the lowest alphas fall in the Opposition half of the Leary model. Uncertain behavior

Table 10.1: Number of Items, Alpha Reliabilities and Typical Item of the QSI-Scales

Scales	Number of items	Typical Item	Alpha
Leadership	8	He or she gives a lot of advice	.83
Helpful/Friendly	6	He or she is some one we can rely on	.79
Understanding	8	If I have something to say s/he will listen	.82
Student Teacher Responsibility/Freedom	10	He or she lets me make my own decisions	.78
Uncertain	6	He or she seems uncertain	.57
Dissatisfied	7	He or she is suspicious	.66
Objecting	7	He or she can get angry	.75
Strict	9	He or she is strict	.69

Table 10.2: Factor Analysis of QSI-Scales

Scales	Factor 1	Factor 2
Leadership	.40	.70
Helpful/Friendly	.61	.65
Understanding	.67	.47
Student-Teacher Responsibility/Freedom	.61	.12
Uncertain	−.27	−.18
Dissatisfied	−.90	.19
Objecting	−.78	.21
Strict	−.47	.48
Variance	45%	22%

yielded the lowest alpha. This may be caused by the relatively low scores, which in turn result in low variances in this scale.

Table 10.2 presents the results of a factor analysis of the QSI's eight scales in which the factors were rotated by hand. The analysis points to two dimensions which differ slightly from Leary's. The first basically resembles the Cooperation–Opposition dimension, and the second the Dominance–Submission. The fact that two factors emerged is an initial indication of the QSI's validity.

The QSI-Items are presented in Appendix 10.1 They are answered on a five-point Likert scale from (one) never to (five) always.

Supervisor Communication Style

Data on the communication style of cooperating teachers collected with the QSI from the 113 student teachers was compared with the profiles of the typology described in Chapter 4. Most of the supervisors belong to the Tolerant and Tolerant/Authoritative types, which often includes behaviors in the Helpful (CD), Understanding (CS) and Student Teacher Responsibility (SC) scales. Communication styles of every category in the typology were represented in the sample.

Figure 10.1: Characteristic Example of a Supervisor Profile that Could Not Be Classified According to the Typology

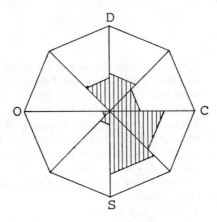

Figure 10.2: Profile of the Uncertain/Tolerant Teacher (from Chapter 4)

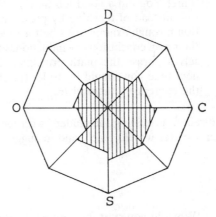

Ten of the profiles, however, could not be classified because they did not resemble any one of the types to a sufficient degree (see note Chapter 4). Most of these profiles are characterized by very high scores on the 'Student Teacher Responsibility' scale. This is a different result than those obtained by using the QTI with secondary teachers and students. It seems plausible that in the supervision situation, similar to the principal–teacher communication described in Chapter 9, a high degree of responsibility of the supervisee may be a more prominent feature than student responsibility in the classroom. As can be seen from a profile example in Figure 10.1 this responsibility is not accompanied by Uncertain behavior on the part of the supervisor. In classroom interaction this is often the case (see Figure 10.2, the profile of the Uncertain/Tolerant teacher).

The following edited excerpts from supervision sessions following student teachers' lessons are presented as an illustration of various types of supervisors' communication styles.

Directive

Supervisor:	'Let's start our discussion by going back to the instructional goals, because I think that some of them were not reflected in the lesson. What were your teaching goals for this lesson?'
Student Teacher:	'I wanted to explain the meaning of multiplication, I wanted the kids to understand that multiplication is a short form of addition, and I gave the example of $4 + 4 + 4 + 4 + 4 = 4 \times 5$.'
Supervisor:	'Do you think you achieved this goal?'
Student Teacher:	'Yes, I do!'
Supervisor:	'How do you know?'
Student Teacher:	'You may have noticed that by the end of the lesson they could easily transform addition exercises into multiplication exercises and vice versa.'
Supervisor:	'Fine! You did a good job on this. However, I think that instead of teaching by presenting new information through examples it's better to let the kids make their own conclusions by induction, so that they themselves phrase the math principles. So, I think that next time you should try to let the students discover the content by themselves.'

This supervisor was direct in providing the student with feedback, in telling her what might have been a better way to teach, and in suggesting what she should do the next time.

Authoritative

Supervisor:	'Why did you start this unit by dividing the class into groups?'
Student Teacher:	'I did it because of the big differences between the students in this class. I don't see how I can teach all of them at the same time in one large group.'
Supervisor:	'You see, it's not effective to start two new experiences or two new topics at the same time. Your class is not used to working in groups. To be able to do that effectively kids need to have some experience in group work, they need special skills. This isn't simply a matter of the way they are seated, but mainly a question of cooperation between them and of communication skills. So, you need to devote some time

to develop the skills needed for group work first. The introduction of a new topic, which in this case is a difficult one, and a new way of organizing the class and studying, all at the same time is too difficult for everyone, including you.'

Student Teacher: 'Well, I agree, I didn't realize how many skills are involved in group work, but I'm pressed for time. I need to teach this before the next holiday and I know that the large individual differences in this class can be better addressed by studying in groups.'

Supervisor: 'Yes, this may be true. But let us stick to the point, which is: Concentrate on one task and go on with another one after you feel that the first task was completed. As I said, it will be easier for you and the kids. Since you agree that group work demands special skills which have to be developed, and you also agree that the topic is difficult, you have to make a decision: either you start a new topic or you introduce a new way of working and change the classroom organization. If you do both things at once neither will be done well enough. I suggest that in this case you first introduce the group work and then the challenge of teaching to individual differences will be easier to achieve. . . .'

In this supervision session the supervisor was task-oriented; her authority seemed to stem from pedagogical knowledge and experience rather than from her hierarchial standing. This, in addition to the pleasant supervision atmosphere, may explain the student teacher's agreement with her feedback and guidance.

Tolerant and Authoritative

Supervisor: 'Let's start our discussion with the question of how the poem should be introduced: should the teacher read it to the class, or should the kids read it by themselves?'

Student Teacher: 'I think the teacher should read it to the class, that's why I read it. I thought that while reading it to them I could better emphasize certain points, so they could understand it better.'

Supervisor: 'OK, I see your point. I would suggest however, to try and let the kids do the poems by themselves. This will help you find out for yourself which way is better.'

Student Teacher: 'Why do you think that's better?'

Supervisor: 'I don't claim one way is better than the other, I just suggest that you try both ways and find out for yourself. You may want to use both for different poems in different circumstances.'

While being tolerant to the student teacher's opinion, the supervisor expressed his position in a pleasant and assertive manner.

Tolerant

> *Supervisor*: 'Could you please tell me why you punished Sarah for not listening? You see, the punishment was not constructive, it didn't help.'
>
> *Student Teacher*: 'I was so mixed up and worried about not being able to control the class, I didn't think at the time if the punishment was constructive or not, I did it on the spur of the moment. . . . it was spontaneous.'
>
> *Supervisor*: 'Well, it seems to me that this was indeed spontaneous. Remembering my first days of student teaching, I can sympathize with you. I was also scared, so your worry is only natural. I'm sure that in time you'll be able to reflect on the process of your decision-making.'
>
> *Student Teacher*: 'How should I react to a student who is not listening?'
>
> *Supervisor*: 'Well, there are numerous ways, I'm sure that in time you'll find out how to react, you'll try various kinds of reactions and find out for yourself which way works best for which types of kids . . .'

In this session the supervisor showed understanding and encouraged the student teacher through sympathy. Though she didn't quite approve of the student teacher's reaction, she was still tolerant and avoided criticism. She also did not offer suggestions.

Uncertain/Tolerant

> *Student Teacher*: 'I thought that the best way to illustrate the concept was by telling a story.'
>
> *Supervisor*: 'That may be a good idea, but I'm not sure that it's the best. You could try other ways as well.'
>
> *Student Teacher*: 'Do you think then that next time I should explain the concept in an abstract way?'
>
> *Supervisor*: 'Actually, that's not my idea, but I agree you may well try it in a more abstract way.'
>
> *Student Teacher*: 'I saw my cooperating teacher illustrate concepts by using stories and I liked it a lot.'
>
> *Supervisor*: 'OK If you like it then go on doing it, but what if some kids don't need any illustrations because they understand the concept? On the one hand you should do what suits you best, but on the other hand you have to consider the students' needs . . .'

This supervisor does not reflect any clear position; he moves back and forth and seems uncertain. Nonetheless, he accepts the student teacher's ideas.

Uncertain/Aggressive

Supervisor: 'I can't understand why you didn't answer Susan's question, it was interesting.'

Student Teacher: 'If I answered her question, I would have to answer all the other questions and that would have taken me away from the subject.'

Supervisor: 'I've told you several times about the damage you might do if you don't answer the kids' questions.'

Student Teacher: 'OK but I think that responding to all questions, which are often irrelevant, at the expense of covering the subject matter is wrong, and I don't want to get behind. So what should I do?'

Supervisor: 'Well, of course it's necessary to meet your goals, but it's also important to answer their questions. I don't understand why you can't try to do both . . .'

In this session the atmosphere was tense. Both supervisor and student teacher were not open to each other's ideas, and there was a sense of uncertainty expressed by both.

Repressive

Student Teacher: 'I couldn't follow my plans because of their questions, which got me off track.'

Supervisor: 'If you can't stick to your plans how do you ever expect to reach your goals?'

Student Teacher: 'Well this doesn't always happen. . . .'

Supervisor: 'Look, if you want to be a good teacher you have to follow your plans. When we meet next month I want you to tell me how you improved in following the plan and avoiding sidetracks.'

Student Teacher: 'Yes, I hope I can do it. . . .'

This supervisor was clearly non-supportive. He strongly stated his opinion and demanded that his suggestions be followed. The student teacher reacted in a submissive way.

Drudging

Supervisor: 'I expected you to invest more time in preparing the materials for this lesson. Teaching is a serious business, you can't do it "off the cuff".'

Student Teacher: 'I really tried to do my best.'

Supervisor: 'It's never enough: you can always do more.'

Student Teacher: 'Well, you know I have to work after school to survive, and it's really exhausting. I stay up real late at night to prepare my lessons.'

Supervisor: 'Look, I understand your problem and appreciate the efforts and energy you invest in your studies.'

This supervisor demands a lot from the student teacher; she expresses the opinion that no matter how much one works, one can always do more. At the same time, however, she seems to understand the student teacher's problems.

Communication in Student Teaching

Over the past two decades a number of studies on student teaching have illustrated several problems which hinder effective supervision (e.g., Griffin, 1986; Hoy and Woolfolk, 1989; Kagan, 1988). The most problematic seems to be the lack of communication between cooperating teachers and student teachers (Southall and King, 1979). Its complexity and longstanding nature does not allow for simple solutions (Hoover, O'Shea and Carroll, 1988).

The research on communication between cooperating and student teachers has largely focused on the managerial and technical domains (Hoover, O'Shea and Carroll, 1988; Killian and McIntyre, 1988). Regretfully, few studies concentrated on the interpersonal aspect of the relationship, the facet which helps determine whether the supervisory atmosphere is supportive or not. Recently, however, there has been an increase in research of this nature (see for an example, Ben-Peretz and Rumney, 1991). One reason for this growth may lie in the recognition that cooperating teachers have a strong influence on what student teachers learn and don't learn. Some authors have described preferred behaviors for cooperating teachers and university supervisors (e.g., Quick, 1967). O'Shea, Hoover and Carroll (1988), for example, mention that supervisors must exhibit respect for the other participants in the supervision triad, communicate in clear concrete and non-judgmental terms and encourage participation in decision-making and goal setting. They encourage the participants to establish a positive relationship with each other in supervisory conferences.

These suggestions for supervisor behavior do not have a strong empirical base (Griffin, 1986). Some related research has been carried out, especially with regard to the supervisors' communication style most preferred by student teachers. The results are mixed. Copeland (1982) states that student teachers would like a direct style at the beginning of student teaching and a more indirect one as the experience progresses. This is not in complete agreement with Blumberg and Amidon (1965) and Blumberg (1980), who suggest that in some instances indirect supervisors' behavior was preferred. Although Copeland (1982) offers possible explanations for the differences in results, they don't really resolve the controversy. Moreover, Copeland's results are based on videotaped supervisory conferences and not actual experiences of student teachers, an aspect which weakens them. Another reason for the inconsistent research findings may be that the distinction between a directive and non-directive style is a false dichotomy. As is clear from the Blumberg studies, supervisors who were high on both direct and indirect behavior were evaluated positively by their supervisees.

The literature, therefore, indicates that the lack of communication between student teachers and their supervisors is an important area of concern. There does not seem to be a clear understanding, however, of the nature of these communication problems. This need provided the impetus for the research described in this chapter. The purpose of the study was to measure the interpersonal relations between student teachers and cooperating teachers, and to analyze student teachers' satisfaction with their supervision.

One problem with previous research efforts was that they resulted in broad dimensions like 'direct' and 'non-direct'. We believed that the systems' communication perspective and the QSI would produce a sharper analysis and description of the supervisory relationship. The QSI's eight scales provide greater specificity in analyzing the various facets of student and cooperating teacher behavior. Further, when combined with measures of student teachers' satisfaction, the QSI may yield a more differentiated view of student-teacher preferences for particular communication styles.

Design of the Study

All the 113 student teachers completed both the QSI and a specially developed questionnaire to measure student teachers' satisfaction with supervision: The Student Teachers' Satisfaction Questionnaire (STSQ).

The STSQ was developed on the basis of discussions with a group of twenty student teachers who were asked to relate to, and elaborate upon, their satisfaction with the supervision. The discussions were protocolled verbatim. The protocol analysis yielded fifteen items which were presented to a second group of twenty student teachers. They judged each item in terms of its validity and relevance to the area of satisfaction with supervision. The entire group agreed on ten items to represent the various aspects of student teachers' satisfaction, a five-point Likert scale was constructed and this became the STSQ.

Data analyses included factor analysis of the STSQ and a series of coefficient correlations to detect the extent to which the various scales of interpersonal relations correlate with different aspects of student teachers' satisfaction. In addition, a series of regression analyses were computed to detect the extent to which the scales of the QSI explain the variance in each of the satisfaction factors. Finally we analyzed the relationship between different supervisor types on the communication style typology (see Chapter 4) and student teachers' satisfaction.

Results

The Student Teachers' Satisfaction Questionnaire

The STSQ yielded two distinct factors after varimax rotation (Table 10.3). One factor represents satisfaction with supervision related directly with teaching (Factor 1), and the second represents satisfaction with several climate attributes in the cooperating school (Factor 2). Cronbach's alpha reliability tests yielded .84 and .74 for the first and second factors, respectively.

Satisfaction with Supervision

Table 10.4 presents the correlations between the interpersonal relationships scales and those for student teachers' satisfaction. Seven of the eight correlations between

L. Kremer-Hayon and T. Wubbels

Table 10.3: Factor Analysis of the STSQ and Alpha Reliability of the Scales Constructed According to the Factors (loadings lower than .40 not marked)

Items	Factor 1	Factor 2
I am satisfied with the relations between us	.87	
I am satisfied with the guidance I get in the cognitive domain of teaching	.96	
I am satisfied with the guidance I get in the affective domain of teaching	.93	
I am satisfied with the guidance I get in the field of classroom management	.69	
I am satisfied with the help I get in the cooperating school		.52
I am satisfied with the teacher interrelationship I observe in the cooperating school		.85
I have the impression that teachers enjoy autonomy in the cooperating school		.76
I have the impression that teachers come gladly to school		.62
The principal of the cooperating school keeps an open-door policy		.60
There is a friendly atmosphere in the teachers' room		.64
Alpha reliability	.84	.74

Table 10.4: Correlations Between Interpersonal Relationships and Satisfaction Scales

Scales	Satisfaction		
	Scale 1	Scale 2	Total Score
Leadership	.67*	.15	.46*
Helpful/Friendly	.81*	.33*	.68*
Understanding	.58*	.16	.45*
Student-Teacher Responsibility/Freedom	.40*	.20*	.38*
Uncertain	−.37*	−.10	−.28*
Dissatisfied	−.35*	−.18	−.33*
Objecting	−.29*	−.30*	−.37*
Strict	.10	−.10	−.05

* p < .01

student teachers' satisfaction with supervision (Factor 1) and the interpersonal scale scores are statistically significant. They are positive and relatively high in the realm of cooperative behavior: Leadership, Helping, Understanding and Student Teacher Responsibility. Objecting behavior, Dissatisfaction and Uncertainty yielded negative correlations. Strictness yielded a low and non-significant correlation.

The correlations for Factor 2 — satisfaction with the school climate attributes

Table 10.5: Results of a Stepwise Multiple Regression Analysis: Beta's and Explained Variance in Satisfaction by Interpersonal Relations Scales

Predictors	Multiple R	RSQ	Beta	p<	Criterion
Helpful/Friendly	.82	.67	.81	.000	
Uncertain	.84	.40	−.19	.006	Satisfaction with Supervision
Helpful/Friendly	.34	.11	.34	.009	Satisfaction with School climate
Helpful/Friendly	.68	.46	.68	.000	Total Satisfaction Score

Table 10.6: Cooperating Teachers' Profiles in the Typology, Mean Satisfaction Scores and Results of Analyses of Variance for Type 1–4

| Type | | Satisfaction with | |
| | | Supervision | School Climate |
	N	(Scale 1)	(Scale 2)
Directive	3	3.0	2.8
Authoritative	9	3.5	2.9
Tolerant and Authoritative	72	4.1	3.7
Tolerant	11	2.5	3.1
Uncertain/Tolerant	2	2.3	3.7
Uncertain/Aggressive #	1	–	—
Repressive	2	2.0	2.0
Drudging	3	1.5	3.7
Impossible to classify	10		
F-value		20.9**	3.7*

#: no satisfaction scores for this one supervisor available
** $p < 0.05$ * $p < 0.01$

— are somewhat different. Only three out of the eight correlations are statistically significant: a positive correlation with Helping and Student Teacher Responsibility and a negative correlation with Objecting behavior. The correlations with the total satisfaction scale scores yield a similar picture. Four interpersonal-relations scale scores are significantly positive and three are significantly negative.

The regression analyses (see Table 10.5) indicate that Helping behavior is a positive significant predictor of both satisfaction scales and total scale scores, and that Uncertainty is a statistically significant negative predictor of Factor 1: satisfaction with supervision. Thus, the more helpful the supervisor the greater the satisfaction; the more uncertain the supervision the less the satisfaction.

Table 10.6 presents the distribution of the supervisors' behavioral styles in the typology, mean scores on the satisfaction scales and results of an analysis of variance for Types 1–4. Because of missing data on the satisfaction scales for Types 5–8 these were not included.

The analyses of variance reveal a relationship between the type of supervisor and satisfaction. It is much stronger for the satisfaction with supervision scale than for the satisfaction with the school climate attributes scale. In general it seems that tolerance on the part of the supervisor, combined with friendliness and guidance leads to student teachers' satisfaction.

L. Kremer-Hayon and T. Wubbels

Conclusion

The results of the study generate some theoretical as well as practical implications.

The Study Instruments

In terms of theoretical implications, it appears that the dimensions of interpersonal relationships borrowed from the Leary model are generic and transcend two specific contexts: one pertaining to the classroom situation which involves 'one to many' relationships (as described in previous chapters), and the other pertaining to the 'one to one' relationship in the cooperating teacher–student teacher setting in the context of professional development.

Practically, the QSI has sufficient reliability and validity to describe the interpersonal style of communication between cooperating teachers and student teachers. It can be used in future research in conjunction with the typology to add insight to the area of supervisor behavior styles.

The satisfaction-scale instrument developed in this study provides some understanding of those aspects which student teachers consider important to their supervision. It is only natural that their satisfaction relates to the guidance they receive in the cognitive and affective domains of teaching, as well as in the field of classroom management. Interestingly enough, however, the student teachers' perceptions included several school-climate attributes that go beyond their direct relationship with cooperating teachers. Their satisfaction with supervision covers a wide perspective that includes the relationships among the teachers in the cooperating school, teachers' autonomy, the atmosphere in the teachers' room, and the principal's management style. Thus, the satisfaction with supervision constitutes an 'inner circle' — the cooperating teachers' interpersonal relationship (Factor 1) — and an 'outer circle' — aspects of the school climate (Factor 2). These perceptions may well be considered by teacher educators in the placement of student teachers. Both the expertise of individual cooperating teachers and school climate should guide this placement. This emerging conclusion is important considering Griffin's (1986) statement that cooperating teachers are often not selected on the basis of their supervising skills. One reason for this may be that these skills are difficult to measure. The two instruments used in this study — the QSI and STSQ — can be used to assist the process of building criteria for the selection of cooperating teachers and schools.

Communication Style and Satisfaction

The correlation between the cooperating teachers' communication style and student teachers' satisfaction with supervision yielded slightly different results for each of the satisfaction scales. The scales that constitute a cooperative style all positively relate to satisfaction, while the opposition scales relate negatively. This finding is not surprising, given our natural preference for a supportive and non-threatening supervisory situation.

Of special interest are the low correlations between Strict and Uncertain behavior and student teachers' satisfaction. Supervisors who employ these styles to enhance the quality of the student-teaching performance should be advised that student teachers may believe they are the result of negative motivation. The low correlations may also be due to varying preferences of different student teachers. Research on student teachers' satisfaction indicates that they differ in their preferences according to individual differences in personality (Kremer-Hayon, Moore and Nevat, 1986). For example, a supervisor may be viewed as uncertain if he or she does not tell the student teacher how to handle a particular situation, but only presents options. Some student teachers may react positively to this behavior, while others will not. Thus, the consequences of Aptitude Treatment Interaction research (Cronbach and Snow, 1977) — in this case, the adaptation of the supervisor's communication style to the attitudinal and behavioral preferences of the student teacher — may well be applied in the context of inter-personal relations in supervision.

There is some question as to why the communication style of cooperating teachers would relate at all to Factor 2 — student teachers' satisfaction with school climate. Since the concept of communication style (or interpersonal behavior) is tied to personality and belief systems via Leary's original research there is no easy explanation for the connection. On the other hand, the school's ethos and climate may indeed influence the interpersonal relations of cooperating teachers, since they themselves contribute to the overall environment. The latter possibility may explain the significant correlations with the second satisfaction factor. Apparently, a more pleasant school climate is related to student teachers' responsibility. If this relation is a causal one it has important implications for the placement of student teachers in schools. However, it should be emphasized that only a few scale scores of the QSI significantly correlated with Factor 2 as compared with Factor 1. This probably occurred because the latter constitutes an 'inner circle' and is more intrinsically related to interpersonal relations, whereas the former constitutes the more distant 'outer circle'.

With respect to the debate on the adequacy of directive or non-directive styles our results indicate that high Leadership (DC) (which is directive) and Student Teacher Responsibility (SC) (which is non-directive) behavior are positively related to student teachers' satisfaction. Negative experiences of student teachers are more related to an oppositional behavior style of the cooperating teacher. As we suspected, directivity or non-directivity do not in themselves explain student teachers' dissatisfaction. Rather, they must be displayed in conjunction with opposition behavior (e.g., strictness, anger, dissatisfaction or uncertainty) to possibly result in student-teacher dissatisfaction with the supervision.

In summary, this chapter suggests that the Leary model can be adapted with a relatively high degree of reliability to the context of teacher education and that most of the QSI-Dimensions are related to student teachers' satisfaction with cooperating teacher supervision and school climate.

Chapter 11

Socialization in Student Teaching

Anne Holvast, Theo Wubbels and
Mieke Brekelmans

This chapter describes research on the relationship between interpersonal teacher behavior and the ideals of both student and cooperating teachers. It sheds light on the cooperating teachers' role in the adaptation of student teachers to the culture of the student-teaching school.

Student Teaching and Professional Growth

Field experiences are an important part of most teacher-preparation programs. The recent educational reform movement has sought to place even more emphasis on them by increasing the amount of time spent in schools by teacher candidates (Guyton and McIntyre, 1990). This is based on the assumption that the more time students spend in classrooms the better prepared they will be upon entering the profession (e.g., Beyer, 1984). For example, Lasley and Applegate (1985) think that field experiences provide time for professional growth and offer prospective teachers opportunities to explore concepts and practice techniques learned in education courses. Studies of student-teaching experiences, however, question the validity of such assumptions (e.g., Feiman-Nemser and Buchmann, 1986).

There are serious doubts whether field experiences indeed promote professional growth. An alternate view holds that they are the initial steps in socializing student teachers into the traditional teaching role. By introducing student teachers to the 'utilitarian perspective', field experiences allow them to forget what they learned in their teacher-training program (e.g., Tabachnick and Zeichner, 1984; Feiman-Nemser and Floden, 1986; Lanier and Little, 1986). Their learning is basically limited to management techniques: getting students through the required lesson(s) on time in a quiet, smooth and orderly fashion and keeping the students on task while maintaining control. In the utilitarian perspective such techniques become an end in themselves rather than means towards some broader educational or social purpose (e.g., Tabachnick, Popkewitz and Zeichner, 1979–1980). Classroom practice tends to place management at the center of teaching, possibly at the expense of student learning (Hoy and Rees, 1977). Innovative teacher-training programs such as inquiry-oriented curricula are in part set up to prevent this adjustment of student teachers to the school (Zeichner and Teitelbaum, 1982).

The notion that student teaching primarily promotes socialization rather than professional growth can only be taken as an hypothesis, however. Zeichner and Gore (1990) conclude that the knowledge base related to the socializing impact of field experiences is ambiguous because studies tend not to focus on their quality and substance.

The Role of Cooperating Teachers

There is no agreement about what influence teacher-training institutions exactly have on the development of habits, attitudes, values, or teaching styles of student teachers. As mentioned, field experiences may promote the socialization of pre-service teachers to school culture (e.g., Fitzner, 1979; Lacey, 1977). The mechanisms of this socialization, however, are not yet completely understood. For example, do novice teachers imitate other teachers and learn acceptable behavior from them, as Feiman-Nemser and Floden (1986) suggest? Although the research generally shows that the cooperating teacher has a much stronger influence on the student teachers' learning than the university supervisor (Boydell, 1991), the role of cooperating teachers in socialization is not clear. In fact, it has not been extensively investigated.

One hypothesis states that the socialization of student teachers is greatly influenced by the instructional style of the cooperating teacher. Griffin (1986) reviews the research on cooperating teachers' influence on student teachers' behavior. He reports mixed results, indicating that such an influence does exist, but that it is probably mediated by characteristics of both groups. The lack of clarity in these results prompted the research described in this chapter. It was thought that such an investigation might lead to improvements in teacher education.

Research Design

Our research on the influence of cooperating teachers on student teachers focused on their interpersonal behavior towards students. We wanted to learn if and how cooperating teachers' behaviors and ideals influence the behavior and ideals of student teachers. We used the theoretical framework outlined in the second chapter to gather QTI-Data on physics student teachers in two Dutch teacher-education programs.

Teacher Education Program

During the study student teachers in both institutions were organized in groups of two or three. Their cooperating teachers were experienced in the classroom and the student teachers both observed and taught their classes. Since the student-teaching experience attempted to maximize instructional time, observations were limited to the first week of the program. Both the cooperating teacher and the student teachers observed all the lessons taught by their peers and discussed these lessons afterward. They also prepared some lessons together. In the early part of the program the student teachers learned how to reflect on the observations of lessons with each other.

Activities in the student-teaching school and on campus alternated and were closely interwoven. The theory presented on campus was intended to provide a structure for student teachers' practice experiences. Student teachers' instructional assignments gradually lengthened and they took more responsibility for their lessons. As a final assignment for the nearly four-month experience, every student teacher developed, planned and independently taught a series of approximately fifteen lessons to one class. Data reported in this chapter on student-teacher communication styles was gathered during this period.

The cooperating teachers were trained for about one week in supervising and counseling skills. In addition, they were intensively introduced to the principles underlying the teacher-education program. Extrapolating from a study by Brouwer (1987), we concluded that most cooperating teachers in this program agreed with these principles. (For a more extended description of the program see Holvast and Hooymayers, 1986.)

Data Gathering

In 1985 and 1986 the QTI was administered to 142 student teachers and the classes they taught in their final assignment. The classes completed the questionnaire at the end of the student-teaching period. As described in previous chapters, class means were used as the students' perceptions of the interpersonal behavior of the student teacher. The student teachers simultaneously completed the QTI for their own behavior in the targeted class (self-perceptions) and they also answered it in terms of their ideal interpersonal behavior. After the student teachers had departed, the same process was repeated between two and four months later with twenty-four cooperating teachers (though not all completed their self-perception and ideal QTIs). Because of the dyad and triad groupings these twenty-four cooperating teachers supervised a total of sixty-seven student teachers.

Every combination of student and cooperating teacher yielded a maximum of six sets of perceptions: student teacher's self-perception (1) and ideal (2), cooperating teacher's self-perception (3) and ideal (4), students' perceptions of the student teacher behavior (5) and students' perceptions of the cooperating teacher behavior (6). No research questions about self-perceptions were proposed and consequently these were not used in the analyses.

A partial replication of this study was performed in the United States (Levy, Wubbels and Brekelmans, 1992). Data was collected from students and teachers in ten classes of five student teachers and their cooperating teachers. Since the sample size in that study was small, results can be reported in preliminary form only.

Research Issue

Our goal was to analyze the extent to which a student teacher's classroom performance is related to the cooperating teacher's way of teaching. We approached

Table 11.1: *Results of Analyses of Variance: Percentage of Variance in the Students'
Perceptions of Interpersonal Teacher Behavior of Student Teachers Accounted for by the
Membership of a Student Teaching Group (two or three students)*

Student's perception of student-teacher behavior scale	Percentage of variance accounted for by the membership of a student-teacher group
DC	69**
CD	52
CS	56*
SC	71**
SO	59*
OS	67**
OD	70**
DO	72**

* = p < 0.05   ** = P < 0.01

this general issue through a comparison of behavior of student teachers placed
with the same or different cooperating teachers. Then the issue was specified into
an investigation of the relationships between students' perceptions of the interpersonal behavior of student teachers and two other variables: their perceptions
of the cooperating teacher and cooperating teacher ideals. Similarly, the literature
about student-teacher socialization prompted us to ask if the student teachers'
ideals are related to cooperating teachers' ideals and actual behavior as perceived
by their students.

Results

Student Teachers' Behavior

To begin to understand the direction of their development, we first investigated
if the student teachers' behavior in the same school is different from student
teachers in other schools. We performed analyses of variance for every scale of
the student-teacher behavior with the membership of the student teacher group
(the dyad or triad) as a factor.

From Table 11.1 it appears that some 50 to 70 per cent of the variance in
the student teachers' behavior is accounted for by their membership in the dyad
or triad placed in the same school. We concluded, therefore, that the school
environment (including their group membership) is related to their classroom
performance.

We next investigated the extent to which similarity of behavior in the same
school as opposed to other schools is due to the influence that cooperating teachers' behavior have on student teachers. Table 11.2 shows the correlations between
the students' perceptions of student teachers and of their cooperating teachers.
While many of the correlations are significant (two tailed test, 5 per cent level),
they are not very high.

Students who see a lot of Leadership (DC), Helpful/Friendly (CD) and
Understanding (CS) behavior in the cooperating teacher see the same in the

Table 11.2: Correlations Between Students' Perceptions of Interpersonal Behavior of Student Teachers and Cooperating Teachers in the Same Class (n = 67)

Students' perceptions of student teachers' behavior scale	Students' perceptions of cooperating teachers' behavior scale							
	DC	CD	CS	SC	SO	OS	OD	DO
DC	.33**	.31*	.28*	x	−.18	−.19	−.25*	x
CD	.27*	.32**	.33**	x	−.21	−.22	−.27*	x
CS	.24	.26*	.35**	x	−.17	−.24*	−.19	x
SC	−.30**	x	x	x	.19	.21	x	x
SO	−.37**	−.23	−.23	x	.27*	.22	.24	x
OS	−.25*	−.24	−.32**	x	.28*	.35**	.23	x
OD	−.16	x	x	x	.25*	x	x	x
DO	.27*	.19	x	x	x	x	x	x

* = p < 0.05;   ** = p < 0.01;   x: −.15 < correlation < .15

student teacher. The less cooperating teachers demonstrate these behaviors, the more their student teachers are perceived as Uncertain (SO) and Dissatisfied (OS). Cooperating teachers who show a lot of Leadership (DC) behavior have student teachers who are quite Strict (DO) and who leave students little Responsibility and Freedom (SC). Uncertain (SO), Dissatisfied (OS) and Admonishing (OD) behavior of the cooperating teacher is positively related to the same behavior of the student teachers and negatively to their Leadership (DC), Helpful/ Friendly (CD) and Understanding (CS) behavior. Finally cooperating teachers' Strictness (DO) and Student Responsibility and Freedom (SC) seem to have no significant relationship with student teacher behavior in the same class. Levy, Wubbels and Brekelmans (1992) corroborated the trend in these results, with stronger correlations (see Appendix 11.1).

In sum, it seems that the cooperating teacher's communication style corresponds to a similar style in the student teachers. It's important to note that student teachers' strictness does not significantly correlate positively to cooperating teacher strictness, but is positive in relation to cooperating teacher leadership. It seems that student teachers may not be able to exactly imitate their cooperating teacher's dominant and cooperative behavior. Once again (see Chapters 3 and 7), we can hypothesize that student teachers mistake oppositional behavior for dominance and thereby behave in a stricter manner than their cooperating teacher.

As an illustration, Figure 11.1 presents the mean students' perceptions for three groups of student teachers. Each group is made up of three classes taught by three student teachers who were supervised by the same cooperating teacher. The figure also presents the mean students' perceptions of each group's cooperating teacher for the same classes. As a reference, Figure 11.2 includes the mean students' perceptions of all the cooperating teachers and student teachers in our sample.

Group 1 has a cooperating teacher who allows students greater-than-average Responsibility and who is more Admonishing, Dissatisfied and Uncertain than the mean. He demonstrates less Leadership, Helpful/Friendly and Understanding behavior. When compared with the average, his student teachers are more

Figure 11.1: *Students' Perceptions of Interpersonal Teacher Behavior of Student Teachers and of their Cooperating Teachers in Three Groups of Student Teachers*

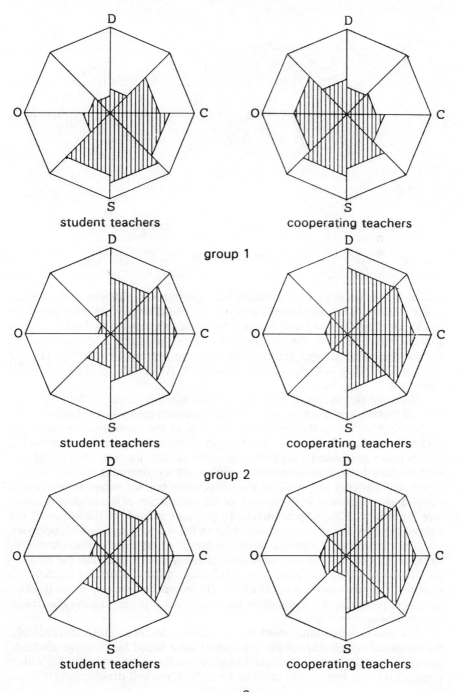

Figure 11.2:   Mean Students' Perceptions of Interpersonal Teacher Behavior of Student
Teachers and of their Cooperating Teachers

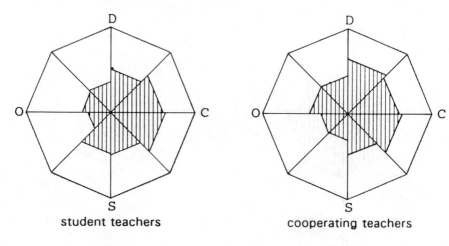

student teachers   cooperating teachers

total sample

Dissatisfied, much more Uncertain and leave greater Responsibility and Freedom
to the students. They are below-average in Helpful/Friendly behavior and show
less Leadership. Groups 2 and 3 have a cooperating teacher who displays above-
average behaviors from the cooperative side of the model and less from the
oppositional. The student teachers show above-average Leadership, Helpful
and Understanding behavior and are less Strict, Admonishing, Dissatisfied and
Uncertain.

We were curious about how much of the variance in the student's perceptions of the student teachers' behavior is accounted for by the behavior of the
cooperating teacher in the same class. Because of the correlations between the
QTI-Scales we could not derive the strength of this relationship from Table 11.2.
We therefore performed a multiple regression analysis for each scale of the student teachers' behavior with forward inclusion of the cooperating teachers' scales.[1]
It appears that only one scale of the cooperating teacher behavior contributes
significantly (5 per cent level) to each of the eight scales of the student teachers
(see Appendix 11.2). Approximately 10 per cent in each of the scales of the
student teachers' behavior is accounted for by the cooperating teacher's behavior.

The percentage of variance of the student teachers' behavior accounted for
by the membership of the student-teacher group is much higher than the percentage accounted for by the interpersonal behavior of the cooperating teacher. We
conclude that the cooperating teachers' classroom behavior in these teacher-
education programs is not the most important factor in the process that molds
student teachers' behavior.

We also gathered data about the cooperating teachers' ideals. Surprisingly,
no significant correlations (5 per cent level) were found between the students'
perceptions of the student teachers' behavior and the cooperating teacher's ideal
Again, this result was corroborated by Levy, Wubbels and Brekelmans (1992). It

seems, therefore, that the way a cooperating teacher teaches influences the student teacher's behavior to a greater extent than the cooperating teacher's ideals.

Student Teachers' Ideals

In the previous section we stated that 50–70 per cent of the variance in every scale of student teachers' behavior was accounted for by their membership in a dyad/triad. To investigate whether the ideals of student teachers in a group were related to each other in the same way, we performed an analysis of variance for every scale of the student teachers' ideal with group membership as the factor. Finding no significant relations, we concluded that although the interpersonal behavior of student teachers is strongly related to the student teaching environment, the ideals of student teachers in one group are more independent from each other.

Because of cooperating and student teachers' interaction in supervisory conferences we might expect a significant relationship between both groups' ideals. This did not occur (5 per cent level). Despite the relationship between the actual behaviors for both cooperating and student teachers, the correlations between student teachers' ideals and actual cooperating teacher behavior were not significant.

Conclusion

This chapter reported on the strong resemblance between communication styles of student teachers who belong to the same group compared to those in other dyads/triads. This finding can only partly be explained by the influence of the cooperating teachers' classroom behavior and not at all by their ideals. It is, however, clear that cooperating and student teachers are somewhat similar in their teaching styles. In the American sample this similarity is stronger than in the Dutch. If we apply a causal interpretation to this relationship, it is most plausible that cooperating teacher behavior influences the student teacher and not vice versa. The study showed that student teachers' ideals are neither influenced by their cooperating teachers' behavior nor by their ideals.

The relationship between cooperating and student teacher's behavior in the US seems to be stronger than in The Netherlands. Though the small sample limits the generalizability of the results, it seems plausible that the grouped Dutch student teachers may be more independent from their cooperating teacher than their American counterparts who are placed individually. The fact that they are in groups also provides them with other examples of teacher behavior. As a result, they may be better able to build a communication style of their own.

Several factors may contribute to the intra-group similarity of student teachers' communication styles. Although the data does not point to the cooperating teachers' behavior as the sole or key reason for the similarity, it is clearly important. Student teachers may try to adopt or imitate their cooperating teacher's style to some extent. The imitation is not absolute, however, and we observed that student teachers often expressed strong disapproval of aspects of their co-operating teacher's communication style.

The systems perspective also points to a possible explanation for the co-operating teacher's influence. Student teachers are in a classroom whose environment has been shaped by the cooperating teacher. The students are used to a particular type of interpersonal behavior. The teacher and class have built a communication system, and characteristics of this system may transfer to the student teachers' lessons. When, for example, a student teacher is placed with a cooperating teacher who has developed a healthy working climate in class (Leadership, Helpful/Friendly, Understanding behaviors), students are willing to listen and to follow instructions more easily than in a class where the quality is lower. As a result, the student teacher is encouraged or even forced to display the same type of behavior. On the other hand, teaching in a class of a very tolerant cooperating teacher where students are continually talking without listening can provoke uncertain behavior in the student teacher. This line of reasoning is in agreement with research results that highlighted the important role of students in determining or even shaping teachers' behaviors (e.g., Doyle, 1979; Zeichner, 1983).

Since the similarity of behavior in a student-teacher group is not completely explained by the cooperating teacher's influence, other factors must be involved. The school environment, including the interaction of student teachers with other personnel in the school, probably influences student-teacher behavior. For the teacher-education programs in this study we do not believe this is the primary factor contributing to intra-group similarity. We agree with Feiman-Nemser and Floden (1986), who suggest that such general socialization pressures are not very strong and that beginning teachers are not easily changed (Lacey, 1977; Zeichner and Tabachnick, 1983).

In addition, the similarity may be a partial consequence of the interaction between the group's members and their characteristics upon entering the program. The groups are comprised of student teachers who, with some limitations have chosen each other. During the student-teaching period they cooperate with and observe each other. These activities may convergently influence their communication style. It is therefore surprising that the ideals of student teachers in the same group are independent from each other. More research is needed to explain this result.

Finally, student teachers' behavior can also be molded by the way the cooperating teacher interacts and guides the student teacher in supervision conferences.

Implications

We believe an important topic for future research is the extent to which students' behavior and student teachers' collaborative activities contribute to the strong relationship between student teachers' behaviors when they work in a group.

The present study may have some consequences for teacher-education practice. The results make us question the appropriateness of individually placing student teachers and cooperating teachers, or matching them in like-minded pairs. This is a common practice in most American teacher-education programs. Bringing student teachers together in dyads or triads, as in the Dutch program, may help them build their own communication styles and apply the techniques learned on campus. This strategy can also counteract possible negative influences of cooperating teachers on the student teacher's professional development.

The results of the study further indicate that when selecting cooperating teachers it is more important to pay attention to their actual behavior than their ideals, since the former are more strongly related to the student teacher's communication style.

Finally we believe that our results justify a need for diversity in student teaching. Given the strong influences of student teachers on each other and of school environments on student teachers we feel it is helpful for the teacher-education programs to place them in different groups and schools.

Note

1   If the effects of all the cooperating teacher scales on one student-teacher scale (square of the correlation) were combined they would total more than one. This combination as a simple addition cannot be allowed, because the effects from certain scales overlap. For example, it is possible that part of the variance in student-teacher behavior attributed to CD cooperating-teacher behavior can also be attributed to CS. While Table 11.2 allows us to compare one student-teacher scale to one cooperating-teacher scale, we cannot derive the effect of all the co-operating-teacher scales on each student-teacher scale. We therefore performed the multiple regression analysis with forward inclusion. 'Forward inclusion' means that the first correlation in the regression equation was the scale with the highest correlation between student and cooperating teacher.

Chapter 12

Teacher Education Programs

Theo Wubbels, Hans Créton and Joost Hermans

Empirical research and different theoretical foundations have produced a variety of orientations to teacher education (e.g., Woolfolk, 1989; Tillema and Veenman, 1987). Since no one has been able to conclusively demonstrate the best method of preparing teachers, we believe in diverse approaches to improve teacher education. This chapter presents our contribution from the systems perspective on classroom communication, building on the research results discussed in the previous chapters. We are aware that this approach has a specific focus and should probably be combined with others which concentrate on instructional methodology or knowledge of subject matter. While recognizing the importance of the various approaches to teacher education (e.g., Lanier and Little, 1986), we devote this final segment to the improvement of teacher education by focusing on interpersonal relationships in the classroom.

The chapter opens by summarizing the descriptions of appropriate interpersonal teacher behavior previously mentioned. We then discuss these descriptions in terms of data we've accumulated in three Dutch teacher-education programs.

The first program is a one-year postgraduate course for university students in different subjects who are preparing to be teachers in the upper level of secondary education. Student teaching and campus activities alternate. Students spend half the time in schools, in a two-phase student teaching period. In the first phase, student teachers are placed in triads with one cooperating teacher; their teaching assignments progress from short lesson segments to whole lessons to a short series of lessons with one class. The second phase is a three-month individual teaching assignment in which they independently teach half-time. They have full responsibility for their classes, and supervision is conducted 'at a distance' (Koetsier, Wubbels and Van Driel, 1992). The cooperating teacher provides feedback concerning the quality of teaching, while the university staff focuses on the learning process of the student teacher. Neither supervisor observes any lessons. Thus, the cooperating teacher has to rely for information about the student teacher's performance on indirect sources such as students and the student teacher. It was decided that the greater responsibility and self-reliance created by not having an observer was more important than the need for observation data. Between the two phases the student teachers study educational theory on campus and are also involved in an action research project.

The second teacher-education program features short courses for students preparing to be teachers in vocational education. The students have extensive work experience and they will be expected to train others about their jobs. They have no formal preparation in teaching. These programs are offered, for example, to veteran technicians, police officers, doctors and lawyers. The courses last between one and two months, and are usually paralleled by half-time teaching practice.

Finally, the third program involved short-in-service courses (two weekly three-hour classes for ten to twenty weeks) for secondary teachers who wish to improve their teaching. These teachers usually have a great deal of classroom experience and firm subject-matter expertise, but are afraid they've become set in their ways. The courses usually focus on improving their relationships with students and communication styles. They consist of theoretical studies based on the teachers' experiences and their applications of course concepts in their classes.

Since we believe the same teacher-education principles apply to both, we don't separate in our discussion pre-service and in-service education. We do realize there are differences, of course, and when these arise they are noted.

Satisfactory Interpersonal Teacher Behavior

Various groups involved in education apply different criteria for satisfactory and successful teaching. Parents, for example, may place primary importance on teachers' capacity to guide their students successfully through school. This criterion is probably also used implicitly or explicitly by many researchers (e.g., Berliner, 1986). Students may expect their teachers to create an atmosphere in which they can feel good and be successful (Hermans, 1981). Teachers will usually agree with these viewpoints, but they may also define expertise in terms of high job-satisfaction and motivation: a good teacher is someone who likes the job and perseveres (Blase, 1982). This book has discussed the qualities of a good teacher from the perspective of interpersonal behavior in class, a criterion that seems related to all the others. They are summarized below, along with an analysis of selected characteristics from our teacher-education experiences.

Communication Style

We concluded in Chapter 3 that teachers and students agree on the nature of appropriate interpersonal teacher behavior based on teachers' ideals and students' views of best and worst teachers. Their image is in agreement with the one derived from the Chapter 5 study on student outcomes and teacher behavior. We believe these results provide a strong indication for the kind of interpersonal behavior that should be promoted in teacher education. Briefly, teachers should be effective instructors and lecturers, as well as friendly, helpful and congenial. They should be able to empathize with students, understand their world and listen to them. Good teachers are not uncertain, undecided or confusing in the way they communicate with students. They aren't grouchy, gloomy, dissatisfied, aggressive, sarcastic nor quick-tempered. They should be able to set standards and maintain control while still allowing students responsibility and freedom to learn. These last two characteristics are partial opposites, and are somewhat controversial for teachers and students. Some people appreciate teachers who are more dominant whereas others want them to be more submissive. The third chapter described this as a preference for a Dominant or a Student-Oriented ideal. In Chapter 5 we stated that these ideals probably reflected different emphases on student performance and attitudes.

Changes During the Teaching Career

Chapter 7 discussed the changes in communication style that teachers undergo during their professional career. Noting the empirical relationship between interpersonal teacher behavior and student outcomes from Chapter 5, we can say that relations between teachers and their students improve in the first four years of their career. This improvement helps raise both student achievement and attitudes. Soon after, however, a steady change takes place which is both welcome and unwelcome. Teachers appear to decline in cooperative behavior and increase in oppositional behavior, a change which negatively affects student attitudes. They also increase in strictness, however, which can heighten student achievement.

Our experiences with in-service programs have demonstrated how difficult it is, even for experienced teachers, to interact properly at the right moment (Hermans, Créton and Hooymayers, 1987). Most of the veteran teachers were able to provide guidance, manage classes and make assignments. They appeared to have no problems in taking initiative, providing structure, lecturing, giving orders and staying on the topic. Many, however, encountered difficulties when they tried to provide responsibility and initiative to students by backing off, actively listening to students' opinions, asking about ideas and paraphrasing students' statements.

Student teachers experience other difficulties. Since they've always received guidance and prescription, it is hard for them to assume an active teaching role, to take charge, to set standards and to assess. Their professional role does not yet seem to fit their developmental stage.

Behavioral Repertoire

While the previous section described relatively stable patterns of teacher communication, it did not specify the behavioral repertoire needed to build such patterns. A successful teacher's communication style does not, for example, include a great deal of admonishing behavior. This does not imply, however, that admonishing behavior should not be part of his or her repertoire. On the contrary, we believe that teaching expertise means that a teacher can suit his or her behavior to situational requirements. He or she must be able to effectively interact in all kinds of educational settings, with students who possess a variety of personal and group characteristics. This requires an interactional repertoire which is both broad and flexible (e.g., Brophy and Good, 1986). 'Broad' implies that he or she has many interpersonal modes, while 'flexibility' means he or she can smoothly switch from one interpersonal category to another.

Effective teachers must display appropriate behavior in all kinds of teaching situations, such as making presentations, leading discussions, and facilitating group and individual work. It is important to note that appropriate interpersonal behavior from one sector of the Leary model may appear differently across teaching situations, and often depends on the instructional method being used. For example, bestowing responsibility on students in group work differs from that when lecturing. All situations require their own specific interactional formula. Being strict and technical might be productive during a grammar lesson, but it can easily kill student motivation while discussing a literary theme.

Interpersonal Pitfalls

On several occasions in this book we've suggested that teachers may mistake opposition for dominance. We have often observed that being strict in class goes hand-in-hand with a certain amount of aggression. Announcing that 'there is no talking allowed here' (DO) is almost always followed by the sanction 'or you'll see what happens!' (OD). The combination of strictness and aggression can easily escalate, and is disapproved of by both students and teachers.

Similarly, we think that providing students with responsibility and freedom can be confused with uncertainty, thus becoming a second interpersonal pitfall. When encouraging students to take responsibility it is imperative that they don't perceive the given freedom as a weakness on the part of the teacher. Uncertain and undecided behavior will often lead to disorder. Many teachers, including those with extensive experience, find it difficult to provide adequate freedom and responsibility for students. For example, when a student poses a critical question, it is hard for a teacher to first ascertain what the youngster is asking (and/or feeling), before reacting. Critical questions can easily invoke teacher uncertainty or aggression, a danger which warns of the need to give students enough opportunity to explain and clarify.

Self-Perception

Chapter 6 presented evidence that effective teachers' self-perceptions were in greater agreement with their students than teachers' who were less effective. The more teachers communicate according to the Leadership, Helpful/Friendly and Understanding sectors, the more they agree with their students about the behavior displayed. This result highlights the importance of teachers knowing how their students perceive them and using that feedback to improve their teaching style.

Goals for Teacher Education

In our view professional teachers have an extended repertoire at their disposal from which they can choose the most effective behavior for various teaching–learning situations. We believe our research clearly outlines the kind of interpersonal teacher behavior that should be pursued in teacher education. Further, it alerts teacher educators to the possible confusion of different behaviors and the need for accurate teacher self-perceptions.

We see three important goals for teacher-education programs related to interpersonal behavior. First, attitudes toward teaching and learning must be based on sound theory and research. Since pre and in-service teachers bring all types of preconceptions to teacher-education programs it may be necessary to change attitude and cognition. Next, teachers must be able to match the appropriate behavior to the situation. Very often teachers have all kinds of skills at their disposal, but consciously or unconsciously choose improper behaviors. Finally, teachers must build a large repertoire of behaviors in the sectors that previously were mentioned as effective in promoting student learning. Each of these goals will be analyzed below.

Goal 1: Change of Attitude and Cognition

At the beginning of our programs (especially in pre-service teacher education) there is usually a stage of attitudinal and cognitive restructuring. It has been shown that novice teachers' ideas about classroom interaction and many other topics are limited and undifferentiated (e.g., Weinstein, 1988). These (student) teachers' preconceptions show a remarkable resistance against traditional attempts to change them (Wahl, Weinert and Huber, 1984; Fiske and Taylor, 1984; Turk and Speers, 1983). We have witnessed both the one-sidedness and the stability. Some examples of these can be seen from the following statements:

— With a new class, you should be very strict right from the start, because it is much easier to loosen the reins than to tighten them.
— Students only learn when I am lecturing.
— One learns from one's mistakes.
— As a teacher I ought to know the answer to every question.

The axiomatic character of these preconceptions (and other examples) is striking. Despite their face validity we feel that they oversimplify a complicated educational reality. We therefore try to instill in beginning teachers the need to diverge from a single approach based on their attitudes, and look at education in a more differentiated way (Weinstein, 1989).

Communicative perspective

Student teachers often see the classroom atmosphere as something that is a result of student characteristics and school culture (Brophy and Rohrkemper, 1981). They cannot easily change the context, however, and we are compelled to demonstrate how teacher behavior influences class atmosphere and how it can be used to improve the learning environment. This is accomplished on campus with the help of group simulations and role plays. We may, for example, have student teachers approach a situation in a number of different ways. We then analyze with them the different communication patterns that evolve from these interventions.

Student teachers do not often see how their own behavior can influence class atmosphere. They also have little insight about how classroom-communication patterns develop and the teacher's role in the process. They often consider the course of events in the classroom as an aggregate of seemingly incidental and haphazard actions. Disturbances, for example are seen as actions of individual students that are unrelated to the behaviors of other students or the teacher. They do not realize that these actions are often part of a rather stable communication pattern, as has been shown by the systems perspective. We therefore let them analyze classroom interaction as a chain of communication messages in which student and teacher behavior are actions and reactions. Instead of analyzing causes and consequences, we identify behavioral interventions that may build a more favorable classroom atmosphere.

Differentiated observations

Teachers' undifferentiated preconceptions are clear from their descriptions of interactions both in classrooms and at campus. Initially, when observing and evaluating each other's lessons, their feedback is rather poor and superficial. They can formulate their observations only in terms of general judgments such as 'she did well' or 'he was confident'. We have tried to broaden teachers' categories by introducing a model for observing classroom behavior, which can be summarized as Progressive Focussing (Parlett and Hamilton, 1976). We first ask them to describe what they have seen. They mostly describe the observation in very general statements ('She related well to the students'). We then teach them to observe more carefully and ask for a description of teaching behavior in concrete terms ('She approached each student with a curious look while verbally formulating a question'). In the last stage of our mini-course on observation we also have them describe students' reactions to the teachers' behaviors. Thus we induce an observation chain that progresses along the following line:

Judgement = >	Description of = >	Description of = >	Description of
about	observed	observed	students'
teaching	teaching	teaching	reactions
behavior	behavior	behavior in	to teaching
	in general terms	concrete terms	behaviors

Integration of new conceptions with preconceptions

We believe that changing preconceptions is only useful if there is a visible effect on the teacher's lessons: new conceptions need to appropriately direct the teacher's behavior. According to Corporaal (1988), new cognitions that effectively direct behavior must be integrated with the teacher's preconceptions. This integration can be seen as a gradual change process in which connections are made between existing and new conceptions. Some of the many strategies proposed in the teacher-education literature to promote this integration are listed below:

— conceptual training (Gliesmann and Pugh, 1987),
— use of action research (Kemmis and McTaggart, 1988),
— strategies to promote reflective teaching (Zeichner, 1987),
— feedback procedures used in skill training (Cruickshank and Metcalf, 1990) or in supervision (Glickman and Bey, 1990),
— workshops seeking to change teachers' perceptions of effective teaching (Hewson and Hewson, 1987),
— use of audio-visual protocol materials (Borg, 1973),
— demonstration of skills and modeling (Putnam and Johns, 1987).

Based on theories from cognitive psychology and information processing theory (e.g., Anderson, 1985; Resnick, 1983; Fiske and Taylor, 1984) Corporaal cites the necessary conditions for these strategies to be successful:

1 The new theories should be presented over long periods of time, and must be moderately incongruous with the existing conceptions; the theories should not be redundant or ambiguous.
2 In training and practice experiences should be immediately and personally relevant.
3 Training activities should not take place under time pressure, and they must not demand too much cognitive activity at a time.
4 Teachers need to have well-developed and accessible cognitive structures and must be motivated to change these structures.
5 Guided skill practice is necessary, but only fruitful if feedback is incorporated into new instruction.

Conceptual change strategies

For many topics it is possible for preconceptions and new themes to gradually become integrated. Sometimes, however, things that teacher educators want pre and in-service teachers to learn conflict to such a degree with the common-sense ideas with which they enter the program that a radical restructuring is needed (Vosniadou and Brewer, 1987).

For example, many pre-service teachers hold a strong, often unconscious, belief that effective teaching in secondary education is characterized by lectures and large-group explanations (e.g., Broekman and Weterings, 1987). This belief may have been assisted by the abundance of conduit metaphors present in the English as well as the Dutch language that describe the transmission of ideas, thoughts and feelings (Reddy, 1979). Pre-service teachers often think that a teacher's real job is to explain things clearly, since this was their own experience as students. Teacher educators, however, want them to realize that the primary aim of education is for students to learn and understand. This notion is almost totally absent in many student teachers' preconceptions of teaching (Weinstein, 1988). Thus, educators might stimulate student teachers to use group work or class discussions, if appropriate, to create learning opportunities for students. To change preconceptions and actions in this way may require a radical restructuring of ideas and skills. Radical restructuring implies that a different cognition has to be built in terms of framework, the domain of phenomena it explains and individual concepts. This process is probably similar to what Schön (1987) refers to as reframing.

We would like to focus on a conceptual change approach which can use Socratic dialogue, described by Posner, Strike, Hewson and Gertzog (1982). It has been applied to teacher education by Stofflett and Stoddart (1991). A person often uses preconceptions to evaluate whether new ideas are intelligible, plausible and fruitful. If they are, then a restructuring or adoption of the new idea takes place. This view has important implications for teaching and teacher education. New and existing conceptions may continuously compete in the student teacher's mind and the existing cognitions will only be replaced if their status is lowered. Thus, not only must the student teacher accept the new ideas, but he or she must also become dissatisfied with the old. This requires that teacher educators have considerable knowledge of student-teacher preconceptions.

While we have found that the intelligibility of theories presented on campus is usually not problematic, we have encountered difficulty in demonstrating their fruitfulness. The power behind the idea of fruitfulness of preconceptions can probably best be understood from the radical constructivist view that knowledge has an adaptive function. Conceptions help us to cope in the world of our experiences (von Glasersfeld, 1991). They obviously have an important survival function, and we will not give them up unless we have a better, more fruitful alternative.

Let us return to the example of the student teachers' view that good teaching requires an emphasis on lecturing and explaining. There may be several (unconscious) beliefs behind this perception. One might be that learning takes place whenever a teacher explains something clearly and without mistakes. Another widespread belief is that the quality of a lesson can be measured by the orderliness of the classroom and the amount of work that occurs, or seems to occur (Créton and Wubbels, 1984). From this belief the adaptive function is clear in that it helps teachers organize their world. Teacher educators might seek to replace these cognitions by others such as: 'Students will learn if they can construct meaning from what is presented and if they can actively engage in working with the knowledge to be learned'. Many things that teachers explain are not incorporated in students' cognitive structures. Further, even if the explanation does pierce the students' cognitive armor, it frequently does so in a way that the teacher did not intend (Osborne and Freyberg, 1985). The intelligibility of this new cognition is relatively easy for student teachers. Plausibility, however, is somewhat more controversial: if a more active role of the learner is better, why do so many teachers always lecture, and why do teacher educators lecture about these topics? And how do we rectify our own experience of learning something when someone explained it very clearly? Student teachers' answers to these questions may be different from those of teacher educators because they have usually not been confronted, until then, with the differences between what the students learn and what the teachers 'teach' (or 'present', since true teaching cannot occur without learning). The most important problem with the new cognition, therefore, is its doubtful fruitfulness in light of student teachers' experiences. The existing (or pre-) cognition seems very fruitful for them from the standpoint that class should be orderly. When they explain the material clearly, the student teachers experience an orderly classroom with attentive students. In this respect the new cognition often appears unfruitful at first: when student teachers use group work or class discussions for the first time, the time on task often seems to decrease and students become noisier and occasionally disruptive. In addition, teachers feel less productive during group work, and this may lead them to project these beliefs onto the class. The disorder is, of course, not desirable; it is due, among other things, to the student teacher's lack of classroom-management skills. The (seeming) unfruitfulness of the new cognition is strengthened when the innovative teaching methods do not initially lead to desired student outcomes.

It is therefore important to attend to the fruitfulness of existing and new cognitions. Special activities should be developed to invalidate the (often unconsciously perceived) plausibility and fruitfulness of the preconceptions of teachers.

A careful analysis of the (student) teacher's preconceptions is required in order to address them properly. Thus, probing into the conceptions of individual teachers should become an important part of teacher-education strategies (e.g., Korthagen, 1992).

Intuitive strategies

In the previous section a rational, analytical and intellectual approach was described for conceptual change. We can also employ more intuitive strategies to influence preconceptions, as suggested by Watzlawick (1978). They are based on the idea that many conceptions can be seen as *gestalts* (Korthagen, 1992) or images rather than as networks of logical connected statements (Wubbels, 1992). The strategies try to convey new ideas in a holistic pattern. Immersion of teachers in experiences, for example, may provide them with real world images far more effectively then secondhand descriptions of reality. Intuitive strategies in theoretical segments of teacher education are not often used, but are possible. An example of an intuitive strategy would be the use of figurative language such as metaphors and proverbs (Korthagen, 1992; Wubbels, 1992; Marshall, 1990; Munby, 1986; Munby and Russell, 1990).

The advantage of using proverbs can itself be explained through a proverb: 'One picture is worth a thousand words'. The Asian proverb 'He who rides the tiger cannot dismount' may create an impressive image of the future for teachers who maintain a repressive climate in class. They are afraid that if they loosen up it will lead to a wave of unruly behavior by students. Their authoritarianism, of course, may severely limit learning, so the teacher may find himself or herself in a no-win situation.

Metaphors such as 'entertainer' or 'captain of the ship' (Tobin, Kahle and Fraser, 1990) succinctly paint a rich image of a teacher's role. In a case study by Créton, Wubbels and Hooymayers (1989), a beginning teacher received feedback that she seemed 'like a lion tamer'. This metaphor provided a number of images about the classroom (it was a cage), her lessons (she tried to get students occasionally to sit still and at other times to do tricks) and the teacher (she could not show any uncertainty for fear of an attack). This kind of feedback helped the teacher see things from a different perspective and led to her reflecting about the type of classroom she really wanted. Her image of her teaching was instantly influenced by the brief mention of this metaphor.

It is possible to use real visual images to achieve the same goals. Photographs and videotapes (such as those used in protocol materials) are obviously powerful ways to convey meaning in a holistic way. A photograph captures an image of reality that is far richer than language used to describe it. English (1988) provides some examples of photographs used in this manner in qualitative research.

Because intuitive strategies employ just a few words — or a single picture — to evoke a whole image they can lead to misunderstandings. Once again, one way to prevent these problems is by the teacher educator having a clear understanding of the pre or in-service teacher's preconceptions. He or she can obtain some information from research on student teacher's preconceptions (Hollingsworth, 1989; Weinstein, 1988). As stated above, it is very important to probe the conceptions of individual student teachers in great detail. Interpersonal skills are necessary to accomplish this (Glickman and Bey, 1990). By actively exploring student teachers' preconceptions the student teacher himself or herself becomes more aware of his or her own thinking. In addition, after using intuitive strategies joint reflection by student teachers and teacher educators on the evoked images can be useful. This will not only analyze if the strategies have been successful in changing conceptions, but will also ensure that they become integrated into reflective practice.

This section discussed changing attitudes and cognitions in teacher-education programs to improve interpersonal teacher behavior. Helping teachers become sensitive to the systems character of communication is the central theme of this approach. Sometimes this involves an integration of new ideas with preconceptions. In other cases conceptual change is needed via an analytical approach or via intuitive strategies.

Goal 2: Satisfactory Use of the Behavioral Repertoire

The following example will illustrate our attempts to help teachers appropriately use their behavioral repertoire. Small changes in teacher behavior can lead to (both positive and negative) communication spirals. A small increase in teacher dissatisfaction with student performance and behavior may decrease their motivation, which in turn may further increase the teacher's dissatisfaction, thus triggering a negative self-reinforcing process. Teachers involved in such a spiral usually see their dissatisfaction as a legitimate reaction to students' behavior. The communicative result is, however, contrary to what the teachers want to attain: more student motivation instead of less. A teacher caught in this pattern is often reluctant to become more friendly because he or she thinks that the students should change first and show greater motivation. This reluctance is not only result but also cause of the unfavorable student motivation. When teachers blame students for demotivation they hinder their ability to select and implement the appropriate behavior to change the undesired pattern. By helping teachers understand these circular processes and the impossibility of solving the problem by blaming the other party, we encourage them to select the appropriate interpersonal behavior. Changing escalated communication patterns (Wubbels, Créton and Holvast, 1988) usually requires (although not exclusively) adequate use of skills that are already part of the behavioral repertoire of teachers. As explained in Chapter 1, escalating communication patterns can often be found in lessons. We have observed the escalating spiral of ever stronger student demotivation and dissatisfied and unfriendly teacher behavior in classes of veteran instructors. Another example occurs more frequently with beginning teachers in disorderly classroom situations. Disruptive behavior of students is followed by corrective behavior of the teacher. The students react to the teacher's admonishing behavior by creating another disturbance. They both then solely focus on each other's aggressive or confronting behavior in order to raise the intensity level notch-by-notch. As described in Chapter 1, this creates an aggressive spiral in which students and teacher strengthen each other's behavior. Watzlawick, Weakland and Fisch (1974) call this 'a game without end', in which the solution is sought in 'more of the same' (dissatisfied behavior or harsh or punitive measures).

In such escalated situations, according to Watzlawick and his colleagues, the solutions chosen only represent a partial understanding of the problem and in fact strengthen the problem's innermost core. We try to help teachers see that in these situations changes for the better often can be reached by implementing what Watzlawick, Weakland and Fisch (1974) call second-order solutions. Second-order solutions are directed at the original (first-order) solution. In the case of the dissatisfied teacher, showing friendly behavior may help to break the communication pattern. This behavior is usually opposite to the teacher's natural reaction and it is therefore not easily displayed. Créton, Wubbels and Hooymayers (1989) describe an example of a teacher in The Netherlands with very severe discipline problems. At first, this teacher reacted with 'more of the same' i.e., with more punitive measures. Since they led to a further escalation of the disorder, this 'solution' actually became the core of the problem. In this case, becoming less strict was the second-order solution that solved the problem created by becoming more harsh. As a result of her new understanding, this teacher acted kinder, quieter, more lenient and less strict toward the students. Second-order solutions radically break the communication pattern and often run counter to common sense, as the following excerpt from an interview with this teacher shows.

> I absolutely did not hit on the idea to decrease the punishments. I didn't realize that decreasing them could make them meaningful again. It would never have occurred to me, although I did realize that all those punishments were of no avail.

The teacher also gave very low grades to students who did poorly on tests. She was convinced that they were a consequence of the students' inattention. The students were indignant about these grades and blamed the teacher's poor explanations for their poor test results. They reacted by becoming even more inattentive and disruptive. This, of course, led to more low grades, more disruptiveness and so forth. Part of the second-order solution, therefore, was to have the students do seat work, hand in their assignments and grade them as high as possible. At first the teacher talked about the grades as follows:

> When I was marking dictations I could of course have been more lenient, but then those who were always noisy and distracted others would not have had an unsatisfactory grade ... I was probably so severe because I wanted to keep them all under control, at all costs, and I used those grades as a means of power.

After the change of behavior she said:

> If it became too disorderly I could always have the work handed in and mark the papers at home. The notes I made were used for rounding off the report card grades. Only in a positive sense, of course, so that a student who worked hard during the lesson would also benefit.

This section provided some examples of helping teachers employ neglected strategies in their behavioral repertoires. Selecting appropriate behaviors which match situational needs often requires cognitive restructuring. This intellectual realignment does not always result from interventions such as instruction or discussion. We have also employed behavioral approaches, and will return to this in the section on methods.

Goal 3: Enlargement of the Behavioral Repertoire

General shortages

The results of our research indicate that inexperienced teachers demonstrate less leadership than very effective teachers and they also may lack an adequate behavioral repertoire in the Strict sector. We believe that their low scores on Friendly and Understanding behavior are related to the similar result for the Leadership scale. As a result, we think that developing these skills should be a prominent goal of pre-service and teacher induction programs. In light of the interpersonal pitfalls, focusing on strict behavior is inherently risky. The training should be sensitive to the need not to combine strictness with aggression.

Older teachers are less friendly and understanding than their students and they themselves want to be. We suppose that the decrease of cooperative behavior during the teaching career is not due to lack of an adequate behavioral repertoire in these sectors. We have noticed that some very experienced teachers tend to become stricter as they get older, and sometimes become unreasonable in their demands. This can provoke student protest that can initially be handled easily, but gradually becomes a real threat to the learning environment. When faced with this difficult problem, the teachers may become even more demanding and corrective, which further stimulates these negative communication spirals. The origin of the decrease in cooperative behavior may therefore be due to an inadequate repertoire in strict behavior and a skill deficiency to giving students responsibility. Training in providing students with freedom and responsibility is therefore a major segment of our in-service education for very experienced teachers. In addition, there is also emphasis on setting norms and standards in a clear, but not provocative way. In showing teachers how to encourage student responsibility and freedom we place special emphasis on behaviors which cannot be interpreted as teacher uncertainty or weakness.

Planning enlargement

When training for new teaching behaviors we follow Joyce and Showers' (1988) model, among others. The activities include theory presentation, modeling by the teacher educator, simulations on campus and in (student) teaching. Feedback is provided by teacher educators, cooperating teachers and colleague (student) teachers acting as peer coaches. There is a close correspondence between activities on campus and the student teaching activities. Student teaching is closely monitored by university staff in order to assess development in the behavioral repertoire and plan further interventions for improvement.

From learning theories and ideas on behavior modification (Bandura, 1969), we assume that enlargement of the behavioral repertoire will best be achieved if at first behaviors are practiced that are not too different from those that teachers already perform. We therefore added one step to the Joyce and Showers model: a stage in which we diagnose the behavioral repertoire which (student) teachers already have, and describe the things they must learn. They can then practice a new approach in a secure environment in which success is expected. Thus, we try to enlarge the behavioral repertoire by starting with the package the teacher already has and helping them find alternatives and plan new strategies.

The development and use of particular skills require different levels of difficulty and are tied to the context where they must be implemented. Teachers' behavioral repertoire is therefore diagnosed in different contexts, e.g., in a variety of classes, using different teaching methods or class settings (in front of a whole class, in groups of students, toward an individual student), and with students of different ability levels and age. We also record aspects of the school culture and climate which may influence the use of particular skills in a given context. On the basis of this diagnosis a program of subsequent training situations is projected following general guidelines such as:

— from easy to more difficult situations
— from well structured into less structured situations
— from very secure into less secure situations
— from simple into complex situations.

The situations follow each other in small progressive steps.

Role of the teacher educator

Such a program puts special demands on teacher educators. They should be able to act in diagnostic, planning and counseling roles. The diagnostic segment includes assessment of behavioral categories which are either already adopted or which need to be developed. In planning, the teacher educator designs a (remedial) training program for each individual (student) teacher, so they can recognize which categories are to be learned and how these can be linked to those that have already been mastered (Hermans, Hooymayers, Créton and Wubbels, 1985). As a counselor, the teacher educator facilitates the future teachers' learning process (e.g., reducing resisting forces and keeping the student teacher motivated to go on). During the training program the diagnostic role often increasingly transfers to the student teachers. In the beginning teacher educators model the process by focusing on the most important observations. At later stages the roles change, and they basically help student teachers analyze and recognize their own behavior. In this sense there is a progression from a more directive role to a more reflective counseling orientation. Here is where a difference between pre and in-service courses appears. In the latter, the participants take more responsibility for their own learning process from the outset.

Enlargement of the behavioral repertoire is a prominent aim in many competency based teacher education programs, and is at least as important as the two purposes mentioned above. Since the approach is largely geared to individuals it must be flexible. The level and depth at which different skills are learned depend upon a person's preferences, interpersonal communication style and other factors. The process requires careful planning and the guidance which is only found in advanced teacher educator skills.

Methods

In previous sections we outlined many issues surrounding the methods used in our programs. We expand on this below by describing the emphasis on behaviors and positive reinforcement.

Emphasis on Behavior

We don't believe much time should be spent on discussions about ideals, values and conceptions about teaching if they are not tied to practice. These discussions are far more realistic and valuable if (student) teachers can relate them to their own classroom experiences. We therefore have our students carry out teaching tasks early in the program.

We may, for example, begin by assigning them short lectures on selected topics such as 'Teaching: experiences, expectations and problems'. These would be prepared in pairs and presented to the rest of the group. The many ideas and learning questions which emerge during these sessions are conscientiously listed by the trainer, photocopied and distributed in the next meeting. This opening activity helps students become aware of notions such as:

— Teaching is a skill and a craft rather than a gift ('Born teachers are also made');
— Teaching can be progressively mastered by practice, evaluation, practice, evaluation, and so on;
— There are many ways to teach effectively;
— The intuitive way in which many teachers teach is not incorrect, but sometimes there are alternative techniques that are more appropriate.

The set of learning questions can become the agenda for the balance of the training program, and can also monitor progress.

We try to have teachers practice new teaching methods as soon as possible, repeating them until they feel in control. At this point they are more willing to realistically reflect on their classroom behavior than before the practice. They seem to be more ready to analyze the preconceptions on which they based their former actions.

In supervising teachers we have benefitted from the use of behavioral suggestions, which help teachers act in a specified way. This behavior potentially allows the teacher to experience a reality that cannot be communicated by mere verbal descriptions or explanations (Watzlawick, 1978). An example was the low-grading teacher's resistance against suggestions to give better grades (in the section on goal 2). This experience made her aware of the effects of her approach to assessment.

An example, similar to one described by Watzlawick (1978) in a different setting, concerns a teacher who thought students couldn't behave responsibly. A minor indication of this belief was that he always wanted to be in the classroom before the students entered. He organized everything and gave them directions and guidance for nearly every activity, including some that they probably could manage themselves. In the end this became a rather undesirable situation, since the teacher became far too busy and the students overly dependent. His view that students lacked competence to take responsibility convinced him there was no other way. A supervisor, confronted with the difficulty of enlarging the teacher's viewpoint, nonetheless encouraged him to behave differently. He finally managed to occasionally have the teacher enter the class after the students had arrived. The teacher was surprised to see that his students had already taken their books out and were ready for work. This made him confront the realization that students were more responsible than he had thought. He consequently allowed them to take more responsibility in other areas. Behaving differently was thus the starting point for a different view of students.

In teacher education, changes of behavior are usually expected after a change in cognition. The previous example demonstrated that (student) teachers' preconceptions can also be changed by first changing behaviors (see also Guskey, 1986; 1989; Fiske and Taylor, 1984; Resnick, 1983).

An important requirement for this behavioral approach is the provision of a secure learning atmosphere and a sophisticated design of what one wants a (student) teacher to do. In our programs for experienced teachers, for example, it appeared that they had to get past their suspicions ('What's wrong with my teaching?'). A trusting relationship between teacher educator and student teacher will facilitate risk-taking by the student, even if he or she doesn't immediately see the benefit.

Positive Reinforcement

The school system uses grades, certificates and diplomas as rewards to motivate students' learning. In the classroom teachers employ all sorts of techniques to stimulate their students, of which positive reinforcement is often considered the most powerful. We have noticed, however, that (future) teachers have problems in positively rewarding each other's classroom behavior. Instead they excel in highlighting other's supposed mistakes and enjoy being critical. They justify this approach with phrases such as 'One learns more from negative than from positive feedback; more from shortcomings than accomplishments', 'I know what I did well; you don't have to tell me. Don't be soft'.

Since skill in delivering positive reinforcement is a requirement for effective teaching (Pintrich, 1990) and coaching of colleagues, we tried to find ways to change this denial. We settled on a combined approach of change of conception and change of behavior. We assign student teachers the task of giving positive feedback after classroom observations. This forces the observer to practice being positive, while the observed teacher has the experience of receiving it. Positive feedback is therefore viewed and practiced as a skill ('Try to formulate what you observed while he or she was teaching and tell it to him or her in positive terms'). In addition, the underlying conception is clarified ('For a professional teacher it is important to be able to point out what a student has already accomplished').

'Being positive but honest' is initially difficult for most of the participants in our programs. Police instructors as well as those with a strong research background seemed to have problems, probably caused by the character of their profession. Police officers are trained to be strict and suspicious in maintaining the law. Researchers are required to be objectively critical, and must search for faults, shortcomings and disconfirming evidence. An initial clash between the pre and new conception was almost inevitable for these participants in our program. Afterwards, however, they felt satisfied that the new idea was better, since their teaching became more effective. In this case, the behavioral approach was once again successful. The idea that being critical was useful for teachers was difficult to change in discussions. After the experience of giving and receiving positive feedback, however, teachers were far more sensitive to unproductive effects of critical feedback. They easily saw that emphasis on failures can lead to uncertainty, tension, fear of failure, resistance, and so on.

Conclusion

We believe that 'educating reflective practitioners' (Schön, 1987) is a valuable, necessary aim of teacher education. Some of the strategies described in the previous sections are contrary to the usual techniques to promote reflective teaching. This places constraints on their use. They can be employed with care and with moderation, but we believe they should be usually followed by a period of reflection.

In this chapter we offered ideas for teacher education to help pre and in-service teachers improve their interpersonal relations with students. We want to stress that an empirical knowledge base about the usefulness of the described strategies is only beginning to emerge. We have enjoyed some success in our programs, but we haven't yet evaluated them rigorously. Research, planned for the future, is needed before the implementation of our strategies can be strongly advocated.

Appendices

Appendix 2.1: Evolution of the Questionnaire on Teacher Interaction

The Questionnaire on Teacher Interaction (QTI), which measures secondary students' and teachers' perceptions of teacher interpersonal behavior, was developed in several studies in the early 1980s (Wubbels, Créton and Hooymayers, 1985). The QTI evolved from Leary's Interpersonal Adjective Checklist (ICL), which we initially tried to transfer to educational settings.

Leary used the ICL (Laforge and Suczek, 1955) as one method of gathering data on interpersonal behavior. The ICL can be used to have someone describe his or her own behavior, the behavior of someone else or someone's ideal. Its 128 items present behavioral characteristics in single words or short sentences. Every item belongs to a sector of the model and is answered either 'yes' or 'no' depending on its applicability. The items are worded according to four levels of behavioral intensity: weak, moderate, strong and extreme. Leary assigned expressions to a level if it was applicable to either 90 per cent (weak behavior), 67 per cent (moderate), 33 per cent (strong) or 10 per cent (extreme) of the population. The wording of the items in a sector runs from behavior with a weak intensity to behaviors with an extremely high intensity. Words indicating a weak intensity are placed near the intersection of axes on the graph, with the extreme-intensity words far away. The following is an example of some items from two sectors of the ICL:

weak	friendly	can be strict if necessary
moderate	affectionate and understanding	stern but fair
	sociable and neighborly	hard boiled when necessary
	warm	firm but just
strong	fond of everyone	sarcastic
	likes everybody	self-seeking
	friendly all the time	impatient with others' mistakes
extreme	loves everyone	cruel and unkind

A number of problems occurred when we initially used the ICL with second-ary students and teachers. First, many of the items (according to students) did not apply to their teachers at all. These included such examples as 'obeys too will-ingly' and 'cold and unfeeling'. Further, we were not able to find expressions with different intensity for every sector. We had great difficulty deciding on expres-sions which indicated extreme intensity for the DC, CD and CS sectors, and weak intensity for SO and OS. This was basically due to the characteristics of the classroom situation and teacher–student relationships. For example, Leadership, Helpful/Friendly and Understanding behaviors are naturally important to a teacher's repertoire. They must be able to show these qualities often and with great intensity. An expression such as 'This teacher is very friendly', which is supposed to indicate extreme behavior, describes more than 10 per cent of all teachers (in fact, students thought it applied to 17 per cent). In the same way, we could not find expressions of uncertainty which appropriately described 90 per cent of all teachers — for example, students thought that 'Can show uncertainty' applied to about 60 per cent of the teachers rather than the necessary 90 per cent.

It was also very difficult for students to answer with just a simple 'yes' or 'no'. They usually preferred a lengthier response, such as 'a little bit' or 'a lot'. Finally, the 128 items included in the questionnaire required a great deal of time to complete. These problems led us to redesign the ICL to make it more appro-priate for the classroom. This resulted in the Dutch Questionnaire on Teacher Interaction (QTI), whose development is described in the chapter.

Appendix 2.2:   The Questionnaire on Teacher Interaction (American version — male teacher)

QUESTIONNAIRE

This questionnaire asks you to describe your teacher's behavior. Your coopera-tion can help your teacher improve his instruction. DO NOT WRITE YOUR NAME, for your responses are confidential and anonymous. This is NOT a test. Your teacher will NOT read your answers and they will not affect your grade. He will only receive the average results of the class, not individual student scores.

On the next few pages you'll find 64 sentences. For each sentence on the questionnaire find the same number on the answer sheet and darken the circle you think most applies to the teacher of this class. Please use only a #2 pencil. For example:

	Never			Always	
He expresses himself clearly	A	B	C	D	E

If you think that your teacher always expresses himself clearly, darken letter E on your answer sheet. If you think your teacher never expresses himself clearly darken letter A. You can also choose letters B, C or D, which are in between. If you want to change your answer after you've darkened a circle please erase completely. Please use both sides of the answer sheet. Thank you for your cooperation.

PLEASE BEGIN
POSSIBLE RESPONSES
NEVER   ALWAYS
A   B   C   D   E

		never		always
1.	He is strict.	A B C D E		
2.	We have to be silent in his class.	A B C D E		
3.	He talks enthusiastically about his subject.	A B C D E		
4.	He trusts us.	A B C D E		
5.	He is concerned when we have not understood him.	A B C D E		
6.	If we don't agree with him we can talk about it.	A B C D E		
7.	He threatens to punish us.	A B C D E		
8.	We can decide some things in his class.	A B C D E		
9.	He is demanding.	A B C D E		
10.	He thinks we cheat.	A B C D E		
11.	He is willing to explain things again.	A B C D E		
12.	He thinks we don't know anything.	A B C D E		
13.	If we want something he is willing to cooperate.	A B C D E		
14.	His tests are hard.	A B C D E		
15.	He helps us with our work.	A B C D E		
16.	He gets angry unexpectedly.	A B C D E		
17.	If we have something to say he will listen.	A B C D E		
18.	He sympathizes with us.	A B C D E		
19.	He tries to make us look foolish.	A B C D E		
20.	His standards are very high.	A B C D E		
21.	We can influence him.	A B C D E		
22.	We need his permission before we speak.	A B C D E		
23.	He seems uncertain.	A B C D E		
24.	He looks down on us.	A B C D E		
25.	We have the opportunity to choose assignments which are most interesting to us.	A B C D E		
26.	He is unhappy.	A B C D E		
27.	He lets us fool around in class.	A B C D E		
28.	He puts us down.	A B C D E		
29.	He takes a personal interest in us.	A B C D E		
30.	He thinks we can't do things well.	A B C D E		
31.	He explains things clearly.	A B C D E		
32.	He realizes when we don't understand.	A B C D E		

PLEASE CONTINUE ON THE NEXT PAGE

		never				always
33.	He lets us get away with a lot in class.	A	B	C	D	E
34.	He is hesitant.	A	B	C	D	E
35.	He is friendly.	A	B	C	D	E
36.	We learn a lot from him.	A	B	C	D	E
37.	He is someone we can depend on.	A	B	C	D	E
38.	He gets angry quickly.	A	B	C	D	E
39.	He acts as if he does not know what to do.	A	B	C	D	E
40.	He holds our attention.	A	B	C	D	E
41.	He's too quick to correct us when we break a rule.	A	B	C	D	E
42.	He lets us boss him around.	A	B	C	D	E
43.	He is impatient.	A	B	C	D	E
44.	He's not sure what to do when we fool around.	A	B	C	D	E
45.	He knows everything that goes on in the classroom.	A	B	C	D	E
46.	It's easy to make a fool out of him.	A	B	C	D	E
47.	He has a sense of humor.	A	B	C	D	E
48.	He allows us a lot of choice in what we study.	A	B	C	D	E
49.	He gives us a lot of free time in class.	A	B	C	D	E
50.	He can take a joke.	A	B	C	D	E
51.	He has a bad temper.	A	B	C	D	E
52.	He is a good leader.	A	B	C	D	E
53.	If we don't finish our homework we're scared to go to his class.	A	B	C	D	E
54.	He seems dissatisfied.	A	B	C	D	E
55.	He is timid.	A	B	C	D	E
56.	He is patient.	A	B	C	D	E
57.	He is severe when marking papers.	A	B	C	D	E
58.	He is suspicious.	A	B	C	D	E
59.	It is easy to pick a fight with him.	A	B	C	D	E
60.	His class is pleasant.	A	B	C	D	E
61.	We are afraid of him.	A	B	C	D	E
62.	He acts confidently.	A	B	C	D	E
63.	He is sarcastic.	A	B	C	D	E
64.	He is lenient.	A	B	C	D	E

THANK YOU!

SCORING PROCEDURE FOR THE QUESTIONNAIRE ON TEACHER INTERACTION

SCALE	ITEMS
Leadership	3, 31, 36, 40, 45, 52, 62.
Helpful/Friendly	5, 15, 29, 35, 37, 47, 50, 60.
Understanding	4, 6, 11, 13, 17, 18, 32, 56.
Student Responsibility/Freedom	8, 21, 25, 27, 33, 48, 49, 64.
Uncertain	23, 34, 39, 42, 44, 46, 55.
Dissatisfied	7, 10, 12, 19, 26, 28, 30, 54, 58.
Admonishing	16, 24, 38, 41, 43, 51, 59, 63.
Strict	1, 2, 9, 14, 20, 22, 53, 57, 61.

Items are scored 0 for A (never), 1 for B, 2 for C, 3 for D and 4 for E (always). To make a profile item scores are added.

Appendix 2.3: Reliability (Alpha Coefficient) for QTI-Scales on the individual and the class level in American (US), Australian (A) and Dutch (D) samples

		Students						Teachers		
		Student Level			Class Level					
		US (1606)	A (72)	D (1105)	US (66)	A (46)	D (66)	US (66)	A (46)	D (66)
DC	Leadership	0.80	0.83	0.83	0.94	0.94	0.94	0.75	0.74	0.81
CD	Helpful/Friendly	0.88	0.85	0.90	0.95	0.95	0.95	0.74	0.82	0.78
CS	Understanding	0.88	0.82	0.90	0.94	0.94	0.96	0.76	0.78	0.83
SC	Student Responsibility/ Freedom	0.76	0.68	0.74	0.86	0.80	0.85	0.82	0.60	0.72
SO	Uncertain	0.79	0.78	0.79	0.96	0.92	0.92	0.79	0.78	0.83
OS	Dissatisfied	0.83	0.78	0.86	0.90	0.93	0.92	0.75	0.62	0.83
OD	Admonishing	0.84	0.80	0.81	0.92	0.92	0.90	0.81	0.67	0.71
DO	Strict	0.80	0.72	0.78	0.95	0.90	0.89	0.84	0.78	0.61

Appendix 2.4: Test-Retest Reliability Dutch QTI (Créton and Wubbels, 1984)

	Scale	
DC	Leadership	.80
CD	Helpful/friendly	.84
CS	Understanding	.80
SC	Student Responsibility/Freedom	.70
SO	Uncertain	.69
OS	Dissatisfied	.65
OD	Admonishing	.76
DO	Strict	.74

Appendix 2.5: QTI Scale Correlations in a Dutch Study (Créton and Wubbels, 1984)

	CD		CS		SC		SO		OS		OD		DO	
	student	teacher	student	teacher	student	teacher	student	teacher	student	teacher	student	teacher	student	teacher
DC	.61	.48	.50	.35	-.12	-.41	-.72	-.72	-.48	-.40	-.33	-.17	.02	.34
CD			.86	.76	.38	.09	-.34	-.37	-.68	-.47	-.60	-.44	-.42	-.19
CS					.44	.30	-.23	-.15	-.69	-.45	-.63	-.57	-.49	-.29
SC							.34	.52	-.24	-.08	-.33	-.40	-.48	-.64
SO									.44	.49	.29	.15	-.03	-.19
OS											.76	.60	.53	.44
OD													.58	.54

Appendix 3.1: Mean QTI-Scores in Dutch, American and Australian Samples of Volunteers

		Teacher's Perceptions			Students' Perceptions		
		US	D	A	US	D	A
DC	Leadership	0.75	0.58	0.73	0.69	0.61	0.69
CD	Helpful/Friendly	0.81	0.62	0.84	0.75	0.65	0.74
CS	Understanding	0.76	0.72	0.81	0.71	0.69	0.72
SC	Student Responsibility and Freedom	0.38	0.45	0.33	0.44	0.45	0.35
SO	Uncertain	0.16	0.23	0.17	0.21	0.24	0.20
OS	Dissatisfied	0.24	0.18	0.21	0.23	0.18	0.22
OD	Admonishing	0.24	0.25	0.21	0.28	0.28	0.23
DO	Strict	0.48	0.33	0.47	0.43	0.32	0.44

Appendix 3.2: Mean QTI-Scores in Dutch, American and Australian Samples for Teachers' Ideals and Students' Perceptions of Best and Worst Teachers

		Teacher's Perceptions			Student Perceptions				
		Ideal			Best			Worst	
		US	D	A	US	D	A	US	D
DC	Leadership	0.95	0.81	0.94	0.82	0.70	0.84	0.28	0.36
CD	Helpful/Friendly	0.95	0.81	0.94	0.84	0.75	0.87	0.19	0.22
CS	Understanding	0.91	0.84	0.93	0.81	0.76	0.84	0.23	0.28
SC	Student Responsibility and Freedom	0.42	0.53	0.39	0.48	0.50	0.46	0.22	0.33
SO	Uncertain	0.06	0.18	0.06	0.16	0.20	0.13	0.45	0.37
OS	Dissatisfied	0.14	0.09	0.12	0.19	0.15	0.15	0.64	0.52
OD	Admonishing	0.08	0.22	0.08	0.25	0.27	0.19	0.70	0.61
DO	Strict	0.54	0.33	0.51	0.46	0.33	0.45	0.62	0.55
	n =	66	66	46	117	357	792	114	341

Appendix 6.1: Path Analyses for the Relations Between Ideal, Teacher Self-Report and (Students' Perceptions of) Behavior

Path analyses were used to investigate whether a teacher's self-report is related only to the students' perceptions or to his or her ideals as well. The analyses were performed separately for best classes, worst classes and for the complete sample. They were performed both for the global QTI-Characteristic and every scale of the QTI separately. The figure below shows the path diagram for this analysis and the path coefficients for the global QTI-Characteristic.

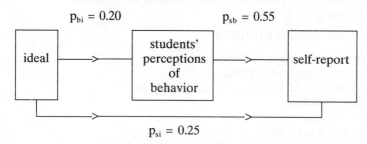

$$p_{bi} = 0.20 \qquad\qquad p_{sb} = 0.55$$

$$p_{si} = 0.25$$

With these path coefficients the correlation between ideal and self-report (0.36) can be split in a direct effect from ideal to self-report and an indirect effect via the actual behavior (Pedhazur, 1982). The direct effect from the ideal to the self-report (0.25) appears to be far larger than the indirect effect via the students' perceptions of the behavior (0.11). Thus, the ideal has a stronger direct relation to the self-report than via the students' perceptions. The analyses for the separate scales and in samples of best and worst classes all have the same results.

Appendix 9.1: The Questionnaire on Principal Interaction (QPI)

DIRECTIONS

This questionnaire asks you to describe your principal's behavior. Your co-operation can help him/her to improve. On the next few pages you'll find 62 sentences. For each sentence on the questionnaire find the same number on the answer sheet and darken the circle you think most applies to your principal. Please use only a #2 pencil.
An example appears below:

	Never				Always
S/He expresses him/herself clearly	A	B	C	D	E

If, for example, you think that your principal always expresses him/herself clearly, darken letter E on your answer sheet. If you think your principal never expresses him/herself clearly darken letter A. You can also choose letters B, C or D, according to your opinion of your principal's clarity of expression. If you want to change your answer after you've darkened a circle please erase completely. Please use both sides of the answer sheet. Thank you for your cooperation.

Appendices

ITEMS

scale: DC LEADERSHIP

4. S/he holds our attention
27. S/he acts in a confident manner
29. S/he is involved in school activities
39. We learn a lot from her/him
46. S/he makes her/himself clear
48. S/he makes the school a pleasant working environment
56. S/he is a good leader

scale: CD HELPFUL/FRIENDLY

1. S/he shows personal interest in us
12. We can depend on her/him
19. S/he helps us in fulfilling our teaching tasks
25. S/he is friendly
32. S/he can take a joke
36. S/he has a good sense of humor
50. S/he is attentive to relationships among teachers

scale: CS UNDERSTANDING

7. S/he is sensitive to misunderstandings
10. S/he identifies with us
15. If needed, s/he is willing to repeat an explanation
21. S/he trusts us
34. S/he is cooperative
42. S/he is patient
53. S/he is a good listener
59. When opinions differ s/he is willing to listen

scale: SC TEACHER RESPONSIBILITY/FREEDOM

6. S/he is permissive
14. Teachers have influence over her/him
22. S/he allows us to teach topics which we find interesting
24. There are some areas in which we can make our own decisions
33. S/he lets her/himself be led by teachers
41. S/he does not follow through on her/his directions
43. S/he creates an atmosphere of ambiguity
52. S/he lets us teach in the ways we choose
61. S/he lets us choose our own content

scale: SO UNCERTAIN

13. S/he is hesitant
17. S/he seems like s/he does not know how to act
38. It is easy to embarrass her/him
44. S/he gives in easily
51. S/he does not know how to react when we do not follow regulations
60. S/he is uncertain in school

scale: OS DISSATISFIED

3. S/he is dull
16. S/he underestimates our knowledge
18. S/he does not reward our behavior
30. S/he seems to be dissatisfied
37. S/he does not trust us
47. S/he is suspicious
55. S/he does not believe we can teach well
58. S/he does not seem happy in school

scale: OD OBJECTING

2. S/he is quick to criticize us if we don't follow her/his orders
5. S/he humiliates us
11. S/he gets angry unexpectedly
23. S/he is irritable
26. It is easy to get into conflict with her/him
31. S/he gets angry easily
35. S/he is sarcastic
54. S/he is impatient

scale: DO STRICT

8. S/he acts harsh
9. S/he is dogmatic
20. We don't feel comfortable in her/his presence
28. S/he expects us to obey
40. We need to get her/his permission for any irregular activity
45. If we don't complete our assignments s/he makes us feel uncomfortable
49. S/he places her/himself on a pedestal
57. It is difficult to fulfill her/his demands
62. S/he is very demanding

Appendix 10.1: The Questionnaire on Supervisor Interaction (QSI)

DIRECTIONS

This questionnaire asks you to describe your supervisor's behavior. Your cooperation can help him/her to improve. On the next few pages you'll find 61 sentences. For each sentence on the questionnaire find the same number on the answer sheet and darken the circle you think most applies to this supervisor. Please use only a #2 pencil.
An example appears below:

	Never				Always
S/He expresses him/herself clearly	A	B	C	D	E

If, for example, you think that your supervisor always expresses him/herself clearly, darken letter E on your answer sheet. If you think your supervisor never expresses him/herself clearly darken letter A. You can also choose letters B, C or D, according to your opinion of your supervisor's clarity of expression. If you want to change your answer after you've darkened a circle please erase completely. Please use both sides of the answer sheet. Thank you for your cooperation.

ITEMS

scale: DC LEADERSHIP

5. S/He talks enthusiastically about teaching.
50. S/He expresses her/himself clearly.
61. S/He gives a lot of advice.
54. I learn a lot from her/him.
29. S/He acts confidently.
1. S/He acts enthusiastically.
21. S/He is businesslike.
36. S/He checks my lesson plans.

scale: CD HELPFUL/FRIENDLY

44. S/He takes a personal interest in me.
17. S/He has a sense of humor.
22. S/He helps me.
51. S/He is friendly.
55. S/He is someone we can rely on.
20. There is a pleasant atmosphere in our discussions.

scale: CS UNDERSTANDING

6. S/He trusts me.
15. S/He is willing to explain things again.
19. If I want something s/he is willing to cooperate.
24. If I have something to say s/he will listen.
10. If I don't agree with her/him I can talk about it.
42. S/He is flexible with me.
38. I can talk with her/him about my difficulties.
26. S/He sympathizes with me.

scale: SC STUDENT TEACHER RESPONSIBILITY/FREEDOM

7. S/He identifies with my way of thinking.
28. S/He lets me make my own decisions.
32. I can influence her/him.
12. S/He lets me decide some things.
52. I am responsible for my own teaching.
11. S/he is lenient.
45. I'm allowed to teach lessons my way.
30. S/He pretends s/he is one of us.
49. I'm allowed to evaluate myself.
59. I'm allowed to make decisions about rules for student behavior.

scale: SO UNCERTAIN

34. S/He seems uncertain.
57. S/He acts as if s/he does not know what to suggest.
40. It is easy to make him/her feel embarrassed.
58. S/He gives in easily.
49. S/He acts timidly.
 8. S/He has a 'wait and see' attitude.

scale: OS DISSATISFIED

39. S/He doesn't seem satisfied.
16. S/He thinks I don't know anything.
27. S/He tries to make me feel unskilled.
53. S/He tries to make me feel small.
37. S/He has a bad temper.
43. S/He is suspicious.
 2. S/He doesn't trust me.

scale: OD OBJECTING

 9. S/He stops me from doing things.
56. S/He gets angry quickly.
48. S/He is sarcastic.
 3. S/He is impatient if I don't get things right the first time.
14. S/He's too quick to correct me.
41. S/He is irritable.
23. S/He can get angry.

scale: DO STRICT

35. If I did not prepare my lessons well I'm afraid to meet with him/her after class.
 4. S/he enforces his/her authority.
18. S/He is critical.
25. If I do something wrong s/he tries to correct me.
31. Her/His standards are very high.
13. S/He is strict.
60. S/He is severe when evaluating.
33. S/He is rigorous in his/her demands.
47. S/He demands that I teach exactly to his/her expectations.

Appendix 11.1: Correlations of Students' Perceptions of Student Teachers and Cooperating Teachers (n = 9)

C.Tch:	DC	CD	CS	SC	SO	OS	OD	DO
St.Tch								
DC	.61*	.72*	.68*	.18	−.84**	−.77**	−.74*	−.26
CD	.49	.61*	.56	.02	−.80**	−.68*	−.62*	−.08
CS	.51	.65*	.63*	.06	−.81**	−.73*	−.69*	−.18
SC	−.40	−.19	−.29	.03	−.19	.12	.15	.28
SO	−.71*	−.78**	−.75**	−.18	.83**	.78**	.78**	.34
OS	−.64*	−.78**	−.75**	−.16	.83**	.83**	.78**	.28
OD	−.60	−.75**	−.72	−.28	.85**	.84**	.80**	.33
DO	−.01	−.19	−.18	.27	−.22	.06	.06	−.05

* = p < .05   ** = p < .01

Appendix 11.2: Percentage of Variance in the Students' Perceptions of the Interpersonal Teacher Behavior of Student Teachers Accounted for by the Behavior of the Cooperating Teacher

students' perceptions of student teachers' behavior scale	percentage of variance accounted for by cooperating teachers' behavior	F	the only supervising teachers' scale in the regression equation
DC	11	18.2**	DC
CD	11	7.9**	CS
CS	12	8.8**	CS
SC	9	6.3*	DC
SO	14	10.2**	DC
OS	12	8.8**	OS
OD	6	4.4*	SO
DO	7	5.2*	DC

* = p < .05   ** = p < .01

References

ADAMS, R.D. (1982) 'Teacher development, a look at changes in teacher perceptions and behavior across time', *Journal of Teacher Education*, **33**, 4, pp. 40–43.

ALLAIN, V.A. (1985) 'Career stages of teachers', Implications for professional development, Paper presented at the annual meeting of the American Educational Research Association, New Orleans.

AMES, R. (1983) 'Teachers attributions for their own teaching', in LEVINE, J.M. and WANG, M.C. (Eds) *Teacher and student perceptions, implications for learning*, Hillsdale NJ, Erlbaum, pp. 105–24.

ANDERSON, C.S. (1982) 'The search for school climate: a review of research', *Review of Educational Research*, **52**, pp. 368–420.

ANDERSON, J.R. (1985) *Cognitive Psychology and its implications*, New York, Freeman.

ASSOCIATION OF TEACHER EDUCATORS (1991) *Restructuring the Education of Teachers*, Boston, ATE.

AU, K.H. and KAWAKAMI, A.J. (1984) 'Vygotskian perspectives on discussion processes in small group reading lessons', in WILKINSON, L.C., PETERSON, P.L. and HALLINAN, M. (Eds) *The social context of instruction*, New York, Academic Press.

BALES, R.F. (1970) *Personality and Interpersonal Behavior*, New York, Holt, Rinehart and Winston.

BANDURA, A. (1969) *Principles of Behavior Modification*, New York, Holt, Rinehart and Winston.

BARRETT-LENARD, J. (1970) *Individual goals and organizational objectives*, Ann Arbor, University of Michigan, Institute of Social Research.

BENNETT, S.N. (1976) *Teaching styles and pupil progress*, London, Open Books.

BEN-PERETZ, M. and RUMNEY, S. (1991) 'Professional thinking in guided practice', *Teaching and Teacher Education*, **7**, pp. 517–30.

BERLINER, D.C. (1986) 'In pursuit of the expert pedagogue', in *Educational Researcher*, **15**, 7, pp. 5–13.

BERTRAND, R. and LeCLERC, M. (1985) 'Reliability of observational data on teaching practices in secondary school mathematics', *Teaching and teacher education*, **1**, pp. 187–98.

BEYER, L. (1984) 'Field experience, ideology, and the development of critical reflectivity', *Journal of Teacher Education*, **35**, 3, pp. 36–41.

BLASE, J.J. (1982) 'A social-pychological theory of teacher stress and burnout', *Educational Administration Quaterly*, **18**, 4, pp. 93–113.

BLOOM, D. and JORDE-BLOOM, P. (1988) 'The role of higher education in fostering the personal development of teachers', in HOOGHOFF, A. and DUSSEN, A.M. VAN DER (Eds) *Teacher Education and the world of work*, Enschede, SLO, pp. 59–71.

BLUMBERG, A. (1980) *Supervision of teachers, a private cold war*, Berkely CA, McCutchan.

BLUMBERG, A. and AMIDON, E. (1965) 'Teacher perceptions of supervisor-teacher interaction', *Administrators Notebook*, **14**, 1.

BLUMBERG, A. and GREENFIELD, W.D. (1980) *The effective principal*, Boston, Allyn and Bacon.

BLUMENFELD, P.C. and MEECE, J.L. (1985) 'Life in classrooms revisited', *Theory into Practice*, **24**, 1, pp. 50–6.

BORG, W. (1973) 'Protocols: Competency-based teacher education modules', *Educational Technology*, **13**, 10, pp. 17–20.

BORICH, G.D. (1988) *Effective teaching methods*, Columbus, Merrill.

BORICH, G.D. and KLINZING, G. (1984) 'Some assumptions in the observation of classroom process with suggestions for improving low inference measurement', *Journal of Classroom Interaction*, **20**, pp. 36–44.

BOYDELL, D. (1991) 'Issues in Teaching Practice Supervision Research: A review of the Literature', in KATZ, L.G. (Ed.) *Advances in Teacher Education*, **4**, Norwood, Ablex, pp. 137–54.

BREKELMANS, M. (1989) *Interpersonal teacher behavior in the classroom*, in Dutch: *Interpersoonlijk gedrag van docenten in de klas*, Utrecht, W.C.C.

BREKELMANS, M., HOLVAST, A. and TARTWIJK, J. VAN (1992) 'Changes in teacher communication styles during the professional career', *The Journal of Classroom Interaction*, **27**, pp. 13–22.

BREKELMANS, M. and WUBBELS, T. (1992) 'Student and Teacher Perceptions of Interpersonal Teacher Behavior: A Dutch Perspective', in FISHER, D.L. (Ed.) *The Study of Learning Environments*, 6, pp. 19–30.

BREKELMANS, M., WUBBELS, T. and CRÉTON, H.A. (1990) 'A study of student perceptions of physics teacher behavior', *Journal of Research in Science Teaching*, **27**, pp. 335–50.

BREKELMANS, M., WUBBELS, T. and CRÉTON, H.A. (in press) 'The Questionnaire on Teacher Interaction', in Dutch: 'De Vragenlijst voor Interactioneel Leraarsgedrag', in GRIFT, W. VAN DER and SIJDE, P.C. VAN DER *Het meten van het school- en klasklimaat*, Almere, Versluys.

BREKELMANS, M., WUBBELS, T. and HOOYMAYERS, H.P. (1988) 'Teacher cognitions and interpersonal teacher behavior', Paper presented at the Conference of the International Study Association on Teacher Thinking, Nottingham.

BRIAR, S. and BIERI, J. (1963) 'A factor analytic trait inference study of the Leary Interpersonal Checklist', *Journal of Clinical Psychology*, **19**, pp. 193–8.

BROEKMAN, H.G.B. and WETERINGS, J.M.J. (1987) 'The prehistory of teacher trainees and the consequences for teacher education', *Journal of Mathematical Behaviour*, **6**, pp. 201–16.

BROOKOVER, W.B. and LEZOTTE, L.W. (1977) *Changes in school characteristics coincident with changes in student achievement*, East Lansing, Michigan State University.

BROOKOVER, W.B., SCHWEITZER, J.H., SCHNEIDER, J.M., BEADY, C.H., FLOOD, P.K. and WISENBAKER, J.M. (1978) 'Elementary school social climate and school achievement', *American Educational Research Journal*, **15**, pp. 301–18.

BROOKS, D.M. (1985) 'The teachers communicative competence: The first day of school', *Theory into Practice*, **24**, 1, pp. 63–70.

BROPHY, J.E. and GOOD, T.L. (1986) 'Teacher behavior and student achievement', in WITTROCK, M.C. (Ed.) *Handbook of Research on Teaching* (third edition), New York, McMillan, pp. 328–75.

BROPHY, J.E. and ROHRKEMPER, M.N. (1981) 'The influence of problem ownership on teachers' perceptions of and strategies for coping with pupil problems', *Journal of Educational Psychology*, **73**, pp. 295–311.

BROUWER, N. (1987) 'Co-operation structures in preservice teacher education programmes and their effects on beginning teachers' classroom performance', Paper presented at the AERA annual meeting, Washington.

BROWN, R. (1965) *Social Psychology*, London, Collier-McMillan.

BRUYN, E.E.J. DE (1979) 'Doceerstijl, schoolse leerprestaties en prestatiemotivatie', in BRUYN, E.E.J. (Ed.) *Ontwikkelingen in het onderzoek naar prestatiemotivatie*, Lisse, Swets en Zeitlinger, pp. 266–304.

BURKE, P.J., FESSLER, R. and CHRISTENSEN, J.C. (1984) *Teacher Career Stages: Implications for Staff Development*, Bloomington, ID, Phi Delta Kappa.

CAMPBELL, J.R. (1974) 'Can a teacher really make the difference?' *School Science and Mathematics*, **76**, pp. 657–66.

CARSON, R.C. (1969) *Interaction Concepts of Personality*, Chicago, Aldine Publishing Company.

CAZDEN, C.B. (1986) 'Classroom Discourse', in WITTROCK, M.C. (Ed.) *Handbook of research on teaching* (third edition), New York, McMillan, pp. 432–63.

CHAVEZ, R.C. (1984) 'The use of high inference measures to study classroom climates: a review', *Review of Educational Research*, **54**, pp. 237–61.

CHRISTENSEN, J.C., BURKE, P., FESSLER, R. and HAGSTROM, D. (1983) *Stages of Teachers' Careers*, Washington D.C., Eric Clearinghouse on Teacher Education.

CLARK, C.M. and PETERSON, P. (1986) 'Teachers' thought processes', in WITTROCK, M.C. (Ed.) *Handbook of research on teaching* (third edition), New York, MacMillan, pp. 225–96.

COPELAND, W.D. (1982) 'Student teachers' preferences for supervisory approach', *Journal of Teacher Education*, **33**, 2, pp. 32–6.

CORPORAAL, A.H. (1988) *Building blocks for a pedagogy of teacher education*, in Dutch: *Bouwstenen voor een opleidingsdidactiek*, Dissertation, De Lier, ABC.

CRÉTON, H.A. and WUBBELS, T. (1984) *Discipline problems of beginning teachers*, In Dutch: *Ordeproblemen bij beginnende leraren*, Utrecht, W.C.C.

CRÉTON, H.A., WUBBELS, T. and HOOYMAYERS, H.P. (1989) 'Escalated disorderly situations in the classroom and the improvement of these situations', *Teaching and Teacher Education*, **5**, 3, pp. 205–15.

CRONBACH, L.J. and SNOW, R.E. (1977) *Attitudes and instructional methods: A handbook of teacher interaction*, New York, Irvington.

CRUICKSHANK, D.R. and METCALF, K.K. (1990) 'Training within teacher preparation', in HOUSTON, W.R. (Ed.) *Handbook of Research in Teacher Education*, New York, Macmillan, pp. 469–97.

References

DECI, E.L., NEZLEK, J. and SHEINMAN, L. (1981) 'Characteristics of the rewarder and intrinsic motivation of the rewardee', *Journal of Personality and Social Psychology*, **40**, pp. 1–10.

DOYLE, W. (1979) 'Classroom effects', *Theory Into Practice*, **18**, pp. 138–44.

DOYLE, W. (1983) 'Academic work', *Review of Educational Research*, **53**, 2, pp. 159–99.

DOYLE, W. (1984) 'How order is achieved in classrooms: An interim report', *Journal of Curriculum Studies*, **16**, 3, pp. 259–77.

DOYLE, W. (1986) 'Classroom organization and management', in WITTROCK, M.C. (Ed.) *Handbook of research on teaching* (third edition), New York, MacMillan, pp. 392–431.

DUNKIN, M.J. and BIDDLE, B.J. (1974) *The study of teaching*, New York, Rinehart and Winston.

EHMAN, L.A. (1970) 'A comparison of three sources of classroom data: teachers, students and systematic observation', Paper presented at the meeting of the American Educational Research Association, Minneapolis, March 1970.

ELLET, C.D. and WALBERG, J.H. (1979) 'Principal competence, environment and outcomes', in WALBERG, H.S. (Ed.), *Educational environments and effects*, Berkeley, CA. McCutchan, pp. 140–64.

EMMER, E., EVERTSON, C. and ANDERSON, L. (1980) 'Effective classroom management at the beginning of the school year', *Elementary School Journal*, **80**, 5, pp. 219–31.

ENGLISH, F.W. (1988) 'The utility of the camera in qualitative inquiry', *Educational Researcher*, **17**, 4, pp. 8–15.

EVERITT, B. (1980) *Cluster Analysis*, New York, Halsted Press.

EVERTSON, C.M. and EMMER, E.T. (1982) 'Effective management at the beginning of the year in junior high classes', *Journal of Educational Psychology*, **74**, 4, pp. 485–98.

FEIMAN-NEMSER, S. and BUCHMANN, M. (1986) 'Pitfals of experience in teacher preparation', in RATHS, J.D. and KATZ, L.G. (Eds) *Advances in teacher Education*, **2**, Norwood, Ablex, pp. 61–74.

FEIMAN-NEMSER, S. and FLODEN, R. (1986) 'The cultures of teaching', in WITTROCK, M.C. (Ed.) *Handbook of Research on Teaching* (third edition), New York, McMillan, pp. 505–26.

FESSLER, R. (1985) 'A model for teacher professional growth and development', in BURKE, P.J. and HEIDEMAN, R.G. (Eds) *Career-long teacher education*, Springfield, IL, Charles C. Thomas, pp. 181–93.

FESTINGER, L. (1957) *A theory of cognitive dissonance*, Evanston, Row Peterson.

FISHER, D.L. and FRASER, B.J. (1983) 'Use of WES to assess science teachers' perceptions of school environment', *European Journal of Science Education*, **5**, pp. 231–3.

FISHER, D.L. and FRASER, B.J. (1990) 'Assessing and improving school climates', *Set, New Zealand Council for Educational Research*, **2**, pp. 1–8.

FISHER, D.L. and FRASER, B.J. (1991) 'School climate and teacher professional development', *South Pacific Journal of Teacher Education*, **19**, pp. 15–30.

FISHER, D.L., FRASER, B.J. and WUBBELS, T. (1992) 'Teacher communication style and school environment', Paper presented at the 1992 ECER conference, Enschede.

FISKE, S.T. and TAYLOR, S.E. (1984) *Social Cognition*, New York, Random House.

FITZNER, K. (1979) *Das Schulpraktikum als soziales System, Eine Untersuchung des Problems der Uebertragung von Systemleistungen in der 1, Phase der Lehrerausbildung*, Weinheim/Basel, Beltz.

FLANDERS, N.A. (1970) *Analyzing teacher behavior*, Reading, MA, Addison-Wesly.

FOA, U. (1961) 'Convergence in the analysis of the structure of interpersonal behavior', *Psychological Review*, **68**, pp. 341–53.

FRASER, B.J. (1986) *Classroom Environment*, London, Croom Helm.

FRASER, B.J. (1989) 'Twenty years of classroom climate research: Progress and prospect', *Journal of Curriculum Studies*, **21**, pp. 307–27.

FRASER, B.J., GIDDINGS, G.J. and McROBBIE, C.J. (1992) 'Science Laboratory Classroom Environment: A Cross-National Perspective', in FISHER, D.L. (Ed.) *The Study of Learning Environments*, **6**, pp. 1–18.

FRASER, B.J. and O'BRIEN, P. (1985) 'Student and Teacher Perceptions of the Environment of the Elementary Classroom', *The Elementary School Journal*, **85**, pp. 567–80.

FRASER, B.J. and RENTOUL, A.J. (1982) 'Relationships between school-level and classroom-level environment', *Alberta Journal of Educational Research*, **28**, pp. 212–25.

FRASER, B.J. and WALBERG, H.J. (Eds) (1991) *Educational Environments: Antecedents, Consequences, and Evaluation*, London, Pergamon Press.

FRASER, B.J., WALBERG, H.J., WELCH, W.W. and HATTIE, J.A. (1987) 'Synthesis of educational productivity research', *International Journal of Educational Research*, **11**, pp. 145–252.

FULLAN, M.G. and STIEGELBAUER, S. (1992) *The new meaning of educational change*, Toronto, The Ontario Institute for Studies in Education.

GENN, J.M. (1984) 'Research into the climates of Australian schools, colleges and universities: Contributions and potential of needs-press theory', *Australian Journal of Education*, **28**, pp. 227–48.

GETZELS, J.W. and JACKSON, P.W. (1963) 'The Teacher's personality and Characteristics', in GAGE, N.L. (Ed.) *Handbook of Research on Teaching*, Chicago, Rand McNally and Company, pp. 506–82.

GLASERSFELD, E. VON (Ed.) (1991) *Radical Constructivism in Mathematics Education*, Dordrecht, Kluwer Academic Publishers.

GLICKMAN, C.D. and BEY, T.M. (1990) 'Supervision', in HOUSTON, W.R. (Ed.) *Handbook of Research in Teacher Education*, New York, Macmillan, pp. 549–68.

GLIESSMANN, D.H. and PUGH, R.C. (1987) 'Conceptual instruction and intervention as methods of acquiring teaching skills', *International Journal of Educational Research*, **11**, pp. 555–64.

GOLDSTEIN, H. (1987) *Multilevel models in Educational and Social Research*, London, Charles Grifth and Company Ltd.

GOOD, T.L. (1979) 'Teacher effectiveness in the elementary school', *Journal of Teacher Education*, **30**, pp. 52–64.

GRIFFIN, G.A. (1986) 'Issues in student teaching: A review', in RATHS, J.D. and KATZ, L.G. (Eds) *Advances in Teacher Education*, **2**, Norwood, Ablex, pp. 239–74.

GUSKEY, T.R. (1986) 'Staff development and the process of teacher change', *Educational Researcher*, **15**, 5, pp. 5–12.

GUSKEY, T.R. (1989) 'Attitude and perceptual change in teachers', *International Journal of Educational Research*, **13**, pp. 439–53.

GUYTON, E. and MCINTYRE, D.J. (1990) 'Student Teaching and School Experiences', in HOUSTON, W.R. (Ed.) *Handbook of Research on Teacher Education*, New York, McMillan, pp. 514–34.

HAERTEL, G.D., WALBERG, H.J. and HAERTEL, E.H. (1981) 'Socio-psychological environments and learning: A quantitative synthesis', *British Educational Research Journal*, **7**, pp. 27–36.

HALEY, J. (1963) *Strategies of Psychotherapy*, New York, Grune and Stratton.

HALEY, J. (1971) *Changing families*, New York, Grune and Stratton.

HALEY, J. (1973) *Uncommon therapy: the psychiatric techniques of Milton H. Erickson, M.D.* New York, Norton.

HALL, G.E. and HORD, S. (1987) *Change in schools: Facilitating the process*, Albany, State University of New York Press.

HALPIN, A.W. and CROFT, D.B. (1963) *The Organizational Climate of Schools*, Chicago, Midwest Administration Center, University of Chicago.

HAMILTON, S. (1983) 'The social side of schooling: Ecological studies of classrooms and schools', *Elementary School Journal*, **83**, 4, pp. 313–34.

HARPER, J.M., SCORCEBY, A.L. and BOYCE, W.D. (1977) 'The logical levels of complementary, symmetrical and parallel interaction classes in family', *Family Process*, **16**, 2, pp. 199–210.

HECK, R.H., LARSEN, T.J. and MARCOULIDES, G.A. (1990) 'Instructional leadership and school achievement: Validation of a causal model', *Educational Administration Quarterly*, **26**, 2, pp. 94–125.

HELMKE, A., SCHNEIDER, W. and WEINERT, F.E. (1986) 'Quality of instruction and classroom learning outcomes; the German contribution to the IEA Classroom Environment Study', *Teaching and Teacher Education*, **2**, 1, pp. 1–18.

HERMANS, J.J. (1981) *Niet voortgezet onderwijs*, Lisse, Swets en Zeitlinger.

HERMANS, J.J., CRÉTON, H.A. and HOOYMAYERS, H.A. (1987) 'Some characteristics of teacher demotivation', in VOORBACH, J.T. and PRICK, L.G.M. (Eds) *Teacher education*, **3**, The Hague, SVO/ATEE, pp. 96–107.

HERMANS, J.J., HOOYMAYERS, H.P., CRÉTON, H.A. and WUBBELS, T. (1985) 'Toward a better preparation of teachers' tasks in the learning and living domain of the classroom', in VOORBACH, J.T. and PRICK, L.G.M. (Eds) *Teacher education: an overview of recent research and developments on teacher education in the Netherlands*, 's-Gravenhage, SVO-ATEE, pp. 180–95.

HEWSON, P.W. and HEWSON, M.G.A.B. (1987) 'Science teachers' conceptions of teaching: Implications for teacher education', *International Journal of Science Education*, **9**, 4, pp. 425–40.

HOFER, M. and DOBRICK, M. (1978) 'Die Rolle der Fremdattribution von Ursachen bei der Handlungssteuerung des Lehrers', in GÖRLITZ, D., MEYER, W.U. and WEINER, B. (Eds) *Bielefelder Symposium über Attributionen*, Stuttgart, Klett-Cotta, pp. 51–69.

HOFER, M. and DOBRICK, M. (1981) 'Naive Ursachenzuschreibung und Lehrerverhalten', in HOFER, M. (Ed.) *Informationsverarbeitung und Entscheidungsverhalten von Lehrern*, München, Urban and Schwarzenberg, pp. 110–58.

HOLLINGSWORTH, S. (1989) 'Prior beliefs and cognitive change in learning to teach', *American Educational Research Journal*, **26**, 2, pp. 160–89.

HOLMES GROUP (1986) *Tomorrow's Teachers: A report of The Holmes Groupe*, East Lansing.

HOLVAST, A.J.C.D. and HOOYMAYERS, H.P. (1986) 'Towards a further professionalization of university teacher education in the Netherlands', in ART, A., EISENDRATH, H. and GRANDJEAN, F. (Eds) *Proceedings of the International Symposium on Physics Teaching*, Brussels, Université Libre, pp. 116–21.

HOLVAST, A., WUBBELS, T. and BREKELMANS, M. (1988) 'Supervising teachers and the teacher behaviour and teaching ideals of student teachers', in VOORBACH, J. and PRICK, L. (Eds) *Teacher education: research and developments on teacher education in the Netherlands*, 4, The Hague, SVO/ATEE, pp. 205–18.

HOOK, C. and ROSENSHINE, B. (1979) 'Accuracy of teachers reports of their classroom behavior', *Review of Educational Research*, **49**, pp. 1–12.

HOOVER, N.L., O'SHEA, L.J. and CARROLL, R.G. (1988) 'The Supervisor-intern relationship and effective interpersonal communication skills', *Journal of Teacher Education*, **39**, 2, pp. 22–7.

HOOYMAYERS, H.P. et al. (1978) *Beginning physics teachers; experiences, opinions, problems and their training*, Utrecht, Department of Physics Education.

HOPKINS, D. (1990) 'Integrating staff development and school improvement: A study of teacher personality and school climate', in JOYCE, B. (Ed.) *Changing school culture through staff development*, Alexandria, VA, Association for Supervision and Curriculum Development.

HORST, P. (1949) 'A generalized expression for the reliability of measures', *Psychometrika*, **14**, pp. 21–31.

HOY, W. and REES, W. (1977) 'The bureaucratic socialization of student teachers', *Journal of Teacher Education*, **28**, 1, pp. 23–6.

HOY, W.K. and WOOLFOLK, A.E. (1989) 'Supervising student teachers', in WOOLFOLK, A.E. (Ed.) *Research perspectives on the graduate preparation of teachers*, Englewood Cliffs, N.J. Prentice Hall, pp. 108–31.

HUBER, G.L. (1982) 'Psychologische modelle der lehrerbildung', *Unterrichtswissenschaft*, **10**, pp. 300–12.

HUBER, G.L. and MANDL, H. (1984) 'Access to teacher cognitions: problems of assessment and analysis', in HALKES, R. and OLSON, J.K. (Eds) *Teacher Thinking: A New Perspective on Persisting Problems in Education*, Lisse, Swets and Zeitlinger, pp. 58–73.

HUGHES, P.W. (1991) *Teachers' Professional Development*, ACER, Australia.

JOYCE, B. and SHOWERS, B. (1988) *Student achievement through staff development*, New York, Longman.

KAGAN, D.M. (1988) 'Research on the supervision of counselors — and teachers-in-training: Linking two bodies of literature', *Review of Educational Research*, **58**, pp. 1–24.

KAGAN, D.M. and TIPPINS, D.J. (1991) 'How student teachers describe their pupils', *Teaching and Teacher Education*, **7**, 5/6, pp. 455–66.

KANFER, F.H. and SASLOW, G. (1965) 'Behavioral diagnosis', *Archives of General Psychiatry*, **12**, pp. 529–38.

KEMMIS, S. and McTAGGART, R. (Eds) (1988) *The action research planner* (third edition), Geelong, Deakin University Press.

KILLIAN, J.E. and McINTYRE, D.J. (1988) 'Grade level as a factor in participation during early field experiences', *Journal of Teacher Education*, **39**, 2, pp. 36–41.

KOEHLER, V. (1985) 'Research on preservice teacher education', *Journal of Teacher Education*, **26**, 1, pp. 23–30.

KOETSIER, C.P., WUBBELS, T. and DRIEL, C. VAN (1992) 'An investigation into careful supervision of student teaching', in VONK, J.H.C., GIESBERS, J.H.G.I., PETERS, J.J. and WUBBELS, T. (Eds) *New Prospects for Teacher Education in Europe II*, Conference Proceedings, Amsterdam, U.L.V.U. and H.H., pp. 245–54.

KORTHAGEN, F.A.J. (in press) 'Techniques for stimulating reflection in teacher education seminars', *Teaching and Teacher Education*.

KOUNIN, J.S. (1970) *Discipline and group management in classrooms*, New York, Holt, Rinehart and Winston.

KREMER-HAYON, L., MOORE, M. and NEVAT, R. (1986) 'Dogmatism in teacher education practices: Aptitude-treatment interaction effects', *Research in Education*, **36**, pp. 19–26.

LACEY, C. (1977) *The Socialization of Teachers*, London, Methuen.

LAFORGE, R. and SUCZEK, R.F. (1955) 'The interpersonal dimension of personality: III, An interpersonal checklist', *Journal of Personality*, **24**, pp. 94–112.

LAFRANCE, M. and MAYO, C. (1978) *Moving Bodies: Nonverbal Communication in Social Relationships*, Monterey, Brooks/Cole Publishing Company.

LANIER, J.E. and LITTLE, J.W. (1986) 'Research on Teacher Education', in WITTROCK, M.C. (Ed.) *Handbook of Research on Teaching* (third edition), New York, McMillan, pp. 527–69.

LASLEY, TH.J. and APPLEGATE, J.H. (1985) 'Problems of early experience students of teaching', *Teaching and Teacher Education*, **1**, 3, pp. 221–7.

LEARY, T. (1957) *An interpersonal diagnosis of personality*, New York, Ronald Press Company.

LEDERER, W.J. and JACKSON, D.D. (1968) *The mirages of marriage*, New York, Norton.

LEITHWOOD, K.A. (1990) 'The principal's role in teacher development', in JOYCE, B. (Ed.) *Changing school culture through staff development*, Alexandria, Association for Supervision and Curriculum Development.

LEITHWOOD, K.A. and MONTGOMERY, D.J. (1986) *Improving principal effectiveness: The principal profile*, Toronto, OISE Press.

LEVY, J., RODRIGUEZ, R. and WUBBELS, T. (1992) 'Instructional effectiveness, communication style and teacher development', Paper presented at the AERA annual meeting, San Francisco.

LEVY, J., WUBBELS, T. and BREKELMANS, M. (1992) 'Student and teacher characteristics and perceptions of teacher communication style', *Journal of Classroom Interaction*, **27**, pp. 23–9.

LEWIN, T. (1936) *Principles of Topological Psychology*, New York, McGraw.

LEWIN, K., LIPPITT, R. and WHITE, R. (1939) 'Patterns of aggresive behavior in experimentally created social climates', *Journal of Social Psychology*, **10**, pp. 271–91.

LIBERMAN, R.P. (1970) 'Behavioral approaches to family and couple therapy', *American Journal of Orthopsychiatry*, **40**, pp. 106–18.

LONNER, W.J. (1980) 'The search for psychological universal', in TRIANDIS, H.C.

and LAMBERT, W.W. (Eds) *Handbook of cross-cultural psychology*, **1**, Boston, Allyn and Bacon, pp. 143–204.

LORTIE, D.C. (1987) 'Built in tendencies toward stabilizing the principal's role', *Journal of Research and Development in Education*, **22**, 1, pp. 80–90.

MAGNUSSON, D. and ENDLER, N.S. (1977) 'Interactional Psychology: Present status and future prospects, in MAGNUSSON, D. and ENDLER, N.S., *Personality at the crossroads: Current issues in interactional psychology*, Hillsdale, Lawrence Erlbaum Associates.

MARSH, H.W. (1984) 'Students' evaluations of university teaching: dimensionality, reliability, validity, potential biases and utility', *Journal of Educational Psychology*, **76**, pp. 707–54.

MARSHALL, H.H. (1990) 'Metaphor as an instructional tool in encouraging student teacher reflection', *Theory into Practice*, **29**, pp. 128–32.

MARSHALL, H.H. and WEINSTEIN, R.S. (1986) 'Classroom context of student-perceived differential teacher treatment', *Journal of Educational Psychology*, **78**, 6, pp. 441–53.

METZ, M. (1978) *Classrooms and corridors*, Berkeley, University of California Press.

MITCHELL, J. and MARLAND, P. (1989) 'Research on teacher thinking: The next phase', *Teaching and Teacher Education*, **5**, 2, pp. 115–28.

Moos, R.H. (1974) *The social climate scales: an overview*, Palo Alto, Consulting Psychologists Press.

Moos, R.H. (1978) 'A typology of junior high and high school classrooms', *American Educational Research Journal*, **15**, pp. 53–66.

Moos, R.H. (1979) *Evaluating Educational Environments: procedures, measures, findings and policy implications*, San Francisco, Jossey-Bass.

Moos, R.H. (1981) *Manual for Work Environment Scale*, Palo Alto, CA, Consulting Psychologists Press.

MURRAY, H.A. (1938) *Explorations in Personality*, New York, Oxford University Press.

MUNBY, H. (1986) 'Metaphor in the thinking of teachers: An exploratory study', *Journal of Curriculum Studies*, **18**, pp. 197–209.

MUNBY, H. and RUSSELL, T. (1990) 'Metaphor in the study of teachers' professional knowledge', *Theory into practice*, **29**, pp. 116–21.

NIALS, J. (1981) 'Teacher satisfaction and dissatisfaction: Herzberg's two factor hypothesis revisited', *British Journal of Sociology of Education*, **2**, pp. 235–46.

NISBETT, R. and Ross, L. (1980) *Human Inference: Strategies and shortcomings of social judgement*, Englewood Cliffs, Prentice Hall.

NUNNALLY, J. (1967) *Psychometric theory*, New York, McGraw Hill.

OSBORNE, R.J. and FREYBERG, P. (1985) *Learning in Science*, Portsmouth, NH, Heinemann.

O'SHEA, L.J., HOOVER, N.L. and CARROLL, R.G. (1988) 'Effective intern conferencing', *Journal of Teacher Education*, **39**, 2, pp. 17–21.

PACE, C.R. and STERN, G.G. (1958) 'An approach to the measurement of psychological characteristics of college environments', *Journal of Educational Psychology*, **49**, pp. 269–77.

PARLETT, M. and HAMILTON, D. (1976) 'Evaluation as illumination: A new approach to the study of innovatory', in GLASS, G.V. (Ed.) *Evaluation Studies Review Annual*, Beverly Hills, Sage, **1**, pp. 140–57.

PECK, R.F., BLATTSTEIN, A. and FOX, R. (1978) 'Student evaluation of teaching', Paper presented at the meeting of the American Educational Research Association, Toronto, Canada, August 1978.

PECK, R.F., OLSSON, N.G. and GREEN, J.L. (1978) 'The consistency of individual teaching behavior', Paper presented at the meeting of the American Educational Research Association, Toronto, Canada, August 1978.

PEDHAZUR, E.J. (1982) *Multiple regression in behavioral research*, New York, Holt Rinehart and Winston.

PETERS, J.J. (1984) Teaching: 'Intentionality reflection and routines', in HALKES, R. and OLSON, J. (Eds) *Teacher Thinking: A new perspective in persisting problems in education*, Lisse, Swets en Zeitlinger, pp. 19–34.

PETERSON, P.L. and BARGER, S.A. (1985) 'Attribution theory and teacher expectancy', in DUSEK J.B. (Ed.) *Teacher expectancies*, Hillsdale NJ, Erlbaum, pp. 159–84.

PINTRICH, P.R. (1990) 'Implications of psychological research on student learning and college teaching for teacher education', in HOUSTON, W.R. (Ed.), *Handbook of Research on Teacher Education*, New York, McMillan, pp. 826–57.

POLANYI, M. (1966) *The tacit dimension*, Garden City, NY, Anchor.

POSNER, G.J., STRIKE, K.A., HEWSON, P.W. and GERTZOG, W.A. (1982) 'Accommodation of a scientific conception: Towards a theory of conceptual change', *Science Education*, **66**, pp. 211–27.

PURKEY, S.C. and SMITH, M.S. (1985) 'Too soon to cheer? Synthesis of research on effective schools', *Educational Leadership*, **40**, pp. 64–9.

PUTNAM, J. and JOHNS, B. (1987) 'The potential of demonstration teaching as a component for teacher preparation and staff development programs', *International Journal of Educational Research*, **11**, 5, pp. 577–88.

QUICK, A.F. (1967) 'Supervising teachers do need special skills', *Education Journal*, **44**, pp. 16–17.

RAMSAY, W. and RANSLEY, W. (1986) 'A method of analysis for determining dimensions of teaching style', *Teaching and Teacher Education*, **2**, 1, pp. 69–79.

REDDY, M.J. (1979) The conduit metaphor — a case of frame conflict in our language about language, in ORTONY, A. (Ed.) *Methaphor and thought*, London, Cambridge University Press, pp. 284–324.

RENTOUL, A.J. and FRASER, B.J. (1979) 'Conceptualization of enquiry-based or open classrooms learning environments', *Journal of Curriculum Studies*, **11**, pp. 233–45.

RENTOUL, A.J. and FRASER, B.J. (1983) 'Development of a school-level environment questionnaire', *Journal of Educational Administration*, **21**, pp. 21–39.

RESNICK, L.B. (1983) 'Mathematics and science learning: a new conception', *Science*, **220**, pp. 477–78.

ROSENHOLTZ, S.J., BASSLER, O. and HOOVER-DEMPSEY, K. (1986) 'Organizational conditions of teacher learning', *Teaching and Teacher Education*, **2**, 2, pp. 91–104.

RUESCH, J. and BATESON, G. (1968) *Communication: The social matrix of psychiatry*, New York, Norton.

RYANS, D.G. (1960) *Characteristics of teachers*, Washington, American Council on Education.

SALLEY, C., MCPHERSON, R.B. and BAEHR, M.E. (1978) 'What principals do: An occupational analysis', in ERICKSON, D. and RELLER, T. (Eds) *The principal in metropolitan schools*, Berkeley, McCutchan.

SANFORD, J.P. and EVERTSON, C.M. (1981) 'Classroom management in a low SES junior high: Three case studies', *Journal of Teacher Education*, **32**, 1, pp. 34–8.

SCHÖN, D.A. (1987) *Educating the reflective practitioner*, San Francisco, Jossey Bass.

SCHULTZ, R.A. (1982) 'Teaching style and sociopsychological climates', *The Alberta Journal of Educational Research*, **18**, 1, pp. 9–18.

SERGIOVANNI, T.J. (1987) *The principalship, A reflective practice perspective*, Boston, Allyn and Bacon.

SHAVELSON, R.J. (1983) 'Review of research on teachers' pedagogical judgements, plans and decisions', *Elementary School Journal*, **83**, pp. 392–413.

SHAVELSON, R.J. and STERN, P. (1981) 'Research on teachers' pedagogical thoughts judgments decisions and behavior', *Review of educational research*, **51**, pp. 455–98.

SHAVELSON, R.J., WEBB, N.W. and BURSTEIN, L. (1986) 'Measurement of teaching', in WITTROCK, M.C. (Ed.) *Handbook of research on teaching* (third edition), New York, McMillan, pp. 50–91.

SIEBER, R.T. (1979) 'Classmates as workmates: Informal peer activity in the elementary school', *Anthropology and Educational Quarterly*, **10**, pp. 207–35.

SIMON, H. and BOYER, E.G. *Mirrors for Behavior III*, (1974) An anthology of observation instruments, Wyncote, Communication Materials Center.

SLATER, P.E. (1962) 'Parental behavior and the personality of the child', *Journal of Genetical Psychology*, **101**, pp. 53–68.

SMITH, W.F. and ANDREWS, R.L. (1989) *Instructional leadership: How principals make a difference*, Alexandria, Association for Supervision and Curriculum Development.

SMITH, L.M. and GEOFFREY, W. (1968) *The complexities of an urban classroom*, New York, Holt, Rinehart and Winston.

SOUTHALL, C. and KING, D. (1979) 'Critical incidents in student teaching', *Teacher Educator*, **15**, pp. 34–6.

STALLINGS, J., NEEDELS, M. and STAYROOK, N. (1979) *How to change the process of teaching basic reading skills in secondary school Phase II and Phase III*, Menlo Park, California, SRI international.

STEELE, J.M., HOUSE, E.R. and KERNINS, T. (1971) 'An instrument for assessing instructional climate through low-inference student judgements', *American Educational Research Journal*, **8**, pp. 447–66.

STERN, G.G. (1970) *People in Context: measuring person-environment congruence in education and industry*, New York, Wiley.

STODGILL, R.M. (1974) *Handbook of leadership*, New-York, The Free Press.

STOFFLETT, R. and STODDART, T. (1991) 'The effects of content instruction on the implementation of science conceptual change strategies in elementary classrooms', Paper presented at the Annual meeting of the American Educational Research Association, Chicago, IL.

STUBBS, M. (1976) 'Keeping in touch: some functions of teacher talk', in STUBBS,

M. and DELAMONT, S. (Eds) *Explorations in classroom observations*, London, Wiley, pp. 151–71.

SUMMERS, A.A. and WOLFE, B.L. (1977) 'Do schools make a difference?' *American Economic Review*, **67**, pp. 639–52.

TABACHNICK, B.R., POPKEWITZ, T. and ZEICHNER, K. (1979–1980) 'Teacher education and the professional perspectives of student teachers', *Interchange*, **10**, 4, pp. 12–29.

TABACHNICK, B.R. and ZEICHNER, K. (1984) 'The impact of the student teaching experience on the development of teacher perspectives', *Journal of Teacher Education*, **35**, 6, pp. 28–36.

TABACHNICK, B.R. and ZEICHNER, K.M. (1986) 'Teacher beliefs and classroom behaviors: some teacher responses to inconsistency', in BEN-PERETZ, M., BROMME, R. and HALKES, R. (Eds) *Advances of research on teacher thinking*, Lisse, Swets en Zeitlinger, pp. 84–96.

TAYLOR, P.C.S. (1990) 'The influence of teacher beliefs on constructivist teaching practices', Paper presented at the Annual Meeting of the American Educational Research Association, Boston.

THOMAS, A.R. (1976) 'The organizational climate of schools', *International Review of Education*, **22**, pp. 441–63.

TIKUNOFF, W.J. and WARD, B.A. (1978) *A naturalistic study of the initiation of students into three classroom social systems*, San Francisco, Far West Laboratory.

TILLEMA, H.H. and VEENMAN, S.A.M. (1987) 'Conceptualizing training methods in teacher education', *International Journal of Educational Research*, **11**, pp. 519–31.

TOBIN, K., KAHLE, J.B. and FRASER, B.J. (Eds) (1990) *Windows into Science Classes: Problems Associated with Higher Level Cognitive Learning*, London, Falmer Press.

TUCKMAN, B.W. and YATES, D.S. (1980) 'Evaluating the student feedback strategy for changing teacher style', *Journal of Educational Research*, **74**, pp. 74–7.

TURK, D.C. and SPEERS, M.A. (1983) 'Cognitive schemata and cognitive processes in cognitive-behavioral interventions: going beyond the information given', in KENDALL, P. (Ed.) *Advances in Cognitive-Behavioral Research and Therapy*, New York, Academic Press, pp. 1–31.

VEENMAN, S. (1984) 'Perceived problems of beginning teachers', *Review of Educational Research*, **54**, pp. 143–78.

VOSNIADOU, S. and BREWER, W.F. (1987) 'Theories of knowledge restructuring in development', *Review of Educational Research*, **57**, 1, pp. 51–67.

WAHL, D., WEINERT, F.E. and HUBER, G.L. (1984) *Psychologie für die Schulpraxis, Ein handlungsorientiertes Lehrbuch für Lehrer*, München, Kösel Verlag.

WALBERG, H.J. (1976) 'The psychology of learning environments: Behavioral, structural or perceptual?', *Review of Research in Education*, **4**, pp. 142–78.

WALBERG, H.J. (Ed.) (1979) *Educational Environments and Effects: Evaluation, Policy and Productivity*, Berkeley, McCutchan.

WATZLAWICK, P. (1978) *The language of change*, New York, Basic Books.

WATZLAWICK, P., BEAVIN, J.H. and JACKSON, D. (1967) *The pragmatics of human communication*, New York, Norton.

WATZLAWICK, P., WEAKLAND, J.H. and FISCH, R. (1974) *Change*, New York, Norton.

WAXLER, N. and MISHLER, E.G. (1970) 'Experimental studies of families', in

BERKOWITZ, L. (Ed.) *Advances in experimental social psychology*, 5, New York, Academic Press.

WAXMAN, H.C. and EASH, M. (1983) 'Utilizing students' perceptions and context variables to analyze effective teaching: A process-product investigation, *Journal of Educational Research*, **76**, pp. 321–5.

WEINERT, F.E. (1978) 'Kommentar zum Beitrag von Hofer und Dobrick', in GÖRLITZ, D., MEYER, W.U. and WEINER, B. (Eds) *Bielefelder Symposium über Attribution*, Stuttgart, Klett, pp. 65–9.

WEINSTEIN, C.S. (1988) 'Preservice teachers' expectations about the first year of teaching', *Teaching and Teacher Education*, **4**, 1, pp. 31–40.

WEINSTEIN, C.S. (1989) 'Teacher education students' preconceptions of teaching', *Journal of Teacher Education*, **39**, 2, pp. 53–60.

WINNE, P.H. and MARX, R.W. (1977) 'Reconceptualizing research on teaching', *Journal of Educational Psychology*, **69**, pp. 668–78.

WISHART, D. (1978) *CLUSTAN, user manual* (third edition), Inter-University/ Research Councils Series, Report no. 47, Edinburgh.

WOOLFOLK, A.E. (1989) *Research perspectives on the graduate preparation of teachers*, Englewood Cliffs, N.J., Prentice Hall.

WOOLFOLK, A.E. and BROOKS, D.M. (1983) 'Nonverbal communication in teaching', in GORDON, E.W. (Ed.) *Review of research in education*, Washington, American Educational Research Association, pp. 103–50.

WUBBELS, T. (1992) 'Taking account of student teachers' preconceptions', *Teaching and Teacher Education*, **8**, 2, pp. 137–49.

WUBBELS, T. (1993) 'Teacher–Student Relationships in Science and Mathematics Classes', *What Research Says to the Science and mathematics teacher*, **11**, Perth, Curtin University.

WUBBELS, T., BREKELMANS, M., CRÉTON, H.A. and HOOYMAYERS, H.P. (1990) 'Teacher behavior style and learning environment', in ELLET, Ch. and WAXMAN, H. (Eds) *The Study of Learning Environments*, 4, Houston, College of Education, pp. 1–12.

WUBBELS, T., BREKELMANS, M. and HERMANS, J. (1987) 'Teacher behavior an important aspect of the learning environment', in FRASER, B.J. (Ed.) *The study of learning environments*, 3, Perth, Curtin University, pp. 10–25.

WUBBELS, T., BREKELMANS, M. and HOOYMAYERS, H.P. (1992) 'Do teacher ideals distort the self-reports of their interpersonal behavior?', *Teaching and Teacher Education*, **8**, pp. 47–58.

WUBBELS, T., CRÉTON, H.A., BREKELMANS, M. and HOOYMAYERS, H.P. (1987) 'Perceptions of the teacher–student relationship' (in Dutch) *Tijdschrift voor Onderwijsresearch*, **12**, 1, pp. 3–16.

WUBBELS, T., CRETON, H.A. and HOLVAST, A.J.C.D. (1988) 'Undesirable classroom situations', *Interchange*, **19**, 2, pp. 25–40.

WUBBELS, T., CRÉTON, H.A. and HOOYMAYERS, H.P. (1985) 'Discipline problems of beginning teachers, interactional teacher behavior mapped out', Paper presented at the AERA Annual meeting, Chicago. Abstracted in *Resources in Education*, 20, 12, p. 153, ERIC document 260040.

WUBBELS, T., CRÉTON, H.A. and HOOYMAYERS, H.P. (1987) 'A school-based teacher induction programme', *European Journal of Teacher Education*, **10**, 1, pp. 81–94.

WUBBELS, T. and LEVY, J. (1991) 'A comparison of interpersonal behavior of Dutch and American teachers', *International Journal of Intercultural Relationships*, **15**, pp. 1–18.

YINGER, R.J. (1980) 'A study of teacher planning', *Elementary School Journal*, **80**, pp. 107–27.

YINGER, R.J. and VILLAR, L.M. (1986) 'Studies of teachers' thoughts-in-action', Paper presented at the International Study Association for Teacher Thinking Conference, Leuven, Belgium.

ZEICHNER, K.M. (1983) 'Individual and institutional factors related to the socialization of beginning teachers', in GRIFFIN, G.A. and HUKILL, H. (Eds) *First Years of Teaching: What are the Pertinent Issues?*, Report N9051, Austin, University of Texas, pp. 1–59.

ZEICHNER, K. (1987) 'Preparing reflective teachers: An overview of instructional strategies in preservice teacher education', *International Journal of Educational Research*, **11**, 5, pp. 565–75.

ZEICHNER, K.M. and GORE, J.M. (1990) 'Teacher Socialization', in HOUSTON, W.R. (Ed.) *Handbook of Research on Teacher Education*, New York, MacMillan, pp. 329–48.

ZEICHNER, K.M. and TABACHNICK, B.R. (1983) 'Teacher perspectives in the face of institutional press', Paper presented at the meeting of the American Educational Research Association, Montreal.

ZEICHNER, K.M. and TEITELBAUM, K. (1982) 'Personalized and inquiry-oriented teacher education' *Journal of Education for Teaching*, **8**, pp. 95–117.

Notes on Contributors

Mieke Brekelmans is an Associate Professor in the Institute of Education (IVLOS) of Utrecht University. She holds a Master's Degree in Chemistry and Psychology. Her Ph.D. was on interpersonal behavior of teachers. At present she teaches in pre-service teacher education (in the field of teacher inquiry). Her research is part of the program 'Education for teachers'. Her research interests include the development of interpersonal behavior during the professional career and the relation between interpersonal behavior and interpersonal cognition.

Hans Créton is an Associate Professor in the Institute of Education (IVLOS) of Utrecht University. He teaches in pre-service and in-service teacher education programs and works in the educational research group 'Education for Teachers'. He holds a Master's Degree in Physics and Adult Education. His Ph.D., was on discipline problems of beginning teachers. He has more than twenty years of experience in school-based teacher development. His major area of interest is the translation of insights from psychotherapy into the supervision of teachers. He specializes in interpersonal teacher behavior from a systems communication perspective.

Darrell Fisher is an Associate Professor and Head of Department of Education in the University of Tasmania at Launceston. Previous to this he was Head of Adult Learning and postgraduate studies in education. His career began as a science and math teacher and following a time as a writer of science materials he became a senior lecturer in a University. His Ph.D. was on the relationships of actual classroom environment and actual-preferred congruence to students' outcomes. His research interests are in the areas of students' perceptions of classroom environment and teacher perceptions of their school environment or climate.

Barry Fraser is Professor of Education, Director of the Science and Mathematics Education Centre and Director of the national Key Centre for School Science and Mathematics at Curtin University in Perth, Australia. His specialities include learning environments, science education and educational evaluation. He is author of *Classroom Environment, Windows into Science* and *Educational Environments*.

Joost Hermans is an Associate Professor in the Institute of Education (IVLOS) of Utrecht University. He holds a Master's Degree in Pedagogy. His Ph.D. was on drop-out in secondary education. He teaches in pre and in-service teacher education and works in the research project 'Education for teachers'. In teaching as well as in research he focuses on student motivation and values and especially on the teacher's role in this motivational process. He has extensive experience in training and counselling in various educational settings.

Anne-Jan Holvast is an Associate Professor at the Centre for Science and Mathematics Education of Utrecht University. He holds a Master's Degree in Physics and has worked for many years in physics teacher-education programs. His research was in the field of teacher education. He is also organizer of the Dutch Physics Olympiad and consultant for development cooperation projects in (Physics) Education between The Netherlands and Third World Countries.

Herman Hooymayers is Professor at the Centre for Science and Mathematics Education of Utrecht University. He holds a Master's Degree and a Ph.D. in Physics. He is the founding father of the research on interpersonal behavior, described in this book. At the present his research field is teacher education and concept development of pre-university physics students. He supervises Ph.D.-students in this field. In addition, he is currently Dean of the Faculty of Physics and Astronomy.

Lya Kremer-Hayon is Professor of Education at the University of Haifa, Israel. She holds a B.Sc. degree in education from the University of Minnesota, Master's degree from the University of Tel Aviv and a Ph.D., from the Hebrew University in Jerusalem. Her practical experience includes elementary and secondary school teaching, supervision of student teachers, university teaching, professional development workshop for teachers. Her administrative position include: Deputy director of the State Teachers' College of Haifa, Head Teacher Education Department and Head Education Department, Head Center of Educational Administration and Evaluation at the University of Haifa. She has written two books on teaching and more than fifty articles in American and European Education Journals.

Jack Levy is an Associate Professor of Education at George Mason University in Fairfax, Virginia, USA. He received a Ph.D., from the University of Southern California in Curriculum/Instruction. During the past two decades he has served as a classroom teacher, secondary administrator, federal government official, professor and consultant.

Rely Rodriguez is an Assistant Principal at J.E.B. Stuart High School in Fairfax, Virginia, USA. She has extensive experience as a secondary science teacher and supervisor. Ms. Rodriguez is a doctoral candidate in Educational Leadership/Language Minority Education at George Mason University.

Theo Wubbels is Professor of Education in the Institute of Education (IVLOS) of Utrecht University. He holds a Master's degree in Physics and a Ph.D. in Education. He was physics teacher and assistant principal in a Montessori High

School, before he became curriculum developer in Utrecht University. He moved to teacher education and is now Head of Teacher Education and of the Research Program 'Education for Teachers'. He specializes in learning environments, classroom communication and methodology.

Address Utrecht University, IVLOS, PO BOX 80127, 3508TC Utrecht, The Netherlands.

Index